UOA 39   H-0160

Institution: **University of Southampton**

Name: **Freedman, JL**

Output Number: **3**

Research Group :

IMMIGRATION AND INSECURITY IN FRANCE

For Stuart, Olivia and Juliette

Critical Security Series

Immigration and Insecurity
in France

JANE FREEDMAN

ASHGATE

Published by
Ashgate Publishing Limited
Gower House
Croft Road
Aldershot
Hants GU11 3HR
England

Ashgate Publishing Company
Suite 420
101 Cherry Street
Burlington, VT 05401-4405
USA

Ashgate website: http://www.ashgate.com

British Library Cataloguing in Publication Data
Freedman, Jane
    Immigration and insecurity in France. - (Critical security series)
    1.Immigrants - France - Social conditions 2.Immigrants - Cultural assimilation - France 3.Social integration - France 4.France - Emigration and immigration - Social aspects 5.France - Emigration and immigration - Government policy
    I.Title
    325.4'4

Library of Congress Cataloging-in-Publication Data
Freedman, Jane.
    Immigration and insecurity in France / by Jane Freedman.
        p. cm. -- (Critical security series)
    Includes bibliographical references and index.
    ISBN 0-7546-3583-X
  1. France--Emigration and immigration--Social aspects. 2. Immigrants--France--Social conditions. 3. Immigrants--Cultural assimilation--France. 4. France--Emigration and immigration--Government policy. 5. Social integration--France. I. Title.

    JV7925.F75 2004
    325.44--dc22

2004004805

ISBN 0 7546 3583 X
Printed and bound by Athenaeum Press, Ltd.,
Gateshead, Tyne & Wear.

Contents

Introduction

In 1983, following the French municipal elections which had been marked by the electoral breakthrough of the extreme-Right Front National, Etienne Balibar remarked that, 'to present those whose existence encompasses the maximum amount of insecurity, immigrant workers, as constituting the principal source of insecurity for France, is a paradox, if not provocation' (Balibar, 1992: 35).

This paradox/provocation was not, however, a passing phenomenon, and the theme of insecurity, and the threat that immigration poses to French society and the French nation, has been a continual leitmotif of political discourse in the years that have followed. Immigration has been interpreted through a prism of security by politicians, police and security services, the media and an important fraction of public opinion (Bigo, 1998). This discourse of security has confused the boundaries between Right and Left and has obscured many of the real social and economic issues surrounding immigration. In arriving at a consensus on the threat to security posed by immigration and the need to tackle this 'threat' through measures of control and repression, many of the realities of the patterns of immigration and of the experience of migrants themselves has been obscured. Although immigration has been a long-term component of French history, the contemporary period has seen a 'problematisation' and 'securitisation' of the issue that is new in its scope and scale. In these circumstances it is necessary to ask how and why immigration has been problematised in this way, and what the implications of the securitisation of the immigration issue are on migrants themselves.

Clearly migration has become a major global issue and one that cannot be ignored. In the post-war years a number of major developments in global migration patterns have placed the phenomenon at the heart of global politics. Firstly, the scale of movements has increased exponentially, so that by 2000 the International Organisation for Migration reported that over 2.5 per cent of the world's population was living outside of their country of birth (IOM, 2000), and virtually every nation was influenced in some way by migration. Secondly, there has been an enormous increase in the diversity of international population movement, with world migration being characterised not only by increased levels of permanent settlement in foreign countries, but also by a myriad of temporary and circular migrations of varying durations and with a rage of purposes. Thirdly there has been an increasing politicisation of immigration both at national and international levels with a dramatic increase in number of regional and global institutions aiming to shape the level and pattern of migration.

France, like other countries of the European Union has seen immigration become an increasingly central and contentious issue in recent years; an issue which has seen both a conceptual and geo-political widening (Geddes, 2003). It is also an issue, which, as argued above has become increasingly securitised. This securitisation has been magnified by processes of European integration, and the opening up of internal borders within Europe. From the start of negotiations over the creation of a borderless Europe, the main security risks were identified as immigration, drug-trafficking and international crime (Kostakopoulou, 2001). The inclusion of immigration in this list coincided with assumptions within the member states about the status of immigration as a threat to national security. Thus 'whereas intra-Community migration was regarded as a fundamental freedom and the cornerstone of European citizenship, non-EC immigration was portrayed by official discourse and policy as an 'invasion' to be feared and resisted (Kostakopoulou, 2001: 52). Large scale inflows of migrants from outside of Europe were perceived as potential economic burdens leading to labour market difficulties and strains on national welfare systems, threats to national security and identities, and to political stability. The framing of immigration as a security issue in this way has meant that national policies of repression and exclusion have been confirmed and justified at the European level.

The mobilisation of immigration as a security issue has justified the intensifying controls placed on immigrants. Immigration control is sometimes conceived only in terms of admittance of non-admittance of immigrants into national territory. However, mechanisms of control are far wider than this and encompass many more subtle and indirect aspects. Brochmann establishes a framework for analysing immigration control in terms of   four variants: external and internal, direct and indirect controls (Brochmann, 1999). Most states employ a varying mixture of external and internal controls in different forms, creating a complex and dynamic system which reflects tensions and dilemmas both within the national political arena and from the broader international context.

The particular contours of the way in which the immigration has become a security issue in France and the way that the immigration control complex has developed, are of course tied up with the particular historical, social and political context of migration to France, and to the philosophies which are the basis of the French state. In particular the ideas of the Republic and of Republican citizenship have been central to the framing of discourse and debate on immigration. This 'myth' of Republican citizenship can be seen to have been mobilised as part of a 'mystificatory discourse' to 'sustain a political consensus that is less and less responsive to the social facts and demands of the situation' (Favell, 1998: 241). This consensus has revolved around the need to integrate or assimilate immigrants into French society through an application of universalist principles which reject any type of recognition of community or ethnic difference. And this insistence on integration has been predicated on the necessity of immigration control as it is has been argued that society can only integrate a certain number of immigrants up to its 'threshold of tolerance'. These Republican principles of integration have been forcibly challenged in recent years by the establishment and settlement of a large Muslim population in France and the continued reiteration of Republican values such as secularism have only served to reinforce the framing of Islam and Muslim immigrants as a threat to French national identity.

Returning to the paradox highlighted by Balibar, it can be argued that the framing of immigration as a security issue has led to the justification of increasingly repressive and exclusionary policies and legislation on immigration and asylum, together with a growing insistence on integration, which have had an important impact on the human security of immigrants within France. Moreover the framing of discourses on immigration and integration within the 'myth' of Republican citizenship has magnified these insecurities by further racialising the immigration issue and adding to exclusionary pressures. Whilst some have argued that a new postnational citizenship is emerging within Europe and that migrants are being granted rights almost equivalent to those of national citizens, this book will argue that on the contrary, repressive immigration policies together with the emphasis on Republican integration, have increased the vulnerability of many categories of migrants within France. In these conditions precariousness and insecurity have become constitutive characteristics of the situation of non-European migrants within France (Lochak, 1999).

The arguments put forward in this book argue that the increasing securitisation of the immigration issue and the introduction of more restrictive and repressive controls, both external and internal, have had a negative impact on the position of immigrants, which in turn undermines the claims of the French state to support universal values of equality and fraternity. The emphasis on the need to control immigration has moved the focus of debate away from the experiences of individual migrants and towards a concentration on flows of migration. That these flows are seen as a threat only serves to reinforce populist anti-immigrant sentiment and to boost the electoral chances of extreme-Right parties like the Front National. Only through a desecuritisation of the immigration issue can a real framework for the development of immigrants' rights and for the tackling of discrimination and racism be established.

Outline of the Book

This book sets out to analyse the way in which immigration and asylum policies and policies for the 'integration' of populations of immigrant origin have developed in France in recent years. In doing so it will highlight the insecurities to which immigrants in France are subjected as a result of the development of these policies. The first part of the book will consider the framework within which immigration and asylum policies have been developed. Chapter 1 will examine conceptions of immigration and citizenship in France, pointing to the development of the idea of immigration as a threat to national identity, and investigating the continuing debate over the assimilation or integration of populations of immigrant origin, whilst in chapter 2 the evolution of immigration policy will be examined in the context of European integration and the development of a borderless Europe. A particular feature of recent attempts to integrate European immigration policies has been the emphasis on creating a unified asylum policy, however this has proved difficult as each country fights to retain control over their national asylum policies. Chapter 3 will look particularly at developments in asylum and refugee policy in France within the context of European integration and will examine the issue of the Sangatte refugee camp and the ways in which this problem highlighted a crisis in the French asylum system and in attempts to harmonise European asylum policy. Chapter 4 deals with another issue which has been the subject of much current debate, namely illegal immigration. The attempts to expel illegal residents from France have led to a large mobilisation around the issues of illegality. This *sans-papiers* movement will be examined in detail in an attempt to uncover the more general issues concerning the treatment of illegal migrants and residents in France and in Europe.

The second part of the book examines more general issues concerning the extent of immigrants' rights and the boundaries of citizenship. This section will argue against those who posit the unfettered expansion of postnational citizenship and will point to the ways in which repressive immigration and asylum policies, the strong emphasis placed on Republicanism in the push for integration, and a failure to deal with discriminations based on gender, race, ethnicity and religion, have acted to restrict the access to and exercise of citizenship rights of both immigrants and populations of immigrant origin. Chapter 5 focuses on the general issue of immigrants' rights, pointing to the exclusionary nature of political citizenship in France, and to the inequalities in social and economic rights between national and non-national residents. In chapter 6, the issue of gender inequality will be addressed directly. This is an issue which is often neglected in analyses of immigration, but as the chapter will aim to show, the construction of a public-private divide forces many migrant women into a situation of dependency on male relatives and colleagues which worsens their situations of insecurity. Chapter 7 will examine another specifically gendered issue, that of the debate over the Islamic headscarf and the exclusion of the Muslim girls from school for wearing a headscarf. This is a problem which has challenged the Republican emphasis on secularism and has been revelatory not only of representations and discourse concerning migrant women, but also of the prevailing attitudes towards Islam and the place of Muslims in French society. The chapter will argue that the way in which Islam has been framed as a threat to the French Republican tradition has in fact only created the conditions for greater exclusion of Muslims from French society. Finally, chapter 8 addresses the issue of racism and discrimination and outlines the ways in which the persistence of such racism and discrimination creates insecurities for populations of immigrant origin in France. The chapter will conclude that the perceived failures of anti-racism in France can be attributed in part to an institutionalisation of racism through the continuing dependence on Republican models of citizenship and rights.

Chapter 1

Conceptions of Immigration and Citizenship

In the May 2002 French presidential election, Jean-Marie Le Pen, the leader of the Front National, running on an electoral platform of which anti-immigration policies were a major part, received almost seventeen per cent of the vote in the first round, eliminating the Socialist candidate, and the then Prime Minister, Lionel Jospin. In beating Jospin in the first round of the elections, Le Pen qualified to go through to the second round run-off against the incumbent president Jacques Chirac. Le Pen was soundly defeated by Chirac in the second round, but his success in the first round shocked and surprised many in France, who had tolerated the Front National as a political presence since the beginning of the 1980s when they first began to have an electoral impact, but had not realised the extent of their popular support. Indeed, that a candidate standing on a platform based largely on anti-immigration measures could gain so many votes, shocked not only the French, but many around Europe and the world. In fact, however, Le Pen's performance should not have come as that great a surprise. Immigration has been a subject of heated debate in France for many years, and it may be argued that both the Left and the moderate Right have contributed to the success of the Front National by their failure to confront Le Pen's anti-immigration diatribes, and further, that they have in fact taken a more and more hard line stance on immigration in response to the perceived electoral appeal of the Front National's policies. The assumption amongst politicians from other parties has been that the Front National poses a real problem in terms of electoral politics because they have addressed the issue of immigration which is a real crisis, and a dangerous one for France. The Socialist Prime Minister, Laurent Fabius, declared in a television interview as early as 1985, for example, that: 'The Le Pen phenomenon comes from real questions, to which the extreme-Right brings the wrong answers' (*Le Monde,* 29 October 1985). Other politicians and the media have echoed this sentiment that the Front National is asking the right questions (even if they may provide the wrong answers) and that immigration is one of the major problems facing contemporary French society. Jacques Chirac, the current President of France, declared in 1991 when he was mayor of Paris, that he felt sorry for the residents of working class districts of Paris who lived next door to immigrants. He talked about the French man:

> who sees his next door neighbour – a family where there is one father, three or
> four wives and twenty-odd kids, getting fifty thousand francs in social security
> payments without going to work: add to the noise and the smell and it drives the

French worker crazy. It's not racist to say we can no longer afford to reunite families (cited in Marcus, 1995: 93).

The use of such blatant racist stereotyping – smelly, noisy immigrant families with large numbers of children, living off the French social security system – may be more typical of the Far-Right, but the fact that such images could be employed by a leader of the largest moderate Right-wing party, then mayor of Paris, and now President of France, demonstrates to what extent the treatment of immigration and immigrants as a 'problem' for the French state and the French people has been normalised. Immigrants are frequently linked with problems of crime, unemployment, and a general 'insecurity' in French society. The number of immigrants, and particular illegal immigrants is consistently overstated, and recently there has been huge debate over the issue of the 'sans-papiers' (literally those 'without papers' who have been resisting deportation from France), and over asylum seekers (and particularly the Sangatte camp which was a subject of controversy between France and the UK). The way in which immigration has been problematised in this fashion, has meant that successive governments have pursued stricter and stricter policies aiming to reduce the number of immigrants coming into France, to return those perceived to be residing in France 'illegally', and to push for the further 'integration' of those immigrants who have a legal right to stay in France. Immigration has become an issue that is now perceived very much in terms of 'security', both in terms of the need to limit entrance to the country and in terms of the push to further integrate settled migrants and ethnic minority communities. The threat to national security posed by immigration is perceived as manifold. Immigration has been linked with economic difficulties – unemployment and deficits in the welfare budget, rising crime, the threat of terrorism. More fundamentally, perhaps, immigration has been seen as a threat to the very basis of national social and political cohesion, undermining French national identity and thus calling the nation-state itself into question. Paradoxically, whilst the debate over immigration, has portrayed policies and legislation designed to limit immigration as safeguarding France's security, it might be argued that these same laws and policies have created an increasingly vulnerable and insecure situation for many of those of immigrant origin currently living in France. And not only has the security of immigrants been affected negatively by increasingly exclusionary policies, the very construction of the discursive boundaries between the French 'us' and the foreign 'them' in current rhetoric and debates over immigration have had an effect in increasing insecurity for migrant and ethnic minority communities living on French territory.

The rest of this chapter will explore the history of France's attitudes to and conceptions of migrants in the post-War period and will go on to examine the ways in which migrants rights and experiences have been shaped by changes in discourse on immigration. It will examine the debate over the creation of a post-national citizenship, and argue that current attitudes and policies towards immigration show in fact the limits of the development of such a post-national citizenship status.

Immigration and the French Nation

The problematisation of the immigration issue and the continuing politicisation of the discourse and debate around immigration and French nationality highlight some seemingly contradictory tendencies within the discourses of nationhood and citizenship in France, and point to discontinuities in the incorporation of non-national residents which would seem to challenge the thesis of a developing postnational citizenship (for a fuller discussion of the concept of postnational citizenship see below). French attitudes to and policies towards immigration can be seen as paradoxical in that whilst in perception and in reality France has been one of the foremost countries of immigration in Europe, it has resisted movements towards multiculturalism or towards any formal acknowledgement of the multi-ethnic nature of its society. As Walzer argues in his study of 'regimes of toleration', France is a complicated case because: 'Far more than any other country France has been a society of immigrants. And yet it isn't a pluralist society – or at least it doesn't think of itself, and it isn't thought of, as a pluralist society' (Walzer, 1997: 38). And although it might be argued that in recent years France has become more and more of a pluralist society, this paradoxical tension between high levels of immigration and an attachment to an assimilationist Republican tradition might be argued to continue, complicating many of the debates surrounding migration and migration policy in contemporary France. Indeed, the debate over immigration can be seen as part of a greater debate about the nature of the French nation-state itself, a nation-state which some have argued is in crisis (Silverman, 1992).

Traditionally France has perceived itself both as a defender of individual rights and a country of immigration, willing to grant citizenship and rights to those who wished to become French. In fact, France has traditionally had greater immigration than other European countries, encouraging immigrants to make up for its low birth rate and lack of workforce. Research published by the Institut National d'Etudes Démographiques (INED), highlights the importance of immigration in the constitution of the French population:

> The proportion of people born in France with at least a parent or grand-parent who immigrated in the past one hundred years is about twenty per cent. Of those of foreign origin, eighty per cent are French from birth. Thus immigration has not only actively supported the demography of France but has also contributed to a greater diversity of the population (Tribalat, 1991: 71).

For centuries, immigrants have made up an important part of the French working class, and in particular the unskilled, industrial workforce (Noiriel, 1988). And from the mid-Nineteenth Century onwards, immigration became a massive phenomenon as the beginning of real industrialisation proved how much France needed foreign workers to supplement its own workforce, with governments as well as industrial leaders actively encouraging immigration. As Georges Mauco, a demographer commented in 1932: 'Only the introduction of new elements, coming from the outside, would be sufficient to nourish the demographic and economic structure of the country. It was clear that immigration, mass immigration, and essentially working-class immigration, was a necessity' (Mauco, 1932).

In fact, although governments took responsibility for organising the diplomatic relations surrounding immigration, and for signing conventions with neighbouring European countries to govern migration into France[1], the actual recruitment of foreign workers was handled by a specialised private organisation, the Société générale d'immigration (SGI) (Weil, 1991). This delegation for the organisation of the practicalities of immigration away from political institutions and towards private labour-market institutions demonstrates the way that immigration was perceived primarily as a labour market issue, and one to be resolved by employers, with government controlling only the very high-level diplomatic issues involves. However, although employers' needs for labour seem paramount in propelling the demand for immigrant labour, immigration was not perceived solely as the importation of labour for French industry, but also as closely linked to the necessity of repopulation of the country – necessary for productivity but also for defence and security. France had continual worries about under-population, and as pro-natalist policies achieved little tangible result, immigration was seen as one solution to the problem of re-populating the country. The migratory phenomenon was so great during the first decades of the Twentieth Century that during the 1920s France was one of the foremost countries of immigration in the world on a per capita basis (Wihtol de Wenden, 1988) and by 1930 France counted proportionally more foreigners amongst its population than the United States (Weil, 1991).

This massive migration created growing difficulties, however, for the French Republican tradition. This tradition which was a product of the 1789 Revolution emphasizes the importance of popular sovereignty, equality and individual rights. Republicanism was favourable to migration in so far as it embraced an open nationalism based on political unity which provided the potential for foreigners to become French citizens if they were willing to adopt French nationality together with language, culture and political traditions. Republican conceptions of the nation also, however, indicated the need for a high degree of cultural unity, and it was here that contradictions began to arise. During the first half of the Twentieth Century, the Republican elements in French politics were attempting to definitively impose their control on the state, and an important part of this campaign consisted in the imposition of cultural unity in the form of a centralised and secular Republic with one language (as opposed to many regional languages) and a unified culture. This campaign was not aided by the introduction of new and diverse populations in the form of labour migrants. As Weil argues, from the second half of the nineteenth century onwards there was a growing contradiction 'between the migratory phenomenon which was becoming massive but necessary – for economic interests, and more particularly for big industries, for the power of the nation faced with Germany, and perhaps also for its socio-political stability -, and a process of social construction of the nation "France" which, in

---

[1] Such conventions were signed with Italy in 1904 and 1906 and 1919, Belgium in 1906, Poland in 1919 and Czechoslovakia in 1920.

order to transcend local specificities and class differences, entrenched common language and homeland in schools, created the identity card, introduced timidly but progressively new social rights reserved for nationals, and thus produced a distinction between national and immigrants' (Weil, 1991: 28).

Post-war migration to France has followed the pattern of many other Northern European countries. This pattern can be described, following Messina, in three broad waves: a first wave of workers including colonial migrants and supposedly 'temporary' guestworkers from the Mediterranean, Africa and Asia, to meet the needs of a rapidly expanding economy; a second wave of spouses and dependents after the closing of doors to labour migration in 1974; and a third wave in the 1980s and 1990s of legitimate and illegitimate refugees and illegal immigrants (Messina, 1996). More recently, as Hansen points out, could be added a new wave, not of inward migration itself, but of mobilisation of illegal immigrants resisting efforts to expel them, and claiming citizenship rights (Hansen, 1999). This mobilisation of the so-called 'sans-papiers' has been central to the contemporary politics of migration in France, prompting widespread discussion about the role of migrants and the nature of citizenship (Terray, 1997).

The first post-war wave of migration lasted from the end of the Second World War until the suspension of labour migration in 1974. During this period, France again experienced massive immigration fuelled both by the recruitment of 'temporary' migrant workers, and by migration schemes and programmes for those from France's (ex)-colonies, the two threads of migration proving complexly interlinked. In the years immediately after 1945 migration was mainly from other European countries – principally Spain and Italy – but the pattern of immigration gradually shifted as more and more immigrants arrived from France's colonies and ex-colonies (particularly Algeria). The regulation of immigration in this post-war period indicates both an expansionist element based on France's continuing need for migrant labour and her desire to boost her population (INED projected that France would need at least 5.3 million permanent immigrants), and also a growing awareness of the ethnic composition of migrant flows and the growing contradictions becoming apparent in the Republican assimilationist view. Some demographers such as Georges Mauco, head of the Haut Comité consultatif de la Population et de la Famille, had already drawn up categorisations of the most and least desirable immigrants based on criteria of their perceived assimilability into French society, thus creating a conceptual model of the demographic analysis of immigrant populations based on notions of assimilation and on ethnic categories (Bertaux, 2000). Mauco's categorisation was officially vetoed by the Conseil d'Etat, but there remained an implicit preference for immigrants from other European countries. The Office National d'Immigration (ONI), created in 1945 to encourage and regulate immigration, located offices outside France in Italy, Spain and later Portugal, to encourage immigrants from these countries. However, the ONI, could not supply the demand for labour quickly enough, and many employers recruited workers directly from other countries, without official checks, or legal papers. Most of these workers were later 'regularized'. In fact, the government recognised the need for 'illegal' immigration outside the official channels of the ONI, to increase immigrant flows and thus to ensure an adequate supply of labour and to ease pressure on wages. In 1963, the Prime Minister, Georges Pompidou, stated clearly that: 'Immigration is a means of creating a certain breathing space in the labour market and of resisting social pressures' (cited in Marie, 1988: 77). And Jean-Marcel Jeanneney, the minister for labour argued in a press release in March 1966 that: 'Illegal immigration is not without its uses because if we stuck to a strict application of international agreements we might face a labour shortage.'[2]

The huge need for immigrants meant that despite the underlying criteria of cultural preference, more and more immigrants came from North and Sub-Saharan Africa and from Asia. This was particularly the case for Algeria, as a law of 1947 had given Algerians the right to French citizenship and the Evian Accords of 1962 which granted Algeria independence, guaranteed free movement and residence for Algerians in mainland France. Successive governments tried to impose restrictions on the influx of Algerians as it became clear that this would be on a massive scale, but these quotas were limited in their effect. Similarly, there were attempts to control the flows of immigrants from France's ex-colonies in sub-Saharan Africa, although these were small at the time. There was a recognition, however, that migration from within Europe would not be enough to meet the needs of French industry and France signed agreements with Morocco and Tunisia to regulate labour immigration from these two countries. Thus in the years between the end of the Second World War and the official suspension of labour migration in 1974, it became clear to all that non-European migration was not only necessary but also inevitable. By 1975, the year after this suspension, the proportion of the immigrant population in France of European origin was only 67.2 per cent of the total immigration population, whilst immigrants from Africa accounting for 28.0 per cent of the total (and Algerians 14.3 per cent) (INSEE, 1997).

The decision to halt labour migration in 1974 can be seen as both an economic and an electoral choice. The decision was taken as a result of the economic recession which followed the 1973 oil crisis, and growing unemployment within France which lessened the need for migrant labour. At the same time there was evidence of growing tension and xenophobia within France and thus electoral pressure for some kind of control of immigration. Already the lack of social infrastructure to cope with immigrant populations was proving problematic, particularly a lack of adequate housing. The fact that many employers had recruited workers directly and not through the ONI meant that they had not been obliged to find accommodation for these workers, and with no houses to go to they were forced to find their own shelter. As a result *bidonvilles* (shanty towns) sprung up on the fringes of cities with large immigrant populations. The construction of public housing to get rid of these shanty towns also caused problems, tending to lead to the concentration of immigrant populations in working-class neighbourhoods (Money, 1999). Anti-immigrant sentiments became increasingly apparent and sometimes resulted in violence. North Africans were attacked in Paris suburbs and anti-immigrant riots broke out in Marseille in 1973 leading to the death of eleven Algerians (Weil, 1991). It was thus a conjuncture of economic and social pressures, together with the desire for electoral appeal which

---

[2] Cited in *Les Echos* 29th March 1966.

led the Secretary of State for Immigration, André Postel-Vinay, to announce a temporary stop on labour migration in July 1974. The suspension was make permanent in October of the same year. The government also attempted to suspend immigration for family reunification but a huge mobilisation of associations defending immigrants' rights convinced them that they could not practically or ethically maintain this ban on family reunification (Weil, 1991). Thus as a report for the OECD suggests, the reasons for the suspension of immigration were complex and went further than simple economic logic: 'These unilateral measures, that to some might appear, over time, to be linked to the energy crisis and to the international financial difficulties, were inspired by essentially political motives … Everything happened as if the approach of a conjunctural recession, more anticipated than felt, as well, constituted an occasion and served to get accepted, restrictive decisions taken based on the social and political situation.' (cited in Wihtol de Wenden, 1988: 191).

However, despite the decision to officially suspend labour migration, and despite government efforts to limit other types of migration and to encourage reverse migration of the supposedly 'temporary' migrant workers, France, like other European countries experienced what Hansen has termed a 'spectacular instance of cross-national policy failure' (Hansen, 1999: 417), in that very few of the migrant workers who had arrived did in fact return to their countries of origin, and moreover, they were in many cases joined by families and dependents. Thus a second wave of migration developed based around the arrival of these families and dependents of the migrant workers who settled in France. Differing explanations have been offered for the way in which patterns of migration developed in Europe, and for the general failure of governments to limit migration or to successfully implement return migration. Hollifield (1992, 1999) has argued that the autonomy of national governments in restricting immigration was limited by an embedded liberalism entrenched in international institutions and agreements and defended by national courts. These embedded liberal values may be argued, for example, to have prevented the French government's attempts to suspend migration for family reunification. A circular passed in July 1974 (immediately following that which suspended labour migration) stopped the migration of families for the purposes of family reunification. However, this circular was annulled because of its questionable legality. As will be argued in more detail below, however, this embedded liberalism clearly has its limits and governments have in other circumstances shown themselves to be less influenced by the strictures of international agreements. Others have stressed that national autonomy is not as limited by international variables, and that governments' failures to limit migration, rather than being the result of an embedded liberalism are the outcome of the domestic political process. Freeman (1995, 1998) for example, has argued that the domestic policy process surrounding immigration has been strongly influenced by the needs of business, and that the incentive structures surrounding these policies favour a modestly expansive policy.

It seems that a complex web of inter-twining factors both guided and constrained successive governments' policies on immigration after the 1974 suspension. Wihtol de Wenden (1988) argues that for the first three years after

1974, immigration politics were focused around the twin necessities of organising what had previously been a relatively anarchic and unregulated phenomenon, and of improving the social conditions of migrant workers and their families. These objectives were quickly replaced, however, by more repressive goals and by a growing involvement of the state at all levels of immigration as it became an increasingly politicized issue. As immigration became increasingly dominated by family reunification, and as immigrant populations stabilised and sedentarised, the issues surrounding immigration policy began to encompass more and more those of ethnic communities. This stabilisation of immigrant populations and the realisation that immigration was not a transitory phenomenon, posed increasingly difficult questions for the French Republican conceptions of nation and citizenship.

A complexity of factors has continued to impact upon immigration policy as well as more generally on French attitudes to immigration, nationality and citizenship. The evolution of this immigration policy since 1974 has also been increasingly affected by the context of European integration, as will be discussed in greater detail in chapter two. As remarked above, even before 1945 and the growth of non-European immigration, the massive influx of immigrants placed strains on the French Republican model of citizenship which gave a central place to both political unity and cultural unity and which aimed for the assimilation of immigrants. These strains have only increased with the increasing ethnic and cultural diversity of migrants in France, to the extent that it might be suggested that this Republican model of citizenship is no longer adequate for the current situation. Instead, it could be argued that France is employing a more and more exclusive model of citizenship, and that far from protecting individual rights, there is a widening gulf in rights and entitlements between national and non-nationals. Whilst it cannot be denied that there is still a concern for the Republican notions of equality and the protection of rights, demonstrated for example by the mobilisation of tens of thousands of people in defence of the *sans-papiers* (for a fuller discussion of the sans-papiers movement see chapter 3), successive governments have been able to enact legislation and to force through various measures to limit the rights of those who are not French citizens, and to make it more difficult to acquire French citizenship. Further, although there has been a move towards dropping the emphasis on assimilation of immigrants in favour of a discourse of integration, there are still important vestiges of the Republican tradition which based citizenship on cultural as well as political unity (Brubaker, 1992). This desire for cultural unity in the face of the growing diversity of the French population has led to particular difficulties for immigrants of Muslim origin as may be evidenced, for example, by the exclusion of Muslim girls from school for the sole reason that they were wearing a headscarf (the so-called affaire des foulards and the particular issues raised by the integration of Muslim immigrants into French society will be discussed at greater length in chapter five).

Brubaker compares French and German ideas of citizenship, arguing that whilst Germany has defined citizenship narrowly as a community of descent, France has employed a more open territorially bounded notion of who is a citizen (Brubaker, 1992). He points to the continually higher rates of nationalisation of foreign residents in France as evidence to support this assertion. It is certainly true that historically France has seemed more willing than other European nations to open up the possibility of foreigners acquiring citizenship and has based its citizenship laws not only on *jus sanguinis* (right of blood) but also on *jus soli* (right of soil) (Noiriel, 1988; Weil, 1991). Yet, it might be argued that this more open territorially bounded notion of citizenship, the idea that those who wish to reside in France may acquire French nationality and become French citizens, has been eroded in recent years, firstly, by the modification of laws regarding the acquisition of French nationality, to make it more difficult for those born in France to foreign parents to acquire nationality, and secondly, and more generally, by a continuing refusal by some elements in society to accept that those who have got French nationality are really French. This refusal to accept as French many who do in fact have French citizenship is indicated by the continuing use of the word 'immigré' (immigrant) to refer to many of the children and grandchildren of immigrants (especially of North African origin), who have always lived in France and have French nationality by law. Further the high levels of poverty and unemployment amongst these sectors of the population show that although they may formally have French citizenship, in reality there is a continuing exclusion of many from the full benefits of this citizenship.

The Stigmatisation of the 'Immigré'

As pointed out above, the use of the term 'immigré' (immigrant) has become highly politicised. One clear indicator of the way in which immigration has been seen as problematic within French political discourse is the way in which the use of the word 'immigré' has come to have very negative implications. The term 'immigré' (immigrant) can be contrasted with that of 'étranger' (foreigner), and the growing use of the former rather than the latter to describe those of foreign origin is a sign of the way in which many in France are rejecting immigrants and refusing to integrate them into French society. As Spire argues: 'without this stereotype always being conscious or explicit, the "immigré" remains associated with a socially dominated position, whereas the "étranger" is more identified with the image of an executive or scientist with a high level of education' (Spire, 1999: 50). But the distinction is about more than merely a distinction in levels of education and type of employment, it is about the unequal political, economic and social relations between two countries and two nationalities (Sayad, 1991). Whereas those from other European countries residing in France (and it must be remembered here that one of the largest group of non-French nationals within the French population is Portuguese) are more likely to be referred to as 'étrangers', the use of 'immigrés' is mainly reserved for those of Maghrebin (North African) or Sub-Saharan African origin. As a perjorative term 'immigré' is reserved for those of Algerian origin more than any other nationality. Moreover, as mentioned, one of the problems involved in the use of the term 'immigré' is that it is applied to those who are not themselves immigrants but merely descendants of immigrants. Many children and grandchildren of North African immigrants in particular, who all have French nationality, still find themselves labelled as immigrants. These 'second' or 'third' generation immigrants are still considered as part of the 'problem' of immigration, whilst those on the extreme-Right blame them for high levels of crime and insecurity, others worry about the failure of integration and the continuing high levels of poverty and exclusion amongst these groups of young people. Thus whether from an exclusionary or an inclusionary perspective, it is difficult to get rid of the label of 'immigré' which as Bonnafous argues: 'marks one out definitively with the seal of exteriority in function of a criteria which is more likely to be that of skin colour, facial features or social condition, than that of one's real origin.'(Bonnafous, 1992: 12). Gastaut (2000) traces the evolution of the language used to describe foreign residents in France and remarks that between 1973 and 1989, the term 'immigré' replaced that of 'migrant' (migrant) or 'étranger' (foreigner), thus indicating a shift in French perceptions of immigrants, from being temporary migrant workers to being a permanent 'social phantom', threatening national unity with unwelcomed cultural, linguistic and religious difference. Further, since the 1960s the use of the word 'immigré' has evolved to designate less and less those coming from another geographic area and more and more those of a different ethnic origin, whether born in France or not. This use of the term 'immigré' to refer to those who are not themselves migrants, but rather the descendants of migrants, has caused disquiet amongst young people whose parents and grandparents were immigrants. As Gastaut points out: 'These younger generations, for the most part born in France, have worked to change this "discriminatory linguistic status", but the French have found great difficulties in finding alternative terms for them: "beurs", "children of immigrants", "second generation" … thus betraying the tensions over identity in public opinion which is ill at ease when defining those which cause it problems' (Gastaut, 2000: 71).

More recently, from the mid-1980s onwards, another term has been added to the lexicography of the debate over immigration, that of the 'clandestin' (clandestine). Gastaut points to an article in *Le Monde* in 1983 which was entitled, 'Les clandestins sont parmis nous' (the clandestines are amongst us) (*Le Monde*, 28 April 1983), and argues that this usage signalled the start of the common usage of the word to describe immigrants (Gastaut, 2000: 73). As more and more of the political discourse around immigration has centred on the need to stem illegal immigration, so the term clandestine has become more and more frequently employed in reference to immigrants, invoking the idea of the immigrant as a threat to the political community, a scapegoat for the imagined collapse of a social order (Weil, 1991). This insistence of the illegality of many immigrants has further pushed the debate over immigration into the territory of security and has served to blur the impact on the human security of migrants of the exclusionary policies being advocated. The line between legal and illegal migration is, in reality a very thin one, both being in some ways parts of the same process (Kostakopoulou, 2001). Indeed, many of the *clandestins* who are the targets of campaigns against illegal immigrants have entered France legally and become *illegalised* precisely through changing policies and legislation on residence status, work permits etc. However, the use of the term *clandestin* implies someone who has transgressed the law and who is thus owed no responsibilities by the French state, someone who may be 'sacrificed to intolerance' (Miller, 1992).

The Myth of an 'Immigrant Invasion'

A constant of the anti-immigration discourse prevalent in France for the past twenty years or more has been a fear that France is being 'flooded' or 'overwhelmed' by immigrants. The work of certain demographers in predicting population trends in France for the years after 2000 has contributed towards a fear of massive migration from the poor countries of the South (Bigo, 1991; Le Bras, 1991, 1998). Thus immigration has been portrayed in terms of an 'invasion' threatening French security. This idea was reflected in an article written by the ex-president Valéry Giscard d'Estaing in 1991 in which he claimed that: 'Although, in this sensitive area, it is necessary to use words with precaution because of the emotional or historical attachments that they may have, the type of problem with which we are now faced has moved from one of immigration to one of invasion.' (*Le Figaro* Magazine, 21 September 1991). This type of language has led to a regular overestimation of the actual number of immigrants present in the French population. Opinion polls have demonstrated that over two thirds of the French public believe that there are far more immigrants in France than is actually the case (Gastaut, 2000). Similarly, most feel that there are too many immigrants. A poll carried out by SOFRES in 1990 showed that 68 per cent of those interviewed felt that there were 'too many' immigrants in France, whilst only 1 per cent felt that there were 'not enough' (*Le Nouvel Observateur*, 13 September 1990).

In fact, statistics from the official censuses reveal an ongoing stability in the proportion of immigrants in the French population since 1975. The census carried out in March 1999 showed that there were 4 310 000 immigrants resident in France, which accounts for 7.4 per cent of the French population.[3] The differences with regard to previous censuses are that the proportion of immigrants from other European countries has diminished, whilst the proportion of immigrants from North Africa (particularly Morocco) and from other parts of the world has increased (INSEE, 2000). The number of immigrants from Sub-Saharan Africa, for example, has increased by 43 per cent since the previous census in 1990. The public belief that there has been an increase in immigration in the past decades may thus be understood, amongst other things, by the perception of an increasing number of non-European or non-white immigrants amongst the immigrant population. This fits in with the growing racialisation of the immigration debate in France, and a belief that some immigrants are more acceptable than others. This 'acceptability' is most often framed in terms of the ease with which immigrants of various nationalities might be integrated into French society. An opinion poll carried out in 1988 shows that whilst European immigrants (from Italy, Spain or Portugal) are rated as integrating very easily, those from North and Sub-Saharan Africa are judged as being very difficult to integrate into French society (*Le Journal de Dimanche*, 14 February 1988). This growing divide in perceptions of European and non-European immigrants has been reinforced by the processes of European integration particularly the opening of borders within Europe and the

---

[3] These figures deal with the population of metropolitan France only and thus exclude French dependent territories overseas.

creation of European citizenship. Thus the perception of the growing visibility of non-European immigrants has reinforced the idea of an immigrant 'invasion' despite the underlying stability in the proportion of immigrants in the French population.

Of course there are always difficulties when dealing with statistics regarding immigration. Firstly, the statistics collected by INSEE during the census, classify an immigrant as someone who was born outside of France. Thus even those who now have French nationality are still immigrants according to this data. In fact, of the 4 310 000 immigrants identified by INSEE in 1999, just over one and half million have French nationality. In other words, over a third (36 per cent) of those labelled as immigrants are actually French in so far as they have French nationality. However, before this proportion of naturalized immigrants is taken as an indicator of successful incorporation of immigrants, it should be noted that rates of acquisition of French nationality differ vastly amongst immigrant groups of differing national origins. In 1999, for example, INSEE found that over 70 per cent of immigrants of Vietnamese origin had acquired French nationality, compared to less than 30 per cent for immigrants of Algerian, Moroccan or Turkish origin (INSEE 2000). Further, as Chemillier-Gendreau argues: 'frequently no distinction is made between two categories of foreigners, those born outside France and those born within our territory. Thus people talk about a global figure of 3 600 000 foreigners' (Chemillier-Gendreau, 1998:24) This synthesis between two different categories of non-French residents means that the figures for immigrants without French nationality include children born to foreign parents within France, and although the rights of these children to automatically acquire French nationality have been restricted under changing nationality laws (see chapter 2 for more detail), they still retain their potential right to acquire nationality under the principles of the 'droit du sol' (right of the soil).

Beyond these issues of classifications and categorisations of who is and who is not an 'immigrant' or a 'foreigner', there is also the question of those who escape any kind of statistical analysis ie 'illegal' immigrants. As will be discussed further in chapters two and three, the whole question of 'illegal' immigrants has been made more complicated by the changes in conditions governing immigration and residence in France which have meant that many who had entered France legally and had been residing there legally have become 'illegal'. The exact number of 'illegal' immigrants in France is impossible to establish, and thus this group of immigrants have provided ample material for the fantasies of the extreme-Right concerning immigrant invasion. Even more moderate politicians and commentators have tended to over-estimate these figures when attempting to use the immigration issue to gain public support. A book published in 1994, for example, contests the statistical methods employed by official organisations and accuses these organisations of using 'camouflage figures' to hide the real scale of immigration. The author, Michel Massenet, suggests that in fact there could be about one million illegal immigrants in France (Massenet, 1994). A similar figure was suggested by two deputies from the RPR-UDF majority who presented a report to the Prime Minister, Alain Juppé, in 1996 (de Courson and Léonard, 1996). In fact, the probable total of 'illegal' immigrants is much lower. A report by the ILO in 1991 estimated that there were about 300 000 people residing in France illegally. This estimate would seem to be born out by the numbers of people asking for regularisation of their papers when governments have offered this. In 1981 when the newly elected Socialist government offered to regularise illegal immigrants, 130 000 people benefited from this regularisation, out of a total of 180 000 who came forward with their papers. In 1997, under the Socialist government of Lionel Jospin, there was again a promise of regularisation of some illegal immigrants and about 150 000 dossiers were presented to the authorities (although as will be discussed in chapter 3, there has been disappointment at the number of people actually receiving regular residence papers following this promise). Although in both cases it must be assumed that there were a number of immigrants who did not present themselves for this regularisation, presuming beforehand that it would not be granted, it would be difficult to imagine that this number was more than double that of those who did present their papers, thus suggesting that the total number of illegal immigrants is far from the million mark suggested by some and much closer to the figure estimated by the ILO. Tribalat makes another important point in respect to the statistics regarding illegal immigrants when she comments that it would be wrong to amalgamate those immigrants omitted from the census with those who did not have legal residence papers. In fact some of those without legal residence papers are included in the census figures of immigrants and thus it would be erroneous to assume that the estimated figure of illegal immigrants should be added on to the figure for immigrants in France arrived at by the official census in order to arrive at the total number of immigrants in France (Tribalat, 1996).

Towards Postnational Citizenship?

Many have pointed to France's particular conception of citizenship, linked to its Republican tradition, and to its willingness to incorporate foreigners and make them into citizens (Brubaker, 1992; Hollifield, 1999). Certainly there is a case for arguing that in the past France has been more open to the inclusion of non-nationals through naturalisation and assimilation into the French state. However, there have been changes in the past decades which suggest an end to this openness, and whilst the Republican aim of assimilation still appears strong in some senses (see for example chapter 7 on the *affaire des foulards*), there has been a growth in exclusionary factors which prevent immigrants from obtaining and exercising citizenship rights. And even the discourse of integration (which has largely replaced the concept of assimilation) can be seen to act as a factor of differentiation and also of exclusion (Lapeyronnie, 1998). As Castles and Davidson suggest, these exclusionary factors are both formal – based on new laws on immigration and the acquisition of nationality -, and de facto – based on different structures of discrimination within French society (Castles and Davidson, 2000). They describe this de facto exclusion from full citizenship which they argue exists in most countries where, 'there are significant groups, usually marked by race, by ethnicity or by being indigenous peoples, who are denied full participation as citizens. They may have the right to vote, but social, economic and cultural exclusion denies them the chance of gaining political representation or of having any real say in the decisions that affect their lives' (Castles and Davidson, 2000: 11). In the context of France, it might be suggested that this second type of de facto exclusion from full participation as citizens occurs particularly with groups marked out by race and ethnicity – the high levels of unemployment suffered by those of African or Asian origin, the lack of access to equal health care, the absence of political representatives are all signs of this de facto exclusion. This type of exclusion contrasts with the belief that France, like other European countries is experiencing the development of a postnational form of citizenship.

There are various different arguments concerning the spread of postnational citizenship, arguments which are both empirical and normative. The argument that will concern us here primarily is the empirical argument that states that as migration has become a greater and greater phenomenon both numerically and in terms of its global scope, then both the sheer scale of migration and also international pressures to establish and defend universal human rights based on personhood and not on national belonging, have lead to the development of new forms of postnational citizenship which extend rights equally to all members of society whether national citizens or not. Based on her observations on the incorporation of migrant workers into European societies, Yasemin Soysal suggests that these countries provide good examples of the development of postnational citizenship. Soysal's notion of postnational citizenship suggests that 'national citizenship is losing ground to a more universal model of membership, anchored in deterritorialized notions of persons' rights' (Soysal, 1994: 3). Resident aliens now have almost identical civil and social rights to nationals, rights which are underwritten by states' agreement to international conventions and treaties on human rights. Further, despite their lack of full political citizenship, these non-nationals have been incorporated into the national state through the operation of immigrant associations and representation of these in political institutions (political rights have also been extended to non-national residents in some European countries through the granting of voting rights in local elections, although this has not happened in France and indeed has been a subject of very bitter debate as will be explained below and in chapter 5). Although Soysal does admit that there may be an 'implementation deficit' with regard to the rights granted to non-nationals she argues that 'though empirical inequalities of race, gender, and class persist, the existence of formally encoded rights has rendered the unequivocal exclusion of migrants from membership unjustifiable and unsustainable' (Soysal, 1994: 135).

This type of argument about the inevitable spread of rights to non-national migrants and the incorporation of these migrants into European societies, might however, seem somewhat over-optimistic. This book will aim to expose the limitations of such an argument by highlighting the continuing exclusion and insecurity faced not only by non-nationals resident in France, but also by many of immigrant origin who have actually acquired French nationality. Indeed, it could be argued that the growing racialisation of the immigration and citizenship debates in countries like France has, if anything, increased the insecurities faced by populations of immigrant origin.

If we examine Soysal's particular argument concerning postnational citizenship, it may be constrained on a general level by pointing out the failure of many states to actually adhere to and apply the international laws and conventions which protect individual human rights. As Castles and Davidson point out: 'international human rights conventions are often not ratified: for example, the 1990 UN Convention on the Rights of Migrant Workers and Members of their Families has only been signed by a handful of emigration countries. Moreover, they may not be implemented where they are ratified' (Castles and Davidson, 2000: 19). It could even be pointed out that some conventions which have been ratified and implemented in the past might now be being undermined by the determination of some states to limit migratory flows. French governments have several times attempted to block the route to migration for family reunification (a principle protected under international law), and although they have not been able to stop family reunification completely, the conditions that they have imposed on this type of migration have made it very hard for migrants to meet necessary criteria. And another example of this undermining of international conventions might be provided by the various new laws governing refugee status that France has introduced which could be argued to be damaging implementation of the Geneva Convention of 1951.[4]

Soysal is not alone in pointing to the role of international laws and conventions in promoting the rights of migrants in Europe. Hollifield (1992) highlights the liberal tendencies of advanced industrial states like France. He argues that whilst up until the mid-70s immigration was fuelled by market forces, at the same time a rights-based system was put in place to protect immigrants. Thus since the oil crisis of 1973 and the subsequent attempts to limit immigration, immigrants have still been able to rely on the rights granted to them under international and national laws. In a more recent article, Hollifield (1999) admits that French governments have tried to limit immigration not only through external border controls but also by 'attacking civil rights and liberties' and by 'going after certain social rights, specifically healthcare'. He still concludes, however, that: 'When the state crossed the invisible line between immigration control (on the one hand), to the point of becoming a threat to civil society and being at odds with the founding (republican) principles of the regime (on the other hand), institutional/judicial, ideological and social checks came into play' (Hollifield 1999: 93). The institutional/judicial checks that Hollifield refers to can be found mainly in the rulings of the Conseil d'Etat (Council of State). However, whilst the role of the Conseil d'Etat in providing an institutional/judicial check on government attempts to limit immigration cannot be set aside, the power of the Conseil d'Etat to guarantee the rights of immigrants is limited and thus immigrants in France cannot rely for their security on national laws any more than they can on international convention. For example, the Conseil d'Etat did force a modification in the 1997 Debré law on immigration, but this modification did not change the overall impact and direction of the law. Such institutional/judicial checks are no

---

[4] The evolution of laws concerning refugee status will be discussed in greater detail in chapter 2.

real safeguard of immigrants' rights against the determination of a government to limit immigration. Further, it may be argued that the fact that the Conseil d'Etat has had to intervene to try and uphold Republican principles of individual rights in the face of government policy, is worrying in itself. Weil affirms that the frequent and continuing intervention of the Conseil d'Etat 'demonstrates clearly the difficulties that politicians have in distinguishing for themselves the Republican rules for action in this domain' (Weil, 1991: 312). In terms of the social checks mentioned by Hollifield as another limitation on the powers of government to exclude migrants and take away their rights, we can point to the huge public mobilisation against certain government legislation and actions, for example a mobilisation in support of the *sans-papiers* (see chapter 4) and against the Debré laws of 1997. However, again it can be argued that there are limits to the extent that these 'social checks' can work against a government's determination to pursue exclusionary immigration policies. Hollifield points particularly to the public objection to the clause of the Debré law which required French citizens to notify the local authorities whenever they received any non-European foreigner to stay in their homes. This article was subject to amendment in the law that was finally adopted. However, other, and some might argue, more restrictive articles of this law, were adopted unchanged. It is interesting to note in this case that the protests about the article of the law which required citizens to notify the authorities if a foreigner was staying with them were challenged on the basis that they infringed the rights and liberties of French citizens. Thus although there was general protest about the ways in which the Debré law would undermine the insecurity of immigrants and foreign residents, the massive mobilisation might be seen to be more the result of a perceived challenge to the rights of French nationals. Further, the admission by many French that they have racist sentiments (see chapter 8), and the widespread support for the anti-immigrant Front National, would seem to indicate that the social checks which might have been assumed to prevent government restrictions on immigrants' rights are not as strong as some have suggested.

Aside from a faith in the role of international and national laws in preserving the rights of migrants in liberal states, others see the market itself and its interactions with the political class as a guarantor of expansionist immigration policies which will tend to grant rights to non-national immigrants in liberal societies. Freeman, for example, contends that liberal states have a built in tendency towards expansive immigration policies because those who advocate such policies e.g. business interests which require migrant labour, are more organised and have better access to government decision-makers than those who oppose immigration (Freeman, 1995). Again, this argument could be said to have been true for France in the period up until 1974 when to some extent, successive governments allowed businesses to take the lead in recruiting migrants and arranging for their entry into France.

Faith in liberal politics and institutions to guarantee citizenship rights to immigrants might also be misplaced in light of the recent developments in European immigration and asylum policy which could be argued to have distanced policy-making from either democratic oversight or judicial control (Geddes,

2000:19). Whilst some have seen the Europeanisation of immigration and asylum policy as a sign of loss of control by national governments over these policies, others have pointed to the ways in which supranationalisation may in fact have allowed governments to pass on unpopular or difficult policy decisions to a higher level. The opening up of internal borders within Europe has certainly led to a greater emphasis on the security of external borders, and it might be argued that this emphasis has had a negative impact both on immigrants trying to enter the EU, and on non-EU nationals already within the EU borders. Further, the instigation of European citizenship rights through the Maastricht and Amsterdam treaties has in some ways only served to highlight the difference between EU citizens and third country nationals within Europe, legitimising various forms of discrimination between these two groups of residents.

The failure of both national and international laws and conventions, and liberal institutions to guarantee the rights of migrants seems to indicate that postnational citizenship is not as close as some might argue. In fact, it may be argued that more and more importance is being placed on the national element of citizenship in many countries, and this might seem particularly true in France. Whilst, as remarked above, France has traditionally made it relatively easy for immigrants to acquire nationality based on the droit du sol (jus soli) rather than just on the droit du sang (jus sanguinis), recent attempts to change the nationality laws and the huge debates that these have provoked serve to demonstrate just how important nationality is in debates over citizenship. Moreover, there is still a clear distinction between the rights of national and non-nationals, and those like Soysal (1994) who postulate a postnational citizenship might be said to be overstating the extent to which non-national immigrants have rights in countries like France. Rights have been granted to immigrants without their having acquired French citizenship, but these rights are fragile and liable to be withdrawn without notice – this creates an increasingly insecure situation for these citizens. In an attempt to deter immigration, for example, the governments of the 1990s made it increasingly difficult for non-national immigrants to receive healthcare. The withdrawal of such a basic right as the right to health illustrates clearly on what fragile grounds non-nationals' rights are based. To claim, as Soysal does that 'the scope and inventory of noncitizens' rights do not differ significantly from those of citizens' (Soysal, 1994: 119) seems barely credible when in France many are denied access to health, social services or education provision for their children. Further these 'noncitizens' may not even have security of residence, being liable to deportation if they are classified as 'illegal' residents. Those immigrants who do not have French nationality are constantly open to such changes in their status. And as the case of the sans-papiers shows, non-national migrants can never even have security in their rights of residence in France. Many of those who found themselves without legal residence papers and liable to deportation from France had in fact been living in the country, working and exercising what they thought were their rights for many years.

A further difficulty with the notion of postnational citizenship is that although non-nationals who have legal residence status may have access to many civil and social rights, they do by any means possess full political rights. The issue of granting political rights to non-citizens in France has been a contentious one. Prior to his election as President in 1981, François Mitterrand had promised to grant non-citizens the right to vote in local elections. This proposal to grant voting rights to non-nationals stemmed from a movement within the French Left which called for a recognition of diversity (*le droit à la différence*) and for a new form of citizenship based upon residence rather than nationality and centred round the granting of political (and particularly voting) rights to immigrants (Favell, 1998). However, this proposition to allow non-nationals to vote in local elections was soon dropped under pressure from the Right-wing, with the Socialist Party seeing it as a potential vote loser. And beyond this rejection of the idea of extending political rights to non-citizens as a potential vote loser, there has been an expression of mistrust of the idea at a more fundamental ideological level, based on the maintenance of republican values of citizenship. As pointed out above, French Republicanism has traditionally involved a political rather than an ethnic conception of the nation, and it is this point which has proved the sticking point for some with regard to the extension of voting rights to non-nationals. Weil, for example, argues that it is precisely because French nationhood is constructed on the basis of the exercise of political rights that it would be wrong to open these rights to non-nationals. To grant political rights independently of the granting of nationality would, he affirms, risk provoking an unwanted counter-effect, namely a retraction to a more closed ethno-cultural conception of nationhood (Weil, 1991: 300). This assertion that the current dependence on nationality for the granting of political rights provides a barrier against encroaching ethno-cultural divisions and inequalities might be convincing by those who are still attached to the model of republican universalism developed during the first half of the century. However, if Republican universalism and discourses of human rights have thus far failed to prevent a growing level of exclusion from full citizenship in an era of growing globalisation and migration, is it then time to re-examine the very essence of French Republicanism and its particular concepts of citizenship and nationhood? Others have argued that rather than providing a barrier against encroaching ethno-cultural divisions, the refusal to grant political rights to immigrants actually intensifies these divisions by reinforcing the exclusions to which non-nationals are subjected. Chemillier-Gendreau, for example, argues in response to Weil's point that: 'However subtle this argument may be, on reflection it is unacceptable. It accentuates the exclusionary character of the nation state and fixes it in an unchanging configuration. The improvement of the lives of all within a community or a region is not conceivable without the participation of those concerned, whoever they may be' (Chemillier-Gendreau, 1998: 77).

A System of Stratified Rights

Rather than claiming universal implementation of post-national citizenship rights, it might be more fruitful and more accurate to examine the rights of immigrants in France in terms of a constantly evolving set of stratified rights which aim to tread a fine line between the exclusion of migrants and the preservation of resources for national citizens, and the need to respect (to some degree at least) the assertion of human rights.

Morris (2002) proposes a framework for the analysis of migrants' rights in terms of civic stratification. Her framework includes three sets of oppositions, between civic exclusion and inclusion, civic gain and deficit, and civic expansion and contraction (this is a slightly amended version of a framework of civic stratification proposed by Lockwood, 1996). Civic exclusion and inclusion refer to the formal denial or granting of rights; civil gain and deficit to the enhancement or impaired implementation of those rights due to informal processes; and civic expansion and contraction refer to 'the shifting character of a regime of rights or of a particular area within its ambit' (Morris, 2002: 410). This model of stratification may be more useful for analysing the ways in which the citizenship status of immigrants has developed in recent years than a model which implies a more homogenous process of extending (or retrenching) the rights afforded to non-nationals. It is also useful in that it takes into account both formal and informal processes for extending or denying rights, thus acknowledging that discriminations in the extension of rights to different groups are not just the result of legal differentiations between categories of residents.

The use of a model of stratified rights allows us, therefore, to take into consideration the ways in which formal and informal divisions have developed between the ways in which different categories are included/excluded from citizenship rights in a variety of areas. Various hierarchies of stratification may be formulated and these vary across different spheres of rights, in other words, different processes of exclusion/inclusion, gain/deficit, and expansion/contraction may relate to political rights than those applying to economic or welfare rights. And whilst it may be argued (in opposition to claims of post-national citizenship), that nationality remains the primary criteria of discrimination with regard to rights, a whole hierarchy of other divisions and discriminations are pertinent, so that, as Lochak suggests: 'Discrimination is truly at the root of the legal conditions of foreigners: the principle of discrimination appearing as the matrix within which all of the past, present and future status of the foreigner is determined' (Lochak, 1985: 86). These discriminations thus operate not only in relation to the division between nationals and non-nationals/foreigners, but also in relation to divisions between French nationals of 'immigrant origin', naturalised nationals, non-nationals from within the EU, foreigners with long-term (ten-year) residence permits, those with short-term residence permits (e.g. students), those with or without a work permit, those with no legal status (the issue of the various categories of 'illegal' immigrants will be discussed further in chapter 4 concerning the *sans-papiers*). All of these divisions and categorisations are relevant to the ways in which various individuals may benefit (or not) from different rights and citizenship status. The ways in which various government's have attempted to limit immigration by using internal controls to 'roll back' the rights (particularly social and welfare rights) of immigrants already in France (see chapters 2, 4 and 5), has only served to increase the stratification present. The attempts of the Chirac/Raffarin government to reform the *Aide Médicale d'Etat* (State Medical Assistance) which provides free health care to all, irrespective of resident/nationality status, provides an example of this (see chapter 4).

The issues of immigrants' political, and social and economic rights will be discussed further in chapter 4, for the moment it is sufficient to note the complexity of the various stratifications of rights in these areas, and to highlight the over-simplification of adopting any model of post-national citizenship which points to a continual process of expansion of citizenship rights to non-nationals. Certainly there are rights which are common to all residents whether national or not, but the increasingly politicised nature of the debate over immigration has meant that some of these rights are now under pressure, and there is a continuing process of flux in the boundaries of rights between different categories of resident. In addition, informal processes linked to the presence of racism and xenophobia might be seen to be contracting the field of exercise of rights of some categories of residents.

Assimilation or Integration: Two-Sides of the Same Coin?

Alongside the debate over the entry of immigrants into France, and the extent of the citizenship rights to which immigrants should be entitled, there has been a linked debate over the 'integration' or 'assimilation' of immigrants. One of the major difficulties in discussing integration is that it is a concept which is almost impossible to measure, and which has been defined in many differing ways, with these definitions varying according to the perceptions of immigration and of the French nation. As Banton argues, the concept of integration rests on 'a mathematical metaphor, which assumes that the social processes of group interaction can be likened to the mathematical processes of making up a whole number' (Banton, 2001: 152). Clearly the various social, political and economic processes encompassed by the notion of integration cannot be resumed as a single progression. Further, the heterogeneity of the populations of immigrant origin in France, makes any attempt to define a single or exemplary course of integration highly problematic. Despite these definitional problems, the notion of integration has been one that has been widely used in terms of research and policy-making with regards to the position of immigrants and ethnic minorities in French society. The concept of integration has also been seen by many as preferable to the more ideologically loaded concept of 'assimilation', although in recent years in France there has been something of a revival in the promotion of assimilation as an ideal, as will be discussed below.

The idea of assimilation is, according to most opinions, a key feature of French Republican ideology, along with universalism, unitarism, and secularism (Hargreaves, 1995). It is a notion which stems from the belief that citizenship should be founded on a high level of cultural cohesion, and that if immigrants wished to become French citizens they should accept French culture and values. The term assimilation fell into disuse in the post-war years, tainted as it was with colonial connotations (Hargreaves, 1995), but has enjoyed something of a revival in recent years, particularly as supporters of this concept have contrasted it favourably with Anglo-Saxon models of multiculturalism. Emmanuel Todd, for example, maintains that the idea of assimilating immigrants is a valuable part of the French tradition, which should not be ceded to the encroaching 'differentialism' of the Anglo-Saxon world (Todd, 1994). Any move that the government might make towards multiculturalism (acknowledging the right to difference) argues Todd, merely creates incomprehension on the part of the citizens thus contributing towards support for the extreme-Right, and means a growing insecurity for immigrants of African origin, resulting in 'the psychological and social disorientation of the second generation' (Todd, 1994: 382). Todd, and other pro-assimilationists, argue that in any case, the process of assimilation is inevitable and is already underway. Christian Jelen, for example, points to the historical example of Polish, Italian and Jewish immigrants who were thought to be inassimilable, but who were in fact well integrated into French society. He argues that: 'Despite handicaps and obstacles of all kinds, the integration of Mahrebis (North Africans) is an irreversible process that has already begun' (Jelen, 1991: 216).

The argument made by those who favour assimilation, that the politics of multiculturalism, and recognition of difference plays into the hands of the extreme-Right, has been commonly adopted in France, even by those who do not openly promote assimilation as such. A short-lived movement in favour of multiculturalism emerged in the 1980s among members of the Socialist party and the intellectual Left, organised around the slogan *le droit à la différence* (the right to difference) (Favell, 1998). However, this movement had little success, running into particular difficulties over the *affaire du foulard* (the headscarf affair) and the debate over secularism in French schools, which led to a heated defence of Republican ideals (see chapter 7). The slogan *le droit à la différence* was also undermined by its adoption in an inverted sense by the Front National. The Front played on the idea of difference, arguing that France and French nationals had the right to be different to preserve their own particular culture from the encroachments of immigrant cultures, globalisation and multiculturalism. In order to counter this extreme-Right discourse, the Left fell back on the defence of the traditional values of Republicanism, arguing that immigrants should be accorded citizenship rights on the basis of their integration into the French nation.

The emphasis on integration in political discourse on immigration, and the perceived need to defend the universalism central to Republican values, has meant that the French state has refused any kind of official recognition of minority groups, either for affirmative or redistributive action (Favell, 1998). Reports of the *Haut Conseil à l'intégration* (the High Commission on Integration) set up by Prime Minister Michel Rocard in 1989, repeatedly state that the French state does not recognise collective rights that are specific to minorities but only universal individual rights (Haut Conseil à l'intégration, 1997). Jennings summarises the French republican philosophy of integration in four propositions, namely, the integration of immigrants must be in accord with the secularism of the state which respects religious beliefs but gives them no special support; it is individuals rather than groups which integrate and support for this integration should not in any way support the constitution of structured communities; integration presupposes rights and duties; immigrants and French nationals should be treated equally, integration should not favour immigrants but should benefit all and create collective cohesion. This philosophy of integration is problematic, however, faced with a culturally, ethnically and religiously diverse population, and a society which is socially and economically divided. Whilst the *affaire du foulard* (headscarf affair) revealed the limits of cultural integration, the continuing economic exclusion of many of the population of immigrant origin together with their lack of political representation seems to demonstrate the failure of the Republican model to propose any real solutions as to the functional integration of immigrants i.e. the ways in which their economic and political participation and rights can be made equal to that of French nationals. In these circumstances it might be right to question the continuing validity of the Republican model, as Castles and Davidson argue:

> The republican model worked well as long as the dominant group was willing to assimilate others, and the economy was able to provide a reasonable level of social integration to all. But how well has the republican model coped with globalization and the immigration of the Other? (Castles and Davidson, 2000: 15).

This (partial) 'failure' of integration is also documented by Dominique Schnapper who concludes that whilst the migrant populations installed in France do not constitute any threat to national unity and whilst their diversity is not a barrier to successful integration, the social and economic conditions of many of the population of immigrant origin do present a cause for concern. Schnapper argues that two considerations in particular must be faced when judging the success or failure of the Republican project of integration. Firstly, the fact that immigrants and their children are over-represented amongst the populations living in poor and dangerous suburbs of big cities, where 'the disappearance of the working-class culture has left a space for the emergence of situations of anomie' (Schnapper, 1991: 203). Children of immigrants, and particularly those of Maghrebin origin, are often faced with social problems, and make up a large proportion of those in special education and of the unemployed. The high visibility of these groups of young people of immigrant origin carries the risk of provoking and accentuating sentiments of xenophobia, which in turn may incite conflicts between groups of different origins. Secondly, there is a risk that the social and economic handicaps and exclusions faced by these immigrants will be multiplied and intensified as the generations progress, leading to further and greater exclusions. This superposition of social and ethnic handicaps will damage any progress towards integration. These difficulties with integration must be addressed not through a culpabilisation of immigrants for their failure to integrate, but through a critical examination of the role of the modern nation (Schnapper, 1991).

Faced with the difficulties of the Republican model of integration (or assimilation), some have proposed other models to promote the inclusion and citizenship of populations of immigrant origin. The movement for the *droit à la différence* was, as described above, relatively short lived. Other conceptions of modes of inclusion have avoided this claim of difference and have anchored themselves instead within the idea of citizenship. Within this perspective it is argued that immigration and its consequences are only one aspect of a more generalised crisis of citizenship in France, and that this crisis needs to be addressed through a re-examination of the meanings of citizenship. Bouamama, for example, has called for a new citizenship based on a shared social project. He argues for a rejection of the 'melting-pot' approach to integration and concludes instead that:

> The new citizenship demands profound cultural mutations which, in their turn, are only possible if the national bond is found in the sharing of a collective project for society and not in a presumed homogeneous and unique national culture. It anticipates inevitable social mutations (Bouamama et al., 1992: 195).

Those who argue for such a new citizenship reject both the right to difference on one hand, and the link between nationality and citizenship on the other. They claim that without social, economic and political equality the right to difference can only be 'a project designed to maintain injustice' (Bouamama, 1994: 19). On the other hand, the continuing link between nationality and access to rights maintains a position whereby the only form of inclusion is through exclusion of those perceived not to belong to this nation. Thus the proponents of new citizenship reject France's opposition to multiculturalism, but at the same time reject communitariansim and call for the acceptation of universalist values based on a community created not from national bonds but from shared social project and goals.

The work of sociologists such as Wieviorka and Touraine has also called into question the French opposition to multiculturalism, by attempting to demonstrate that the reclamation of an ethnic identity, particularly amongst young people, does not signify an attachment to a fixed community identity, but is rather a modern expression of individual subjectivity. Wieviorka supports what he calls a medium position between a total recognition of the right to difference and a resistance to any type of differentialism. This middle way would involve a valorisation of ethnic difference within the limits of universalist principles (Wieviorka, 1993a).

Conclusion

The new theories of integration proposed by the proponents of new citizenship and by supporters of a French multiculturalism show the ways in which the French Republic might deal with the fact that ethnic difference is now, whether desired or not, a reality for French society. However, the practical adoption of such conceptions by policy-makers would depend on a shift in the discourse on immigration and integration, a shift which will be difficult to make. In fact, as the problems of integration are posed more and more acutely it seems that policy-makers have fallen back to a greater and greater extent on the old rhetoric of Republicanism, 'making dogmatic stands about sacred national values, virtues and ideals' (Favell, 1998: 248). As Favell has argued with regard to the integration policies of both France and the UK, 'instead of addressing the causes of integration failure – notably poverty, declining welfare and inequality – these states promote an increasingly centralised ideological consensus around cultural and value issues' (Favell, 1998: 252). The result of such a failure to address real and practical problems of integration can only be the boosting of populist and xenophobic sentiments, and the creation of greater insecurities for immigrants and their descendants. The following chapters will examine the ways in which immigration policy has been increasingly driven by this ideological consensus around French cultural values, and the ways in which these policies have served not to widen access to citizenship rights but on the contrary to create new forms of exclusion and insecurity.

Chapter 2

The Development of Immigration Policy in a European Context

In the years since the official suspension of labour migration in 1974 France has introduced a whole series of new laws to regulate immigration and the acquisition of nationality. These policies are specific to France with its particular history of immigration and conceptions of nationhood and citizenship. However, there are also growing external pressures which influence policies, particularly those emanating from continuing European integration. Immigration policies thus need to be considered within the context of France's membership of the European Union, and the continued attempts of the EU to agree on common immigration and asylum policies that they can enforce. The difficulties involved both in agreeing common immigration and asylum policies for all the member states of the EU, and then in implementing such policies if they were agreed, have been well-documented (Geddes, 2000). There is a growing tendency amongst European countries, however, to commit to ever-more restrictive targets on immigration, leading to the creation of what some have termed 'Fortress Europe'. One of the contributory elements to the maintenance of restrictive immigration targets has been their perceived electoral appeal, with governments thus wanting to appear 'tough' on immigration issues. As Geddes remarks: 'It is a sad fact that there are few votes in being nice to immigrants.' (Geddes, 2000: 26). Further, immigration has been seen more and more in terms of security, and this rationale has encouraged tighter and tighter controls being put in place. Immigration and asylum are seen as threats to the 'societal security' of states (Waever et al., 1993), posing a threat to national identities and hampering governments in their quest to control their populations. Increasingly also, immigration and asylum have been linked with the security threat posed by terrorism (Koser, 2001). This perceived relationship between immigration and security was highlighted by the effects of the terrorist attacks of September 2001 in the USA, and their aftermath on the treatment of immigrants (particularly Muslim immigrants) in the EU. The links between immigration and security were drawn explicitly in the French presidential and election campaigns of 2002, when both the Far-Right Front National and the moderate Right-Wing RPR and UDF emphasized the issue of insecurity in their campaigns and linked this to the need for greater control of immigration. Following the victory of Jacques Chirac in the presidential elections, and the moderate Right in the legislative elections, the new government has acted quickly to instigate reform in immigration and asylum policies.

Amongst the first actions of the new Interior Minister, Nicolas Sarkozy, was to reach agreement with the British Government over the eventual closure of the Sangatte Camp for asylum seekers near Calais, as well as the installation of tighter controls and higher security around the Channel Tunnel. The issue of Sangatte also highlights one of the real driving forces behind the growing supranationalisation of European immigration and asylum policies i.e. the need to sustain the principle of free movement of goods and people within the EU which is one of the central tenets of European integration. One of the elements at stake in the Sangatte controversy has been the perceived impediments to the free movement of goods through the Channel Tunnel created by asylum seekers' attempts to smuggle themselves through the tunnel. The UK put pressure on the French government to close the camp and to reinforce security round the entrance to the Tunnel, both to discourage asylum seekers from entering the UK, and also to protect the movement of goods through the Tunnel. This issue illustrated the ways in which continued European integration and the opening up of internal borders was seen as a threat to national security, and it is thus clear how states have pushed for tighter controls on immigration and movement of third country nationals within the EU. The putting into place of a system of free movement of goods and of people in the EU has had clear legal and political implications for the movement of third country nationals both into and within the EU, but it may be argued that these third country nationals are largely overlooked by the provisions of the various EU Treaties which enshrine free movement, and that in fact, their existence somehow disturbs the basic philosophy of the European Union. As Brochmann remarks: 'The legal status of third country nationals living in an EU memberstate (resident aliens) was not contained in the Single European Act, even though this group now constitutes the majority of the immigrant population in Western Europe.' (Brochmann, 1999: 18).

France, like other EU members seems to be in the process of reinforcing the 'fortress' against unwanted immigrants. This must be done, however, within the structures put in place by the EU. As remarked above, attempts to agree on a common European immigration and asylum policy are closely linked to the moves towards creating European citizenship and guaranteeing free movement of European citizens within the EU. In order to open up internal borders within Europe, member states have felt the need to impose stricter controls on the external borders of the EU. One of the most significant steps towards opening internal frontiers was the Schengen Agreement of 1985, of which France was one of the initial signatories (along with Belgium, Germany, Luxembourg and the Netherlands). The Agreement was implemented in 1995 and the Schengen system included within the full EU structure in the Amsterdam Treaty of 1997 (with provision for the UK and Ireland to continue to opt out of the Schengen area). Although there have been many difficulties in implementing the Schengen acquis, the agreement and its implementation remain important as a key to understanding the direction in which European border control is moving. The Agreement of 1985 stated that:

In regard to the free movement of persons, the Parties shall endeavour to abolish the controls at the common frontiers and transfer them to their external frontiers. To that end they shall first endeavour to harmonise, where necessary, the laws and administrative provisions concerning prohibitions and restrictions which form the basis for the controls and to take complementary measures to safeguard security and combat illegal immigration by nationals of States that are not members of the European Communities.[1]

The emphasis here is clearly on the need to install further safeguards on external borders in order to realise the opening of internal borders. Immigration is thus placed firmly in the realms of security. The implementation of Schengen should have had some benefits for non-European citizens – principally the right to free movement for third country nationals who have entered the Schengen area legally. However, this right to free movement within the Schengen area has not been full realised because of the difficulties they have encountered in receiving and using their Schengen visas. And even in this supposed right of free movement, a clear distinction is made between EU and third country nationals with the latter being subject to myriad conditions on their movement, including, for example, the obligation to report to the appropriate authorities within three days of their arrival in another country. Further, the granting of such a right to free movement for third country nationals within the Schengen area has been balanced by the imposition of more restrictive conditions on entry into the Schengen area and an increasing internal controls through the Schengen information system (a vast computerised database) and greater police powers to stop and control identity. France has been one of the most vocal countries in the Schengen area in terms of demanding greater border controls and amplified efforts to reduce 'illegal' immigration from all the other partners (Brochmann, 1999). This use of the Schengen area as a way of attempting to increase border controls and limit immigration more strictly can be seen as part of a general trend whereby France, like other European states, has used the EU and the supranationalisation of immigration policy as a way of reasserting control over 'unwanted' migration (Geddes, 2001). And this use of the EU to reduce 'unwanted' migration can be seen to be extending to the areas of refugee and asylum policy as well. As Lavenex argues with regard to refugee and asylum policy in Europe: 'European integration does have an important impact by providing a forum for the pursuit of predominantly restrictive policies' (Lavenex, 2000: 179). Thus the 'communitarisation' of immigration and asylum policy through its move to the first pillar of the EU under the Amsterdam Treaty of 1997, should not be seen merely as a loss of control for European states as immigration moves from the intergovernmental to the supranational policy-making arena. In fact, rather than penalising the individual member states through a loss of control over immigration and asylum policy, this change might be seen as useful in advancing the 'selfish' interests of these member states in limiting immigration (Van Selm, 2002). This pursuit of the interests of member states through supra-nationalisation of immigration and asylum policy might be seen as advancing

---

[1] Article 17, Schengen Agreement.

further through the summits at Tampere in 1999, Laeken in 2001, Seville in 2002, and Thessalonika in 2003. These summits re-affirmed the necessity of putting in place common European policies on asylum and immigration and strengthened the commitment to further measures to ensure the security of the EU's external borders. However, the outcomes of these summits might also be seen as demonstrating the maintenance of intergovernmental control over the very sensitive issues of immigration and asylum, with a failure to reach final agreement on many questions under discussion. As in many areas of EU policy-making, a hybridity between supranational and intergovernmental influences remains, but within this complexity of decision making processes can be seen a process whereby the changing relationship between European states has created a new understanding of 'good' and 'bad' forms of migration (Geddes, 2003), and where the opening of internal borders and the creation of European citizenship has reinforced worries about the security of external borders and the status of non-citizens within the European area.

French immigration policies since 1974 can thus be seen in the context of a general consensus within the EU on the necessity of imposing stricter controls, and whilst some might regard European integration and the creation of the Schengen Area as having removed some of France's internal security with regard to border controls, at another level it is useful to see the moves toward supra-nationalisation of immigration and asylum policy as another tool by which national governments have been able to advance their goal of limiting inward migration into France. The rest of the chapter will analyse the various developments and reforms in nationality and immigration policy in France in the context of this larger European framework.

Immigration Policy After 1974

Following the suspension of labour migration in 1974, immigration policies were centred around the imperatives of further reducing migratory flows, encouraging return migration to reduce the numbers of foreigners in France, and at the same time 'integrating' those immigrants who wished to remain. The goal of reducing immigration – and even a wish expressed by some to reach a target of 'zero immigration' – has met obstacles in that the French state has been unable to ban immigration for family reunification, and for asylum seekers, and in the inability to stop 'illegal' immigration. However, successive governments, of both the Right and the Left have introduced measures aimed at further limiting and controlling immigration.

Between 1974 and 1981, under the presidency of Giscard d'Estaing, the issue of immigration was placed firmly onto the main political agenda, with the two principal aims announced of control and integration. Following the official suspension of migration in July 1974, another circular was issued which suspended immigration for family reunification. This second circular was judged unconstitutional by the Conseil d'Etat, and was reversed in May 1975. However, the new circular introduced strict criteria for the granting of family reunification which were designed to severely limit the numbers entering through these means. Alongside these measures of control, attempts were made at integration mainly through improving the living conditions of foreign workers and their families who were already settled in France. In October 1974, the Secretary of State for Foreign Workers (a newly created post under the Giscard presidency), announced a package of twenty five measures regarding immigration. As well as promising greater control of migratory flows, these measures aimed to provide better housing for immigrants, to organise a structure to help immigrants adapt and integrate, to provide education and professional training, to put in place organisations to help with the social integration of immigrant workers, and to progressively grant immigrants the same rights as those of French nationals. In a meeting of the Council of Ministers, Giscard promoted this new programme by arguing that 'French brotherhood should extend to immigrant workers who contribute to our productivity and our progress' (cited in Wihtol de Wenden, 1988: 195). However the rhetoric of integration and of improving the lives of immigrant workers proved to be far removed from reality, particularly once the issue of the costs of these steps to integration emerged as a major theme of discussion (Wihtol de Wenden, 1988). Indeed, the fact that the first Secretary of State for Migrant Workers, Postel-Vinay, resigned after only six weeks because insufficient money was allocated to improve the housing of immigrants may be seen as a sign that, from the beginning, the discourse on integration was intended to remain at the level of rhetoric (Silverman, 1992). Both the housing and training programmes for immigrants remained severely underfunded, whilst little progress was made on the extension of immigrants' rights.

A confirmation that this policy of control and integration was not judged successful was provided by a change in policy direction from 1977 onwards. A new government was formed in this year, with a new Secretary of State for Migrant Workers, Lionel Stoléru. This period was marked by the growing public nature of the debates over immigration and over the place of foreign residents within France, provoked partly by increasing evidence of the sedenterisation of the migrant population. This sedenterisation was marked by a feminisation of the migrant population as more and more women came to join their husbands already in France, as well as generational changes as the second and even third generation of children were born to these migrant parents. With these changes came the realisation that migration was a permanent phenomenon, but also a growing pressure for a reversal of this migratory process, and policies which seemed designed to make these immigrants invisible as political or social actors. Quickly the focus on integration and pluralism was dropped and political discourse centred on the notions of repatriation. It was argued more and more openly and forcefully that immigrants were a cost rather than a benefit to the French State, that at a time of increasing economic crisis, immigrants took the jobs of French workers and deprived the French economy of resources by sending money back to their relatives in their countries of origin. Stoléru announced his intention to tighten control on rights of entry and residence, to try and substitute French workers for foreign workers, and to remove immigrants from France voluntarily through state aided repatriation. In 1977 a scheme known as 'aide au retour' (help to return) was introduced which offered ten thousand francs to those immigrants willing to return to their country of origin. To obtain this ten thousand francs immigrants had to return their residence permits to the French authorities, renounce their rights to any welfare payments, and return to their country of origin with all of their family. The aim of the government was to encourage one million immigrants to return to their countries of origin within the following five years. However, less than 60,000 foreign workers eventually took up the offer, and most of these were Spanish and Portuguese workers, not the Algerians at whom the scheme was primarily aimed. A second measure aimed at reducing the number of immigrants was a law known as the Bonnet law, after the Minister of the Interior, which was passed in January 1980. This law imposed further limits on the entry and residence of foreigners which together with the creation of new conditions on the renewal of residence permits[2], would act to make more immigrants liable to expulsion on the grounds of the irregularity of their residence status. The criteria established for renewal of residence permits were closely linked to employment status, reinforcing the discourse on the costs/benefits of immigrants to France, and creating an increasingly insecure position for many migrant workers who were often employed in sectors where the risk of unemployment was high.

The Socialist Government and the Promise of Reform

Following the election of the first Socialist Government of the Fifth Republic in 1981, under the Presidency of François Mitterrand, there was a hope of reform and relaxation of some of the strict immigration policies and laws adopted by the previous regime. Mitterrand had included in his electoral manifesto three propositions (out of the total 110) specifically relating to immigration. These promised to remove discriminations affecting migrant workers, to grant immigrant workers equal rights with French nationals including the right to vote in municipal elections, and to 'democratise' the organisation of the Office national d'immigration (ONI).

The beginning of the 1980s did mark a period where there was the greatest distance between Right and Left over immigration policy, and where initially the Left did introduce some reforms which would increase the security of migrants, however, this was followed by a gradual shift towards a restrictive consensus which would be maintained more or less for the next twenty years. Although the Socialists had promised in their election manifestos to adopt a far more lenient immigration policy and to grant many more rights – including the right to vote in local elections – to immigrants, a variety of pressures, and significantly the mounting electoral success of the Extreme-Right Front National, caused a shift in their policy back towards a more restrictive agenda. Thus whilst

---

[2] Residence permits would no longer be renewed if the immigrant was seen to pose a threat to public order, if they had insufficient or irregular revenues, if their work permit was not renewed or if they were unemployed, or if they came back late from holidays outside of France.

the Socialists described their immigration policy as 'new', and there were certainly some new elements present in their policy, these might be interpreted more as a change of emphasis than a real change in policy direction. The ultimate goals of limiting new immigration and of integration of immigrants already present lent a continuity with the policies of the previous Right-wing government. The first years of the new Socialist regime did see some changes, particularly at the rhetorical level, but in fact the underlying continuity of policies meant that it was fairly easy for the Socialist governments in the latter half of the 1980s to shift back to more restrictive policies in line with their predecessors. As one political commentator remarked in 1985, with regard to immigration: 'the positions of the major political parties are far closer than one would think' (*Le Monde*, 8 June 1985).

The first measures taken by the new government concerning immigration did appear to chart a different course from the previous government, and in doing so set the scene for a confrontation between Left and Right on the issue. Whilst immigration policies in the years after 1974 had increased the insecurity of immigrant populations with their emphasis on expulsion and repatriation, the new Socialist government promised to try and make these populations more secure. Soon after their election, in May 1981, the government stopped the programme of voluntary repatriation that had been put in place by the previous administration, and launched a programme to regularise the situation of many of those residing illegally in France. Any foreigner who had been born in France, or had lived in France since before the age of ten was made 'inexpulsable' by two circulars issued in July and August of 1981, whilst another circular of August 1981 regularised the status of all foreign workers who had entered France illegally before 1 January 1981. Under the terms of this latter circular, around 140,000 illegal residents were granted legal residence papers. In addition, foreign residents were granted the right of association, which was a step towards bringing their rights into line with those of French nationals, and provided a boost to their political mobilisation through the formation of immigrant associations (for a fuller discussion of the role of immigrant associations see chapter 4).

These measures were accompanied by a discourse which privileged the ideas of increasing the security and rights of immigrants. Nicole Questiaux, the Minister for National Solidarity declared that: 'it is solidarity with everyone, French and immigrants alike, which will guide our action' (cited in Weil, 1991: 213). Whilst Claude Cheysson, the Minister for Foreign Relations, on a trip to Algeria, made a speech expressing the recognition and debt that France owed to Algerian workers and announcing that the government was intending to grant immigrants the right to vote in the 1983 municipal elections (*Le Monde*, 9 August 1981). Although this declaration was quickly contradicted by François Autain, the Secretary of State for Immigration, who announced that any precipitate action regarding the extension of voting rights would be against the long-term interests of immigrants, and that more basic rights pertaining to their integration into French society should be guaranteed before the issue of voting rights was discussed, the declaration caused a storm of opposition. The Right-wing opposition capitalised on this issue to accuse the Socialists of 'laxity' with regard to immigration, a charge which was used continually to imply that the Left was undermining French security through its weak immigration policies. This was also an issue from which the emergent extreme-Right Front National sought to capitalise, with its leader Jean-Marie Le Pen declaring that any project that extended voting rights to immigrants would begin 'a process of *défrancisation* of France' (*Le Monde*, 12 August 1981).

Under attack from the Right on this issue, and with opinion polls showing public opinion clearly against the extension of voting rights to immigrants[3], this proposition was quickly dropped by the Socialist government.

The government's failure to honour Mitterrand's pre-electoral proposition to extend the right to vote to immigrants, together with only partial reforms in other areas and a continued emphasis on blocking illegal immigration and preventing the influx of greater numbers of immigrants (the number of expulsions in fact rose from 2861 to 8482 between 1981 and 1984, meant that whilst the Right accused the government of laxity, for many immigrants there were more elements of continuity than of rupture with the policies of the preceding government (Cordeiro, 1984). This impression of elements of continuity with the repressive policies of the previous government was reinforced by a policy change in 1983, when, faced with an ongoing economic crisis, together with the electoral progress of the Front National (see below), the government decided to take a harder line on immigration, clamping down on illegal immigrants, and introducing a new scheme of voluntary aided repatriation. Attempts were made to differentiate this latter scheme from the *aide au retour* introduced by the previous government and abolished by the Socialists in 1981. The new scheme was entitled *aide à la reinsertion* (help for reinsertion) and it was planned that it should be organised through agreement and cooperation with the immigrants' countries of origin. However, these countries refused to negotiate agreements for the repatriation of their nationals, and finally the scheme was introduced unilaterally by France.

As well as trying to clamp down on illegal immigration, the government introduced measures to limit immigration through other means – family reunification and asylum. A decree of December 1984 imposed stricter conditions for family reunification, demanding that immigrants who wished their families to join them must show proof of adequate housing and financial resources. These conditions made the right to family reunification far more tenuous as many of those immigrants already residing in France lived in poor housing and had little or no financial resources. Meanwhile, a proposed reform in the asylum system had the intention of putting in place a quicker selection process to avoid 'false' asylum seekers benefiting from welfare payments and social protection (Wihtol de Wenden, 1988). Thus by the time of the legislative elections in 1986, the underlying theme of the need to limit and control immigration had resurfaced and had overtaken the Socialist government's initial rhetoric on the need to increase the security of immigrants. It can be argued that a series of factors including the emergence of the Front National as a major political actor (see below), have continued to emphasise this theme in French immigration policy.

---

[3] A poll carried out by BVA on the 12 and 13 August 1981 revealed that 58 per cent were hostile to extending voting rights in local elections to foreigners, 35 per cent were favourable, and 7 per cent did not express an opinion.

The Front National and the Popularisation of Anti-Immigrant Sentiment

One of the evident motivations for the continual efforts to limit immigration is the supposed electoral appeal of such policies. As remarked in the introduction to this chapter, politicians do not see the vote winning potential in being nice to immigrants, and thus across Europe, parties from across the political spectrum are introducing stricter immigration controls and aiming to create an image of being 'tough' on illegal immigrants, 'bogus' asylum seekers etc. This is very obviously true of France where, despite a promise of security for immigrants from Socialist governments, both Right and Left-Wing governments have introduced stringent new policies and legislation on immigration, asylum and nationality. Whilst the Left have been slightly more reluctant than the Right to resort to the 'charter flight' solution to illegal immigration, all sides of the political spectrum have talked about the 'problem' of immigration and the need to find solutions to that problem. Indeed, the French Communist Party (PCF) was one of the parties placing immigration on the national political agenda in their campaign for the 1981 presidential elections when they supported the Communist mayor of Vitry (a suburb of Paris) who ordered the demolition of a hostel for immigrant workers from Africa in December 1980. And faced with increasing economic difficulties and a wave of strikes, particularly by immigrant workers in the car industry in 1982-3, several Socialist ministers talked about their belief that the strikers were being encouraged by Muslim groups and Islamic fundamentalists (Hargreaves, 1995; Kepel, 1987). One of the key factors, however, in ensuring the politicisation of the immigration issue and in encouraging the instigation of stricter and stricter immigration policies and laws has been the electoral rise of the far-Right Front National with its anti-immigration platform. The emergence of the Front National as a constant electoral presence since 1983 has pushed immigration firmly to the centre of political debate and has encouraged a belief that a policy of stringent immigration control will be electorally successful.

The Front National was founded by Jean-Marie Le Pen in 1972, amalgamating a variety of extreme-Right groups and parties. From its inception, anti-immigration policies were the central core of its platform, advocating mass repatriation of non-French citizens, preferential treatment for French residents in terms of employment, housing and benefits, and restrictive reform of nationality laws. The party had little electoral success in its first decade, but made a major breakthrough in municipal elections in 1983 in the town of Dreux, near Paris. These municipal elections were marked by the emergence of immigration as a key vote winning (or losing) issue, which was taken up by all major parties. For example, the Socialist mayor of Marseille, Gaston Defferre, fought these municipal elections on a platform of his being particularly well-placed both to expel illegal immigrants and to fight delinquency, thus reinforcing the association that had been made between the two issues (Silverman, 1992). Indeed, during these elections the general theme of insecurity was linked to the issue of immigration in various ways, with a whole host of problems being amalgamated and linked to the presence of immigrants residing in France. Anti-immigrant discourse was often couched in very open terms. The mayor of Toulon, Maurice Arreckx, who was a member of the centre-Right UDF, wrote in a national news magazine, for example that:

> As an elected politician it is my duty to say out loud what everyone is thinking to themselves but does not dare to say. France has, and must preserve, a great tradition of welcome, but she does not have the vocation of being the refuge of the unemployed of Europe and Africa. Our country has become a dustbin where revolutionaries, delinquents and anarchists of every sort have collected. We must get rid of them (*L'Express*, 28 January – 3 February 1983).

This theme of linking immigration to insecurity was employed to great effect in the town of Dreux, near Paris, where in a municipal election at the end of September 1983, the Front National candidate, Jean-Pierre Stirbois, scored 16.7 per cent in the first round of the election and was invited to form a coalition by the RPR mayor. The success in the municipal elections of 1983 was repeated in the European elections of the following year when the Front National gained 11 per cent of the vote. And from the mid-1980s onwards, despite a damaging split in 1998[4], the Front National has remained a significant electoral presence, particularly at the municipal level. Moreover, in national elections, although the Front National has not succeeded in becoming a party of government, their continuing high levels of electoral support have had a clear impact on the strategies of other parties (see figure 2.1 below).

Immigration has been the single most important issue through which the Front National has mobilised support, 'a matrix through which most other issues could be channelled' (Hainsworth and Mitchell, 2000). Immigrants have been linked to a host of problems present in French society including unemployment, crime, delinquency, drugs, problems with housing and education, even the spread of AIDS. Immigration is thus for the FN a useful tool for explaining all the ills of French society (Soudais, 1996). As Marcus points out: 'Le Pen has skilfully picked up and manipulated the issue of immigration, using it as a focus for the Front's appeal. The immigrant has been resurrected as the traditional scapegoat for all France's ills' (Marcus, 1995: 27). The Front's policies include forced repatriation of non-European immigrants, the restrictive reform of nationality laws, and national preference in allocation of employment, housing, education and social security benefits. They painted a picture of immigrants, and particularly Muslim immigrants, as inassimilable, and therefore a threat to the values of the French nation. Despite the primitive nature of the Front's discourse and policies, some of the themes elaborated by them have had an important influence on the political debate over immigration. As Wihtol de Wenden argues:

> The Front National imposed the tone of the debate, using a pseudo-economic discourse (for them the halting of immigration and the use of repatriation are an

---

[4] In 1998 after a dispute between Jean-Marie Le Pen, and Bruno Mégret, the deputy leader of the party, the latter left to form his own party, the Mouvement National Républicain. The MNR espouses similar views to the Front National, but has so far been much less successful electorally.

end in themselves rather than a way of managing an economic crisis as they are for the Left) to mask arguments which are grounded in emotional and cultural values, and in appeals to the negative aspects of immigration (Wihtol de Wenden, 1988: 332).

Indeed, an opinion poll carried out following the success of Le Pen in the 2002 presidential elections indicates that widespread acceptance of some of the core ideas of the Front National. Over three-quarters of those surveyed expressed the opinion that politicians did not do enough to defend traditional French values, whilst two-thirds felt insecure and believed that more power should be given to the police. Regarding immigration, 59 per cent expressed the opinion that there were too many immigrants in France (SOFRES, *Le Monde*, 30 May 2002). It might be argued that these type of results show an increasing 'banalisation' of the ideas of the extreme-Right, as they become more and more acceptable to French public opinion. As well as demonstrating the impact of the Front National on French political discourses and ideologies, these type of figures may also be seen to indicate that many of the ideas put forward by the Front were already present in French political consciousness and beliefs. Nonna Mayer points to the ideological proximity between the Front National/Mouvement National Républicain and the traditional parties of the Right, arguing that the popularisation of the Front's ideology has been made easier by the fact that these opinions were already widespread within the traditional Right in France (*Le Monde*, 2 June 2002). What these results demonstrate is that across the electorate, a significant body of 'ethnocentric' voters has emerged, voters whose electoral behaviour is motivated above all by a dislike of immigrants. The presence of these voters cannot but influence the policies adopted by different governments with regard to immigration.

Figure 2.1 The vote for the Extreme-Right in national elections 1974 – 2002 (% of votes cast in the first ballot in two-ballot elections)

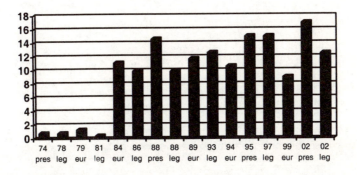

(Figures for 1999 european elections and 2002 legislative elections include votes cast for the Front National and the Mouvement National Républicain in the first ballot)

The continuing electoral success of the Front National seems to indicate that despite what some commentators may have hoped, the vote for the FN is not merely a protest vote, but also a vote in favour of the policies that they advocate (Eatwell, 1998). As Taguieff argues: 'The Front National vote is no longer only a vote against (against the Left, then against the Right), it is also a vote for' (Taguieff, 1996: 44). The size of this vote 'for' anti-immigration policies can be attributed to the astute tactics and charismatic leadership of the party, but it could not have been achieved if some of the ideas espoused by the Front were not already embedded within French opinion. The parties of the Left and of the mainstream Right can also be held answerable for their failure to respond adequately to the rise of the Front National, and for their promptness in adopting anti-immigrant policies which they thought might gain them votes.

The Pasqua Laws: Reinforcing Control

As outlined above, the emergence of the Front National as a major player on the French political scene was one of the contributing factors to the continuing politicisation of the immigration issue, and their anti-immigrant discourse was an influence in the shaping of the immigration policies of other parties. The issue of immigration figured largely in the campaign for the 1986 legislative elections, and the role of the Front National was also central in these elections after the Socialist government had changed the electoral system from a majoritarian two-ballot system to a proportional system. The new electoral system meant that the Front National won thirty-five seats in the new National Assembly and posed a problem for the moderate-Right government which had just been elected. In response, and as a tactic for regaining the votes lost to the Front National, the new Right-wing government, under Prime Minister Jacques Chirac, set out to dramatically reform immigration and nationality policies.

The reforms were managed by the Minister of the Interior, who would lend his name both to these laws and to subsequent immigration laws passed in 1993. A sign of the increasing securitisation of the immigration issue were the measures taken by Pasqua to increase the powers of the police, both at the borders and internally, to carry out random identity checks and to detain and deport individuals without the correct identity papers. The increasing police controls were legitimised by a series of terrorist bombs in Paris in 1986 which were linked to the Middle East, and therefore, in political discourse, to Muslim immigrants in France. The first Pasqua law, passed in September 1986, extended the restrictions concerning entry and residence rights that had been defined by previous laws. It also attempted to remove some of the control over the immigration process from the judiciary by stipulating that decisions to deport immigrants could be taken by local prefects rather than judges. This decision was designed to speed up the process of expulsion of illegal immigrants, but also to make the decision part of an administrative process rather than a judicial one. Many of the restrictions on expulsions put in place buy the Socialists were also lifted. As a result of these changes the number of foreigners expelled from France in the following three months doubled (Voisard and Ducastelle, 1988). One incident which attracted particular attention was the deportation of 101 Malians on a 'charter' in October 1986. This was the first time that a charter flight was used to expel immigrants who had been arrested after a police raid in application of the new Pasqua law. Although many expressed horror at the wholesale deportation of immigrants in this manner, public opinion seemed in general to be in favour of this tough new policy. A poll carried out by BVA in November 1986 found that 67 per cent of those surveyed approved the expulsion of the Malians in this manner, whilst only 19 per cent disapproved (Gastaut, 2000). This idea of 'charters' for deporting illegal immigrants, although introduced by the Right-wing government, has also been advanced by some on the Left. Famously in July 1991, Socialist Prime Minister, Edith Cresson, announced on television that she was not averse to re-introducing charters to fight against the problem of illegal immigration. Although a portion of the Left reacted strongly against this statement, again it seemed that public opinion was favourable to the idea, with 66 per cent of those surveyed supporting Cresson's statement (Gastaut, 2000).

The effects of the Pasqua law could have been even more far-reaching if the government had succeeded in its attempts to carry out a corresponding reform of the French nationality laws. This reform was one of the clearest signs of the influence of the extreme-Right on the debate over immigration. The discussion of nationality and national identity was a key element of the discourse of new-Right groups such as the Club de l'Horloge, and the mid-1980s had seen the publication of a series of books on the issue (Griotteray, 1984; Le Gallou, 1985). A central tenet of this discourse was the idea that the current processes of acquiring French nationality through the *droit du sol* (*jus soli*) were too easy. French nationality, it was argued, should only be accorded to those who deserved it, and who could prove that they merited the honour of being naturalised as French citizens. The reforms of the nationality laws proposed in a bill presented to the National Assembly in October 1986, went in the direction of these arguments by removing some of the rights to the acquisition of nationality which currently existed. The major element of this reform proposed that children born in France of foreign parents should no longer automatically acquire French nationality at the age of eighteen. Instead they would have to make a voluntary request for French nationality (accompanied by an oath of loyalty to the French Republic) which could be refused on certain grounds e.g. if the person had been sentenced to prison for longer than six months. The thrust of this proposed reform was clearly to reinforce the idea that French nationality was not an automatic right but a privilege which had to be earned. The effects would have been far-reaching both on the children it affected and their parents. The proposal provoked a huge outcry, and was rejected by the Conseil d'Etat, leading the government to temporarily shelve the bill and to set up a commission to look into the whole area of nationality. The Commision de la Nationalité, headed by the vice-president of the Conseil d'Etat, Marceau Long, reported in 1988, and re-affirmed the importance of the *droit du sol* as part of the French Republican tradition (Long, 1988). Although the government might have been seen to have failed in their bid to reform the nationality laws, the lessons of this defeat were used to introduce reforms more effectively when the Right returned to power in 1993.

In the interval between the Right-wing administration of 1986-88 and the return of the Right to power in 1993, the intervening Socialist government effectively returned to the policies that they had been following up until 1986, aiming to further limit immigration and at the same time to push for the integration of immigrants already in France. The Haute Conseil à l'Intégration (High Council for Integration) was set up by the government to further this latter aim, whilst a variety of decrees and laws enacted further modifications in the conditions of entry to and residence in France. Hopes of de-politicising the immigration issue and removing it from the centre of public debate were foiled, however, by the emergence of the controversy over the *affaire des foulards* (the headscarf affair) in 1989. This debate over the rights of Muslim girls to wear headscarves in secular French schools provoked new polemics over the place of Muslim immigrants within France, and over the capacity of the French Republic to integrate/assimilate these immigrants (see chapter 5 for more details). The Right-wing returned to power in 1993 with a determination to finish the reforms that the government had started in 1986 and had not been able to see through to completion. Pasqua was again named Minister of the Interior, and proclaimed his determination to reach a goal of 'zero immigration'. In a stronger position this time, due to large Right-wing majority in the National Assembly and the weak Left-wing opposition, the government resolved to reduce all forms of immigration, including asylum seeking, to an absolute minimum, and to cut down massively on the number of foreigners being naturalised and receiving French nationality. A set of laws were immediately passed to try and achieve the target of zero immigration. What can be seen to distinguish these policies from previous immigration policies was that they set out with a clear focus on 'rolling back the rights of foreigners across the board' (Hollifield, 1999: 74). These laws set new conditions for the entry and residence of foreigners in France, making it easier for police and prefects to prevent foreigners from entering France and to expel them from French territory, limiting the residence rights of many immigrants, making the conditions for family reunification more strict (imposing, for example, a wait of two years before any family members could be brought to France to join a relative who was already resident there), giving local mayors the power to refuse to marry or to annul marriages that were suspected of being marriages of convenience. The reforms also attempted to exert controls over immigration through constraining immigrants' social rights and access to the social security system, particularly health care and education. This shift in focus to limit immigration through limiting immigrants' social rights can be seen in part as a result of the perceived failure of external controls. In addition, with the parallel development of European integration and a perceived loss of control over external borders through the development of the Schengen area, using such internal controls could be seen as a way of the French government re-gaining control of the immigration system. Rolling back immigrants' rights in this way also engenders debates about the nature of citizenship and nationality, and thus puts extra emphasis on demands for changes in nationality laws. The laws changing the conditions of entry and residence of immigrants in France were accompanied in 1993 by a law changing the conditions of acquisition of French nationality, a reform which had previously been attempted in 1986 (see above). For Pasqua, the importance of this reform of the nationality laws was clear, it was a vital aspect of sustaining the French Republic and its values of integration and assimilation. As he argued in a speech in 1993:

> The reform of the Nationality Code is far more important than is sometimes imagined. We cannot hope to integrate or assimilate in our Republican melting-pot those who do not really, in full consciousness, choose to be French. The counterpart to the absence of an ethnic criterion in the French conception of the Nation is that this Nation can only be founded on adhesion. When Michelet proclaimed that 'France is a spiritual principle', he called out to those who wished to be citizens to make this their principle. Thus in subordinating the acquisition of French nationality to a voluntary act, we have laid the foundations of a grand policy of integration (Pasqua, speech to UNESCO, 14 October 1993).

The 1993 reform of the nationality laws again took away the automatic right to acquisition of French nationality of children born in France to foreign parents. These children would have to make a request for nationality between the ages of sixteen and twenty-one, and this request might be denied under certain conditions such as having a criminal record. In addition parents of minors would no longer be able to claim French nationality for their children, thus placing all of the responsibility for claiming naturalisation on these children when they reached the age of majority. The inability to claim French nationality for children had important consequences for the citizenship rights both of these children themselves, and of their parents. The rolling back of rights in this way, and the changes in nationality law also had important gendered consequences which will be discussed further in chapter 6.

The result of all these reforms was to create a highly insecure position for many immigrants living in France. As Lochak concludes:

> The consequences that might be expected from the application of these laws were not slow to materialise: destabilisation of young people born or having grown up in France who were deprived of the assurance of being able to live there in the long-term; a throwing into irregularity of thousands of people whom up until then had legally been guaranteed the right to remain in France; a brutal restriction on the right to family life; a denial of the right to social protection and to a minimum standard of living to all persons who were no or were no longer in possession of a residence permit, even if they had previously worked and made social security payments; reinforcement of a repressive police system of which the whole of the population, nationals included, felt the consequences, whether through an intensification of identity checks, or through the involvement of the police, under the pretext of detecting fraud, in the private lives of individuals (Lochak, 1997: 44).

The adoption of the second Pasqua laws can be seen as an indication of the determination of the French government to halt immigration and to limit immigrants' rights. The reforms were not adopted without opposition, however, and the creation of increasing numbers of 'illegal' of 'clandestine' immigrants led to a rebirth of the *sans-papiers* movement, with protests, occupations and hunger strikes by those who had no legal residence status and were at risk of expulsion from France (for a fuller discussion of the *sans-papiers* movement see chapter 4). This movement was supported by many French nationals, worried at the extent to which immigrants' rights were being challenged by the French government, and about the ways in which nationality and citizenship were being called into question by these reforms. The government pointed to the apparent success of their reforms in limiting immigration – inward immigration into France fell from a total (including asylum seekers) of 135,000 in 1992 to 68,000 in 1995 – thus justifying the harshness of some of the measures by their effectiveness in achieving their goals. However, the apparent fall in immigration flows may be deceptive, as many of the previously legal flows were pushed underground, swelling the ranks of the 'illegal' *sans-papiers*. For example, the increased restrictions on family reunification meant that many who would previously have immigrated under these provisions realised that they would be refused, and came into France on a tourist visa, hoping to extend their stay with their families and obtain legal residence papers once they had arrived. In addition, the numbers trying to cross the borders illegally with no visas rose steadily from 1993 onwards. Thus the clampdown on immigration could be seen to have contributed to a rise in the illegal smuggling and trafficking of migrants which the government in fact wished to counteract. The supposed success of the reforms in cutting immigration should therefore be qualified.

Patrick Weil (Weil, 1995) has established a schema for examining the evolution of immigration policy between 1974 (the year of the suspension of immigration) and 1993 (the year of the second Pasqua laws). This schema, shown below in table 2.2, is based on three fundamental policy areas with regard to immigration: policy concerning 'illegal' immigrants who wished to become regularised; policy with regard to legal immigrants and their relationship to the French state; and policy with regard to the return migration of legal migrants. For each of these policy areas he defines three 'solutions' adopted by governments and demonstrates the ways in which combinations of the three have been put into action.

Table 2.2 Evolution of Policies and Strategies with Regard to Immigration, 1974 – 1993

Phases	Problem		
	A	B	C
June/July 1974	A3	B1	No measures in this area
July 1974 – March 1977	A3	B1	C2
March 1977 – May 1981	A3	B2 and B3	C3
May 1981 – March 1983	A2	B1	C1
March 1983 – March 1986	A3	B1	C2
March 1986 – May 1988	A3	B2 and B3	C2
May 1988 – March 1993	A3	B1	C2
March 1993	A3	B3	C2

A.   Policies regarding illegal immigrants who wished to become regularised
  ➤   Open access to different categories of legal status
  ➤   Regularisation of those illegal immigrants who had been on national territory for a certain period of time
  ➤   Prevention of movement from illegal to legal categories of immigrant
B.   Policies regarding legal immigrants in their relationship to the French State
  ➤   Increase resources and rights for legal immigrants
  ➤   Maintain the same level of resources and rights
  ➤   Diminish resources and rights
C.   Policies with regard to the return migration of legal migrants
  ➤   Non-interference with natural migratory flows
  ➤   Encouraging voluntary repatriation
  ➤   Provoking forced repatriation

This schema demonstrates the gradual evolution of immigration policy towards a more restrictive and repressive agenda, culminating in the acceptance with the Pasqua laws of an agenda of blocking paths to regularisation of illegal immigrants (and indeed creating new forms of illegality), rolling back the rights of immigrants already in France, and encouraging return migration as far as possible. This restrictive agenda, as has been argued above, may have seemingly been successful in cutting immigration, but in the long-term has created growing problems of illegality and insecurity for many immigrants. Developments since 1993 have seen a continuation of the trend outlined above towards greater restriction, and to some extent this has been facilitated by attempts to integrate European immigration and asylum policies, allowing some externalisation of controls, which have been paired with further internal control mechanisms.

The immediate follow-up to the Pasqua laws were the Debré laws of 1997 (named after the new Minister of the Interior, Jean-Louis Debré). The adoption of these laws was influenced by the same concerns about immigration as had accompanied the Pasqua laws, but in circumstances where greater emphasis was placed on the need to increase security. This increased emphasis on security was reinforced by two factors. Firstly, France's relationship with Algeria was proving increasingly problematic following an intervention to prevent the Islamic radical party (FIS) winning power in the 1992 elections. Anger at this intervention led to a number of terrorist attacks by Islamic radicals in France, provoking the French government to increase the powers and the presence of police and military in an operation known as the plan *vigipirate*. The focus on the threat of terrorism by Islamic radicals clearly had a negative impact on Muslim immigrants living in France, particularly after one of the bombers was found to be a second-generation Algerian living in France. This young man's life story was covered in detail in the French press, and used as an example of the failure of French society to integrate Algerian immigrants, and of the continuing threat they posed. Secondly, in addition to this heightened public concern over the supposed threat posed by Muslim immigrants in France, the continued mobilisation of the *sans-papiers* against the Pasqua reforms, led the government to seek to introduce further reforms to solve this problem of the *sans-papiers* once and for all. The Debré law of 1997 reinforced the repressive dimension of immigration policy and increased the insecurity of non-nationals through various measures including the restriction of the power of judges concerning the detention of suspected illegal immigrants (thus giving greater control to the police) and the creation of new conditions in which the non-renewal or removal of a residence permit was possible. The law also stipulated that children under the age of sixteen would need to prove that they had been resident in France for over ten years to apply for nationality, and that foreign wives/husbands of a French national would have to wait at least two years before they could obtain a residence permit. One of the most controversial elements of this law, and one which provoked a huge mobilisation against the law (see chapter 3), was the requirement that French citizens should notify the local authorities whenever they received a non-EU foreign citizen as a guest. This clause provoked a massive mobilisation from French civil society, denouncing the infringement of civil liberties and the intrusion of the State into individual's private lives. The clause was eventually amended after opposition from the Conseil Constitutionnel, but the generally restrictive direction of this new law was maintained.

The 'New Republican Pact'

When President Chirac called early legislative elections in May/June 1997, the gamble backfired, and the Left again took control of the National Assembly with Lionel Jospin forming a government. For many immigrants and their supporters, the return of the Left brought hope of a reversal of some of the repressive and restrictive legislation that had been passed in the previous years. The discourse of the new government certainly augured well for a more open immigration policy with the emphasis on a return to the core Republican values, particularly a defence of the *droit du sol*. He argued that:

> France is a country with ancient Republican traditions, which was built in layers
> that flowed together into a melting pot, creating an amalgam which is strong

because of the diversity of its component parts. For this reason the *droit du sol* is an inseparable part of the French nation .... France must define a firm and dignified immigration policy without renouncing its values or compromising its social balance (*Libération*, 20 June 1997).

During the campaign Jospin had promised to repeal the Pasqua and Debré laws if his party was elected, and once in power he set out an immigration, nationality and citizenship policy comprising four elements, namely, a new republican integration policy which welcomed immigrants and respected their human rights but at the same time combated illegal immigration; a new policy of co-operation with sending states; a review of nationality law which would be undertaken by a new commission set up under the direction of the migration scholar Patrick Weil; and steps to resolve the problem of the *sans-papiers* through a new regularisation policy (Hollifield, 1999).

Whilst this new 'Republican pact' seemed to hold out promise of a substantial change in direction in immigration policy, for many the subsequent reforms were in fact '*beaucoup de bruit pour rien*' ('much ado about nothing') (Alaux, 2001b). In trying to find policies that would move towards the demands of pro-immigrant groups and lobbies, and of their Communist and Green coalition partners, whilst at the same time not alienating Right-wing voters too much, the government risked enacting policies which did not in fact have any great effect on the situation regarding immigration.

One of the major stated aims of the Republic pact was to reinstate the rights to citizenship for those having been born in France, the *droit du sol*, and this was done through the Guigou law of December 1997 which amended the Pasqua and Debré laws to state that anyone born in France could acquire French nationality at the age of eighteen as long as they could show that they had been resident in the country for at least five years after the age of eleven, and that any minor could request naturalisation as early as the age of thirteen provided that their parents agreed and that they had resided in France for at least five years since the age of eight. The law also created a Republican identity card which would be given to any child born in France of foreign parents before they gained naturalisation to ensure that the cases of stateless children produced by the Pasqua and Debré reforms did not re-occur.

A second piece of legislation designed to amend the Pasqua and Debré laws was the Chevènement law of 1998. The passage of this bill was difficult, meeting opposition from both Left and Right. Whilst the Right criticised the bill for being too lax with regard to immigration and called for a referendum on the new reforms, the Communist and Green parties, together with the extra-parliamentary Left, were angry that the bill only amended the Pasqua and Debré laws, rather than repealing them completely. In fact the Chevènement law made some amendments to the previous legislation by eliminating a number of the conditions imposed on potential immigrants to France, particularly with regard to family reunification. It also stated that one-year residence permits should be issued to certain categories of foreigners including all those who entered France before the age of ten, anyone who could prove that they had been living in France for over fifteen years, foreign spouses of French nationals and foreign parents of French children. Further, special consideration in the issuing of work and residence permits would be given to foreign scientists and scholars invited to work in France and to anyone who had special personal or familial reasons for wanting to migrate to or remain in France. The bill also created a new form of 'territorial asylum' (discussed below).

Although the reforms introduced by the Socialist government and the new 'Republican pact' might be seen as a temporary respite in the rolling back of immigrants' rights instigated under previous governments, the effects of the reforms were limited. Critics pointed to the utilitarian motivations and structures of these reforms, arguing that whilst the Pasqua and Debré laws had attempted to close French borders to all immigration apart from that protected by international law (refugees and immigrants coming for family reunification), the Chevènement law opened up other modes of legal immigration, but only for those who were seen as useful to France (Alaux, 2001b). A particular cause for debate was article 12b of the law, which allowed for the regularisation of *sans-papiers* under certain circumstances. This article, it was argued, held out false promises, and was in effect neutralised by a circular which accompanied it and which specified the conditions of application of this regularisation. Although around 80,000 residence permits were delivered as a result of these reforms, many *sans-papiers* found their claims for regularisation rejected, and the *sans-papiers* movement continued to be active, demanding a general regularisation, rather than a consideration of individual cases under strict, and often seemingly arbitrary criteria (for a fuller discussion of the *sans-papiers* movement see chapter 3).

The Socialist reforms did little to assuage the heated debate over immigration, and indeed, the issue became central to the election campaign of 2002, when the Right-wing campaign centred on the issue of security, and the need to reinforce the security of French citizens through a tighter control on illegal immigrants and 'false' asylum seekers. The success of the Front National leader, Le Pen, in reaching the second round of the presidential elections, and thus eliminating Jospin, the Socialist candidate, can be seen as testimony to the importance of these issues and the new Right-wing government formed following the election has been quick to capitalise on the popularity of its policies on security by introducing new laws on internal security, on the management of immigration, and on asylum.

The Right and the Promotion of Security

As noted above, the Right-wing campaign for the 2002 elections played on the 'insecurities' faced by the French people, and promised to tackle these insecurities through new legislation on immigration and asylum, amongst other measures. The new government acted on these electoral promises quickly, introducing three pieces of legislation which will have an impact on immigrants and asylum seekers. The full effects of these laws which deal with internal security, the management of immigration, and the reform of the asylum system, have yet to be felt in full, but it has been argued that they will act to increase the insecurities faced by many groups of immigrants and asylum seekers, further restricting their rights and creating new categories of 'illegality' and new tougher policies on deportation of immigrants. In addition, the government has acted to try and reduce still further the rights of those without legal residence status to any form of health-care, with a reform of the *Aide Médical d'Etat* (AME), a move which has received strong opposition from many pressure groups worried about the threat to human rights, in particular the human right to health, posed by such a reform.

Introducing his law on the management of migration, the Minister of the Interior, Nicolas Sarkozy argued that the failures of previous governments to adequately control migration had caused a rise in xenophobia and racism. In his speech to the National Assembly he asserted that:

> The French people are not hostile to foreigners. They are on the other hand, at best exasperated by, at worst despairing of, the incapacity of the State to manage migratory flows. Xenophobia and racist sentiment are the fruits of this powerlessness and laxity of the State (speech delivered to the National Assembly, 3 July 2003).

The new law he argued, would reassure the public of the government's control of migration and counteract these tendencies towards xenophobia, thus facilitating the integration of migrants legally resident in France. Amongst the reforms proposed by this law is the introduction of a record of fingerprints of all those issued with visas for entry into France to make it easier to trace those who had outstayed the period of validity of the visa. In an additional attempt to discourage those who outstay their visa, anyone who wishes to invite foreign (non-EU) relatives or friends to stay with them will be asked to engage beforehand to cover the costs of return of this visitor if necessary. Moreover, the period of detention for those arrested without legal residence papers will be increased from twelve days to thirty two days, to try and ensure that more of those arrested are expelled from French territory.

The law also contains proposals for trying to prevent the installation of 'illegal' immigrants in France. One of the articles has the aim of countering marriages of 'convenience' by stipulating that if either of the partners can not prove that he or she has a legal residence permit then this will be seen as a primary indicator of the absence of consent for the marriage (i.e. the mere fact of being without legal residence papers will case doubt on the sincerity of the marriage whatever the other indicators and circumstances). Illegal work will also be targeted with a reform to criminalise and penalise workers who are employed without the requisite residence and work permits (for a fuller discussion of illegal employment see chapter 4).

As well as fighting against illegal immigration and residence in France, the law introduces the idea of formally requiring 'integration' as a criterion of residence in France. Sarkozy announced in his address, his intention to fight against a certain communitarian vision of French society within which 'communities of immigrant origin organise themselves to resist Republican integration' (speech to the National Assembly, 3 July 2003). To this end, a formal contract of integration will be introduced which will be the basis for the issuing of ten-year residence permits. These ten-year permits should only be issued to those who have 'proved a real willingness to integrate into French society' (Sarkozy, speech to the National Assembly, 3 July 2003). The contract of integration to be signed by new arrivals in France will entail an engagement to 'respect the fundamental values of the Republic'.

The intention of this law, to reduce immigration and to ensure that those immigrants who do remain in France are fully 'integrated' echoes the intentions of many previous governments. The determination of the new government, however, might distinguish it from some of its predecessors in its willingness to override concerns over immigrants' rights and freedoms in order to achieve its objectives. Sarkozy has not been slow to translate into action his determination to reduce the number of immigrants in France, pushing for a doubling of the numbers of illegal immigrants expelled from French territory. Three new detention centres for illegal immigrants are planned and should be completed by 2006, whilst the capacities of those detention centres already in existence have been doubled. Sarkozy announced in March 2003 that he intended to send a 'charter' flight full of expelled immigrants every week (*AFP*, 26 March 2003). In an address to local prefects in September 2003, he reinforced the message that he wished to see the number of expulsions of illegal immigrants doubled even before the new law on immigration came into operation. And in October 2003, France and Belgium agreed to cooperate to send joint 'charters' via Paris and Brussels to expel illegal immigrants (*Le Nouvel Observateur*, 29 October 2003). It is probable that this initiative on joint 'charters' might be joined by other EU countries. In the first nine months of 2003, over 25,000 foreigners were expelled from French territory, a 12.9 per cent increase on the previous year. This determination to track down and expel illegal immigrants is accompanied by a similar determination to enforce 'integration' and to reject any form of 'communitarism' or multiculturalism. The proposed introduction of integration contracts has been accompanied by a re-opening of the debate over the 'foulard' (see chapter 7), a debate which has been emblematic of the French Republic's refusal of multiculturalism.

In addition to the law on the management of immigration, there have also been new laws introduced on internal security and on the reform of the asylum system. Whilst not directly addressing immigration, the law on internal security, in seeking to rid French society of some groups that the government perceives as a threat to security, has affected various groups of immigrants. One of the major targets of this law, for example, is prostitutes, and particularly immigrant sex workers. Under the terms of this law any immigrant found guilty of active or 'passive' soliciting may be immediately expelled from the country (see chapter 6 for more details). Finally, a new law on asylum seeks to reforms the system of asylum in France in order to reduce the numbers granted refugee status. These proposed reforms of the asylum system, which will supposedly make it more efficient, have been criticised by many as putting the whole system into crisis, and of plunging many asylum seekers and refugees into states of great insecurity. The full extent of these reforms to the asylum system will be discussed in the following chapter.

Conclusion

The politics of immigration in France has been marked by two overarching goals in the years since the closure of borders in 1974 – that of control of the number of immigrants reaching France, and that of integration of those immigrants that are residing permanently in the country. Further, these two goals have been inextricably linked by the premise that any successful integration requires a limitation on the number of immigrants entering the country otherwise a perceived 'threshold of tolerance' with regard to immigrants will be exceeded. The development of these immigration and asylum policies have been played out within the context of attempts to create a unified and integrated European immigration and asylum policy; attempts which, as noted above, have been only partially successful. What the process of European integration of immigration and asylum policy has done is not to remove control from nation states within Europe but rather to construct new forms of power which can increase the regulatory capacity of states (Kostakopoulou, 2001). This power has increasingly been used to assert the rights of states to exclude non-EU nationals from its territory, and this is true of France as elsewhere. This assertion of the right of exclusion has been justified by the invocation of the threat to France's security posed by immigration, both in terms of the threat of terrorism, the economic threat to French jobs and to the social security system, and the threat to French national culture and identity. In these terms the restrictions on immigration may be seen as legitimate 'self-defence', but the costs engendered by such a restrictive policy are not taken into account. These costs can be measured in terms of the insecurity, vulnerability and hardship inflicted upon immigrants and would-be immigrants due to the restrictive policies in action and upon the negative impact this has upon the scope and nature of the principles underpinning the French polity. As Kostakopoulou argues, such a restrictive immigration policy can 'undermine the future of democracy for all' (Kostakopoulou, 2001: 128).

Chapter 3

Refugee and Asylum Policy: Heading for a Crisis?

A key area on which European countries have tried to gain agreement and cooperation is that of asylum and refugee policy. Under the terms of the Schengen agreement, member countries could and should refuse to grant asylum to any asylum seeker having passed through a safe third country, whilst the Dublin Convention of 1990 signalled that an asylum claim could only be made in one country of the EU – the country that the asylum seeker had arrived in, unless they had relatives in another EU country – and that once a decision was made on this claim that decision should stand for all of the EU countries. The aim of the Dublin Convention was to avoid one person making multiple asylum claims in different countries and asylum seekers being sent, or trying to move from one country to another to find one which would grant them refugee status. The discourse amongst the member states of the EU has talked of a communitarisation of asylum issues, which together with other immigration issues have been moved from the Third to the First Pillar of the Maastricht Treaty and are thus liable to a more supra-national and less intergovernmental approach. In reality, however, there has been little agreement on reaching a common asylum policy with all states attempting to minimise their commitment to sharing the burden of receiving refugees. A significant example of the failure to reach any agreement over the treatment of asylum seekers has been the continuing dispute between France and the UK over the Sangatte camp (see below). The problem of Sangatte is clearly linked to the absence of a real unified European policy on asylum which has meant that: 'hypocrisy and lack of cooperation prevail with each country trying to get rid of asylum seekers judged undesirable by moving them on to a neighbouring country or by shifting the burden of protection outside of the EU thanks to readmission agreements' (Wihtol de Wenden, 2002: 9). France has been no exception to this general rule, and has pursued a policy of trying to reduce the number of asylum seekers within its territory, cutting the number to whom refugee status is granted, and attempting to remove all of thus whose claims are judged unfounded. Further there has been an increasing tendency amongst both politicians and the media to focus on the issue of so-called 'bogus' asylum seekers and to condemn them as 'economic migrants' rather than true political refugees. This may be seen as one of the damaging effects that has arisen as immigration and asylum have been treated as one and the same issue (Joppke, 1997). As European states like France have closed their borders to labour migration and have at the same time reduced or stopped completely resettlement programmes for political refugees, asylum seeking has become one of the major routes of legal migration into Europe, and consequently politicians have begun to treat immigration and asylum as one single issue. However, the perception of many that most asylum seekers are in fact economic migrants ignores both data on the outcome of asylum claims, and also the fact that for many asylum seekers there are both political motivations for leaving their own country and also economic and social reasons for choosing a particular country in which to claim asylum. As Koser argues, the perception that most asylum seekers are 'bogus', 'fails to take account of data showing that consistently across the European Union over the last decade up to fifty per cent of asylum applicants are granted either refugee status or some kind of temporary protection. It also confuses motivations for leaving with motivations for selecting a country of asylum. It is reasonable to expect that someone fleeing persecution will at the same time try to apply for asylum in a country where he or she has an existing social network, understands the language and has a chance to work' (Koser, 2001: 88).

This type of observation of the behaviour of France and other European states towards asylum seekers tends to undermine the belief in the privilege of asylum as a form of migration. Soysal, for example, argues that: 'Despite restrictive regulations, asylum remains a privileged form of migration. Attempts to stop or repatriate asylum seekers receive international attention, and are heavily debated within and outside Europe' (Soysal, 1994: 24). A closer examination of the French example of the treatment of asylum seekers would seem to demonstrate, however, that the privilege of this form of migration is being quickly undermined, and that asylum seekers in France, as elsewhere in Europe, are finding their security more and more in question. And in the face of state's unwillingness to receive refugees, the security of asylum seekers cannot be guaranteed either by national law or by the actions of international organisations. In fact, the right to asylum is written into France's constitution, and in 1993 the Constitutional Council ruled that the French authorities should not be able to deny access to the asylum process on the grounds that the asylum seeker could have lodged a claim elsewhere. This ruling implied that the French government could not constitutionally implement the provisions of the Schengen and Dublin Conventions. However, as has been argued previously in this book, the liberal perspective on the protection of migrants' rights by national and international law, cannot be maintained in the face of strong political pressure to restrict those rights. Following the 1993 Constitutional Court ruling, the Right-Wing government was quick to introduce a new article into the Constitution which gave French governments the rights to conclude international agreements with other European countries concerning the rights of asylum (Lavenex, 2000). The Schengen and Dublin Conventions could thus be fully implemented which allowed the government to restrict the numbers of those it would allow to apply for asylum in France. Similarly, international organisations have not been very successful in defending the rights of asylum seekers in France, despite making their concerns known to the French government. In December 2000 the United Nations High Commission for Refugees (UNHCR) noted its worries over 'access to the territory and procedure for determination of refugee status' in France. This type of concern, however, seems to have had little impact on French governments who have continued to pursue a hard line policy in their attempts to deter asylum seekers. The conditions for asylum seekers in France have become so insecure that in July 2001, the National Consultative Commission on Human Rights issued a report in which it concluded that: 'The current situation does not correspond to the basic demands of respect for human rights which are essential to our country' (CNCDH, 2001: 36).

The institution responsible for adjudicating on the granting of refugee status in France is the Office Français de Protection de Réfugiés et Apatrides (OFPRA), set up in 1952 for this purpose. In the first twenty years of its existence the number of claims dealt with by the OFPRA was relatively small and the rate of refusal of asylum claims was negligible (Legoux, 1995, 1996). The number of claims began to increase after the suspension of immigration in 1974, and as the number of claims increased, the criteria for granting refugee status became stricter, although there were exceptions to this. Chilean asylum seekers fleeing the Pinochet regime were generally welcomed, and quotas were established for receiving South-East Asian asylum seekers who were thus accorded refugee status automatically. The numbers of asylum seekers of other nationalities increased gradually, and as it did so, the proportion of those whose claims were rejected also increased. The increasing numbers of asylum seekers at a time when governments were trying to limit the number of immigrants to France was seen as a challenge to government policy and gradually the suspicion of asylum seekers as being 'economic migrants' attempting to exploit the asylum system to gain residence status in France began to grow.

Fears of an ever increasing flow of asylum seekers – the total number of asylum applications in France peaked at 61,372 in 1989 – led to successive governments throughout the nineties enacting measures with the aim of making France a less attractive destination for asylum seekers. In 1989 housing grants to asylum seekers were suspended, meaning that they had to turn to specialized housing provided either by the government in reception centres or by charitable associations, or else rely on help in finding lodging from community support networks already in place. Family allowances for asylum seekers were also suspended making their financial situations even more precarious. Then in 1991 asylum seekers' right to work was revoked. This created an intolerable financial situation for many. The government provided an extra 2500 places in reception centres, but this was not sufficient for the needs of all those arriving to seek asylum in France. The results of these reforms was to create an impossible financial and social situation for many asylum seekers. As Brachet comments: 'From the start of 1992, the new arrivals who did not find a place in a reception centre, were objectively incapable of surviving on their legal allowances. The meagre minimum allowance (about 1300 francs at the time) that was granted to adults for twelve months only, irrespective of the number of children dependent on them, was evidently not sufficient to live on' (Brachet, 2002: 55). Many asylum seekers were thus forced to work illegally, leaving them vulnerable to exploitation in the labour market, and also allowing governments to confound the issue of asylum seekers with that of illegal employment and to label many asylum seekers as mere 'economic migrants' who were taking advantage of the French system. Officially the reasoning behind this decision to remove the right to work from asylum seekers was that participation in the labour market would favour integration into French society and thus make removal more difficult if the asylum claim failed (ProAsile, 1999). The consequences of the decision, however, have been very difficult for many asylum seekers. A study of Kurdish asylum seekers who arrived in France in 2001, pointed to not only the economic costs of this ban on working, but also the moral and psychological difficulties which it had provoked (Mohseni, 2002).

Despite the difficult social and economic consequences for asylum seekers, French governments in the first half of the 1990s were pleased with the supposed success of their dissuasive tactics. As figure 3.1 shows, the number of asylum claims fell sharply in the first half of the 1990s from its high of 61,372 in 1989 to only 17,405 in 1996, and with it fell the number of persons granted refugee status in France (figure 3.2). This reading of the fall in the number of asylum claims as a direct result of the toughening of conditions for asylum seekers in France has been shown, however, to be rather simplistic. Following the low of 1996, the number of asylum claims has again been rising (table 3.3), reaching 47,291 in 2001, and 51,087 in 2002. These numbers are for those who claim conventional asylum and do not include those claiming territorial asylum (discussed below). If the figures for those claiming territorial asylum are included then the total number of asylum seekers making claims in France in 2002, is estimated at around 90,000 including children.[1] The proportions of asylum seekers from different regions has also altered in recent years, and part of the reason for the recent re-growth in the number of claimants is the growing number of asylum seekers arriving from Africa. In particular the number of asylum seekers from the Democratic Republic of Congo and from Mali has increased rapidly. Despite France's efforts to discourage asylum seekers, the numbers they receive are still rising. The exact reasons for which people seek asylum in one particular country rather than another are still the object of speculation in many cases (as can be seen by the debate over those trying to reach England from Sangatte as described below), but the policies of making life harder for asylum seekers has not had the desired effect of permanently reducing the number of asylum claims in France, in fact it may be argued that it has merely created extra social problems which charities and refugee support associations have been struggling to deal with.

---

[1] The exact figure of the number claiming asylum is hard to calculate in part because a person can present a claim both for conventional and territorial asylum and thus there is some overlap between the two figures.

Figure 3.1 Evolution of requests for (conventional) asylum 1992 - 2001

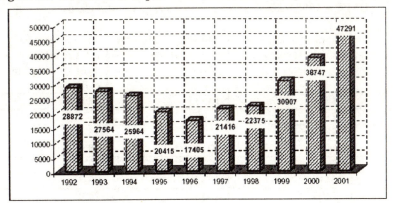

Source: OFPRA, 2003

Figure 3.2 Number of requests for (conventional) asylum granted 1992 - 2001

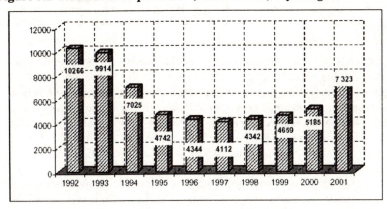

Source: OFPRA, 2003

A second part of the strategy for reducing the number of people granted refugee status in France has been to apply stricter criteria to those asylum applications which are received, so that fewer of these are successful. The total number of persons granted refugee status in France has fallen continually in the last decade, in real terms and as a percentage of asylum claims received, as shown in table 3.3 below:

Table 3.3　Total number of persons granted refugee status by the OFPRA 1990 – 2002, and as a percentage of total claims

Year	Number of asylum claims received	Number of persons granted refugee status	Number granted refugee status as a % of total asylum claims
1990	54813	13537	24.6
1991	47380	15981	33.7
1992	28872	10266	35.5
1993	27564	9914	35.9
1994	25964	7025	27.0
1995	20415	4742	23.2
1996	17405	4344	24.9
1997	21416	4112	19.2
1998	22375	4342	19.4
1999	30907	4659	15.1
2000	38747	5785	14.9
2001	47291	7323	15.4
2002	51087	8495	16.6

Source: OFPRA

　　　　Officials have argued that the fall in the number of those being granted refugee status is due to changing political situations in the main countries of origin of refugees to France, and also as a result of changing countries of origin of refugees. However, if the numbers granted refugee status are considered as a percentage of the total numbers seeking asylum in France then there is clearly evidence of a mounting number of refusals. The rate of refusal of asylum applications rose from 57 per cent in 1985 to 84 per cent in 1995 (Hollifield 1999: 68). And critics of French asylum policy have pointed out that contrary to what the OFPRA has claimed about changing countries of origin of asylum seekers there is in fact a remarkable continuity in the main nationalities seeking asylum in France, and that in fact, the situation in these countries has not evolved far enough to warrant such a dramatic decrease in the numbers receiving refugee status. It might thus be argued that rather than changing circumstances in the countries of origins of asylum seekers, the decrease in the number of claims that are granted might be a result of a tightening of the criteria for granting refugee status and demands for proof of persecution that are increasingly difficult to meet. A study published in 1988, which examined the decisions emanating from the OFPRA, and from the Appeals Commission to which claims rejected by the OFPRA may be taken, concluded that the level of proof required from a person in order to be granted refugee status had not ceased to rise, and that judges were becoming excessively rigorous in their treatment of asylum claims (Tiberghien, 1988). The figures for the years since 1988 would seem to demonstrate a further tightening of the criteria for judging asylum claims as the numbers granted refugee status have continued to fall.

These figures are at the centre of a continuing political debate about the nature of asylum and the adequacy of the French laws concerning asylum seekers. Whilst some have claimed as above that the criteria employed for judging asylum claims have become more rigorous and are used to exclude those to whom the French state should in fact protect, others maintain that the asylum system needs to be made even more rigorous to exclude those 'false' asylum seekers who are merely 'economic migrants' and who pose a supposed threat to the security of the French nation. The Right-wing government elected in 2002, condemned the inadequacy of the existing laws, and introduced a new law which was passed by the National Assembly in June 2003, and which modified the existing law on asylum of 1952. In a report prepared to support the new legislation it was argued that the high-rate of refusals of asylum claims was a result of the fact that most of the claims received did not adequately meet the criteria laid down by the Geneva Convention for the granting of refugee status. The asylum system, it claimed, was being abused by people more interested in 'economic migration' than in 'political refuge'. As a result, 'the French asylum system which has been in place for the last half century is faced with overload and must be reformed' (Leonetti, 2003: 9). The full implications of the new law on asylum will be discussed in greater detail below, but it is clear that the political debate on asylum has moved away from a focus on guaranteeing the human security of asylum seekers and refugees, to one of reducing their number in order to protect the French system from these supposed abuses by 'economic migrants'.

Territorial Asylum – A New Alternative?

In 1998, the Socialist government created a new status for refugees, a 'territorial asylum' which could be granted to those who had been persecuted not by their state but by members of civil society in their country of origin. Territorial asylum would be granted to those 'whose life is threatened in their country of origin' or who is exposed to 'inhumane and degrading treatment'. This status was designed to deal especially with Algerians seeking asylum in France because of persecution by Muslim groups in Algeria. The status of territorial asylum, unlike refugee status under the Geneva Convention, gives only temporary and discretionary protection which may be removed when the prefecture finds it appropriate to do so. The 1998 law was the first time that this temporary asylum was codified, but was in fact the culmination of a gradual move away from formal refugee protection procedures towards more informal and ad hoc treatment of asylum seekers – this move towards more informal and temporary procedures for dealing with refugees was initiated both by the situation in Algeria and by the influx of refugees from the former Yugoslavia (Bosnia and then Kosovo) in the 1990s. The creation of this new status was proclaimed by the government as an advance in helping to speed up the decision process on asylum and to extend France's protection to those who might not have otherwise received it. In fact, many have seen the new law as a way of reducing the numbers granted refugee status in France, and have pointed to the very high level of rejection of demands for territorial asylum (Wihtol de Wenden, 2002).

The number of people claiming territorial asylum has increased rapidly since its introduction. In 1998 only 1335 people claimed territorial asylum, whereas by 2002 this number had reached 28372. The majority of those claiming territorial asylum are of Algerian origin, as predicted in the formulation of the new status. In 2001, 82.8 per cent of all claims for territorial asylum in France came from Algerians. However, the majority of these claims have been rejected. In 1999, only 6.1 per cent of claims for territorial asylum were granted, and by 2001 this figure had fallen to 1.5 per cent. Some critics of the new territorial asylum have argued that the creation of this provision was not an real attempt to extend humanitarian protection, but in fact a more cynical part of a utilitarian immigration policy which seeks to create procedures where immigrants may be accorded legal status if this is judged to be beneficial to the French state at a particular time (Alaux, 2001b). The fact that decisions on territorial asylum were to be taken by the prefectures under the direct responsibility of the Minister of the Interior, added to the impression that claims for territorial asylum would be subject to a political rather than merely a humanitarian judgement.

New Reforms of the Asylum Laws

The reforms introduced by the Socialist government in 1998 to try and solve the asylum 'crisis', have not been enough, however, for the current Right-wing government. Immediately following their victory in the presidential elections of April/May 2002 and the legislative elections of June 2002, the new government affirmed its commitment to reform asylum law as part of its aim of achieving greater security. Nicolas Sarkozy, the Minister of the Interior in the new Right-Wing government, affirmed to the press that he believed that the current legislation on refugees and asylum was too 'lax' (*Le Monde*, 31 July 2002), and that strict reform was needed to reduce the time spent considering asylum claims, and to remove those whose claims were unfounded from French territory as quickly as possible. Whilst the government has attempted to put a humanitarian spin on this reform, pointing to the long delays in the processing of asylum claims as adding to the insecurity of asylum seekers – Jacques Chirac, for example, explained in a television interview that he found it absurd that some asylum seekers had to wait eighteen months for their demands to be processed -, it is clear that the main objective in the reform is to try and reduce the number of asylum seekers and refugees on French territory. And the government claims that this need for reform of the asylum system is not new, pointing to an internal memo produced by the Foreign Office under the previous (Socialist) government which talked about 'flagrant deviations' in policies on asylum and warned that the French authorities 'were not filtering out manifestly unfounded claims' (*Le Monde*, 15 January 2002). In labelling many of those seeking 'asylum' as 'false' asylum seekers with manifestly unfounded claims, governments have attempted to shift the responsibility for any failure in the asylum system on to the asylum seekers themselves. This type of rhetorical manoeuvring is echoed in the claim of the Minister for Social Affairs, François Fillon, who claimed that his budget for responding to situations of poverty and social distress was at risk of being saturated by the huge numbers of asylum seekers in France (*AFP*, 17 October 2003). These type of declarations about the incapacity of France to cope with the number of asylum claims it receives echo the fears of an immigrant 'invasion', and provide supposed justification for the tough new law on asylum, deflecting any criticisms that there might be of this law for its infringement of international conventions on asylum and refugees.

This new law, modifying the 1952 law relative to the right to asylum was passed in a first reading by the National Assembly in June 2003. The reforms envisaged by the new law will unify the procedures for processing the two types of asylum claims (conventional asylum and territorial asylum) under the direction of the OFPRA, rather than leaving police prefectures to deal with territorial asylum claims as the system has done up until this point. The logic for this move is to remove the possibility for those who have had their claim for statutory asylum rejected by the OFPRA then presenting a new claim to the prefectures. The unification of all asylum procedures under the direction of OFPRA would have the advantage of ensuring that those staff dealing with asylum claims should have had the appropriate training – this will please those associations which have criticised the lack of training of the prefectoral workers who have been given the task of dealing with territorial asylum claims. However, moving the whole process into the domain of the OFPRA might also limit the chances of those who have failed to receive statutory asylum and have tried again to get territorial asylum.

A second measure envisaged is the augmentation of the number of countries which are included in an exception clause from the terms of the Geneva Convention. Under the terms of the Convention states are authorised to designate countries in which they believe the political situation has evolved such as to no longer justify according protection to persons originating from there. The French government has signalled its intention to try and increase the number of these 'safe' countries to whose nationals it will not grant protection – anyone from one of these countries who does try and claim asylum will have their claims processed within forty eight hours without a full hearing, and will normally not receive refugee status. Any asylum seekers from these countries are not entitled to a provisional residence permit or to any lodging or benefit. They will usually be kept in detention until they can be deported. Among the countries to be added to this list of exceptions are Mali, Bangladesh and Ghana, each of which produced a non-negligible number of asylum seekers in France in 2001 (2940 from Mali, 825 from Bangladesh and 121 from Ghana). This measure seems to fit in with the general trend that has been established – namely to dismiss as many asylum claims as 'manifestly unfounded' as quickly as possible in order to limit the number of those who might obtain refugee status in France.

Finally, the government intends to prolong the period for which asylum seekers whose claims have been rejected may be kept in detention. At the moment those whose claims have failed can legally be kept in a detention centre for a maximum of twelve days. Sarkozy has announced his intention of increasing this period of legal retention in order to ensure that the maximum possible number of failed asylum seekers are sent back to their country of origin and that fewer escape deportation. The number of available places in detention centres will be increased, and the government has announced that it intends to use more and more 'charter flights' to deport failed asylum seekers en masse. All of these measures indicate a strong desire to reduce again the number of those who are granted refugee status by the French state, and to remove from France as quickly as possible anyone whose demand is judged 'unfounded'. These new laws could signal a real crisis for the right to asylum in France (Wihtol de Wenden 2002).

Sangatte

One the most widely publicised debates over asylum seekers arose in connection with the Red Cross camp at Sangatte, near Calais. The existence of this camp was a point of contention between the French and British governments, with the British arguing that the French authorities did not do enough to prevent asylum seekers from the camp trying to smuggle themselves into Britain on board freight trains and Eurostar train services through the Channel Tunnel. The French, on the other hand, argued that it was not entirely their problem if asylum seekers wished to try and enter Britain, and pointed to the supposedly more 'friendly' conditions for asylum seekers in Britain – such as the right to work of asylum seekers waiting for their case to be processed – which, they argued, exerted a pull factor across the Channel. The existence of the camp was also seen as a challenge to European integration, an impediment to the free movement of goods through the EU, one of the founding principles of European integration, enshrined in the Maastricht Treaty. The resolution of the issue of Sangatte was therefore not only of interest to France and the UK, but to the rest of Europe, as a question of the way in which EU countries would deal with the issues of asylum seekers.

The Sangatte centre was opened by the Red Cross, with funds from the Ministry of Social Affairs, in September 1999 to deal with the emergency of refugees fleeing from the war in Kosovo. The original purpose of the centre was to offer shelter to some of these refugees – it was designed to receive between two hundred and three hundred people. By 2002 the centre was holding up to one and a half thousand refugees, most of them from Afghanistan and Iraq. The weekly turnover of inmates could reach up to one third of the total, and thus the centre was seen as a place of transit both by the residents and by those who ran it (Laacher, 2002). The status of those who stayed at Sangatte was uncertain, they were not strictly 'refugees' in the sense that they had not been granted refugee status by the French state, neither had they made an asylum claim in France. They therefore had no legal right to stay in France, but at the same time they had not been placed in detention centres with a view to deporting them back to their countries of origin. Sangatte was thus described as a 'grey zone', with neither France nor the UK willing to take responsibility for those who were living there. The fact that the French authorities applied seemingly 'exceptional' legal conditions to the Sangatte

Camp indicated the creation of a zone within French territory but outside of the reach of normal French law. This situation was compared by some to that of an eighteenth century general hospital 'where the sick, the mad, and the poor were piled together' (Collectif Cultures et Conflits, 2002: 56). The existence of this 'no man's land' where potential asylum seekers collected demonstrated the State's unwillingness to tackle the issues of asylum seekers and refugees, perhaps hoping that if they ignored them for long enough they would go away. It seemed, in fact, that the French authorities assumed that all those who stayed at Sangatte would eventually attempt to reach England, and thus no explanation was provided to them of the possibility of seeking asylum in France. This idea was explicitly discouraged – when the International Organisation for Migration (IOM) visited the camp to try and make the inmates aware of the dangers involved in trying to reach England, and of the obstacles that they would face if they got there, the French Ministry of the Interior warned the IOM officials not to mention the procedures for claiming asylum in France. Similarly, when associations supporting asylum seekers parked a van outside the camp gates in order to distribute leaflets in various languages advising on the rights of asylum seekers in France, they were moved away by the special police forces guarding the camp (Carrère, 2002: 17). This type of behaviour by the French authorities indicated a clear desire to discourage those staying at Sangatte from making asylum claims in France, an attitude which may have been explained by the main nationalities present in the camp – Afghans and Iraqis. An analysis of the asylum claims treated by the OFPRA in 2001 shows that 76.4 per cent of the Afghans and 46.8 per cent of the Iraqis who claimed asylum in France were granted refugee status. These figures are much higher than those for other nationalities. Thus 'not informing the Afghans or the Iraqis in the camp at Sangatte about these rates of recognition, which are completely out of the ordinary in terms of the asylum statistics in France, demonstrates clearly a desire to avoid too many of them availing themselves of this right' (Carrère, 2002: 17).

In focusing on whose responsibility it was to deal with the residents of the Sangatte camp and on what should be done with them, the debates often neglected to enquire into the processes that had brought so many people to the camp in the first place. This failure to try to understand the global processes behind the production of the asylum seekers at the camp led many to label them all as 'economic migrants' whose unjustified claims for refugee status should be rejected by both France and the UK. One detailed study of the residents at the camp diminishes this argument, however. The author of this study Smaïn Laacher (2002) argues against the labelling of asylum seekers at Sangatte as 'economic migrants'. His study at Sangatte enquired into the reasons the asylum seekers gave for leaving their country of origin. The results, detailed in table 2.6 below, show that the principle reasons given by the asylum seekers themselves for leaving their countries are war and political persecution.

Table 3.4 Reasons given by asylum seekers in the Sangatte camp for leaving their countries of origin

Reason for leaving	Per cent
War	39.4
Political persecution	34.2
Unemployment	7.4
Other	15.8
No reply	3.2
Total	100

Laacher concludes that: 'For all those who come to Sangatte the general context is the same: they have come from countries at war, or which are experiencing unnamed civil wars in certain parts of their territories, countries where military, social and economic insecurities, the negation of rights, and the (often violent) imposition of dominant cultural and religious models, is a permanent structural reality. It is important to note that the different elements that make up this general insecurity are objectively and subjectively indissociable' (Laacher, 2002: 26).

The study also demonstrates the mechanisms that operate to bring these asylum seekers to Europe, and to France, and shows that the attempts to limit the number of immigrants and asylum seekers reaching Europe seem to have had the effect of creating a growing market for the services of people smugglers who can charge high prices for bringing these asylum seekers across the borders into the EU. Seventy-five per cent of those interviewed at Sangatte had paid between five and ten thousand dollars to reach Europe. This tends to confirm the observation made by other researchers which shows that the price of entry into French, or European, territory is becoming increasingly difficult and expensive (Chemillier-Gendreau, 1998).

The interviews also reveal that contrary to what many believed, the asylum seekers at Sangatte had not set out from their countries of origin with the intention of trying to reach England but had arrived at Sangatte after finding out about the possibilities of getting to England from others in Europe, often from the smugglers who would offer to get them there. Almost 90 per cent of those interviewed said that they had only found out about the existence of Sangatte after arriving in Europe, and 52.5 per cent of these had only found out about the camp once they had arrived in France. Neither were they drawn to the UK by perceived advantages for asylum seekers there. In fact, the only 'pull' factors drawing these asylum seekers to England was the existence of friends or relatives there. Their perceptions of conditions for asylum seekers in the UK had little to do with their choice – in fact most admitted that they knew little or nothing about England –, neither did the fact that they spoke English – again, few spoke English, and whether or not they spoke the language made little difference to their decision to try and reach the UK. The comments of a young man from Afghanistan are typical: 'I found out about Sangatte from the smugglers in Paris. I don't have any real project. I'll just do whatever I can to stay safe' (cited in Laacher 2002: 53). Thus whilst some argued that the very existence of a centre for asylum seekers at Sangatte acted to create new migrants who would leave their home countries with the intention of reaching the camp, it seems rather that these people would have left their countries of origin whether or not the camp existed, and that the Sangatte centre merely served to provide a vivid illustration of the problems of asylum seekers in Europe. As Laacher argues: 'These general observations authorise us to conclude that, contrary to dominant discourse, the Sangatte centre is in no way a mechanism creating or favouring a migratory influx' (Laacher, 2002:64).

But whilst the goal of getting to England remained prevalent amongst those staying at the Sangatte camp, the means of achieving this goal became more and more difficult and dangerous during the period of the camp's existence – many were killed whilst attempting the crossing from France to England and others had limbs amputated. The pressure on France to put tighter and tighter controls on the camp and to increase the security surrounding the entrance to the Channel Tunnel, meant that those trying to reach England often had to try several times before making a successful attempt, many never made it. And the asylum seekers trying to get to England found that due to the increasing security measures in place, they could no longer attempt the crossing on their own but became completely reliant on smugglers to achieve the trip. Thus a paradoxical situation arose whereby the French desire to prevent these people from claiming asylum in France coupled with the British insistence that security at the Sangatte camp and around the Channel Tunnel be tightened to prevent these people arriving in England created a situation which benefited the people smuggling networks which the states of the EU have consistently condemned and proclaimed their determination to eliminate. As Carrère remarks: 'If at the beginning those who wished to reach England could try by themselves to slip aboard one of the existing means of transport, it is much more difficult today, and this situation has opened up the market to smugglers of all types. States have thus been responsible for the creation of channels and networks which they claim to be opposing, and for placing asylum seekers in the hands of those who see in them a source of abundant profits' (Carrère, 2002: 20). Thus, as in many other cases, the goal of increasing the security of state boundaries only served to reinforce the insecurity of those who were attempting to cross those boundaries and who became reliant on trafficking and smuggling networks set up to take advantage of the increasing securitisation of immigration and asylum issues.

Following the election of the new Right-wing government in 2002, a Franco-British agreement was finally reached over Sangatte. The French government promised to close the camp by April of 2003 and in return they sought assurances that the UK would impose stricter conditions on asylum seekers to mitigate some of the supposed 'pull' factors attracting people to the UK. The Sangatte camp was in fact closed earlier than the date agreed, in December 2002. The British and French governments decided that 70 per cent of the residents of the camp on the date of closure would be allowed to enter the UK, with France allowing the rest to remain in France and receive a work permit and a temporary residence permit. The deal between the two governments also involved the installation of new high-tech security equipment at Calais, and other French ports, to try and detect and stop any other migrants attempting to reach the UK through these routes.

The closure of the Sangatte centre has not, however, put an end to the influx of migrants into the area around Calais. Even before the camp was closed many came hoping to gain a 'badge' that would signal that they had been resident in the centre and that they were therefore entitled to travel to England with the other residents. A report in *Libération* described the living conditions of some of these people:

> It's a line of old cement pipes at the side of road, surrounded by mud. At the entrance to these pipes hang a curtain of damp clothes and wet blankets. Nine people live here. By day they crouch round a fire, at night they hide inside the icy pipes ... They know that on Tuesday night about 80 of their compatriots managed to negotiate entry to the Sangatte centre, getting a badge and a probable safe-passage to London. While the others wait they hide. 'When we go to a church to try and get some dry clothes and some food, the police are waiting for us', sighs Shoghi, 25 years old. 'As we haven't got a badge they'll take us to prison' (*Libération*, 6 December 2002).

Many similar reports told of the hundreds of migrants camping out in the hope of gaining a badge and a passage to the UK. And once Sangatte was finally closed at the end of December these migrants began to gather around other Channel ports, still hoping to reach England. The closure of the Sangatte centre has not, therefore, resolved the problem of these migrants who wish to cross the Channel to claim asylum, and in a wider sense it can be argued that the issue of Sangatte demonstrated a failure of the European agreements on asylum seekers and refugees. The fact that the various EU conventions on asylum seekers have stipulated that these migrants must claim asylum in the first country they reach in the EU, means that those who wish to have a choice in the matter of their destination will find themselves obliged to find illegal means to cross internal European borders. Some of those seeking to reach the UK from Sangatte and from other French ports, have family and personal ties in the UK which make this a favoured destination, others have been promised by traffickers and smugglers that they will be taken to the UK. Whatever the reasons, these people are desperate to cross borders and will taken many risks to reach their destinations. In addition, as individual European states look for internal controls and restrictions which will deter asylum seekers from making claims in their country, there is greater incentive for these asylum seekers to try and cross into another country to make their claim there. Many of those trying to cross to the UK know little or nothing about the conditions for asylum seekers there, but feel that they must be better than the conditions they have encountered in France. One Afghan woman seeking to enter Sangatte echoed feelings expressed by many others about why she would not seek asylum in France:

> I don't expect anything from France. The police set their dogs on us, spray tear gas at us. When they arrest us they let us go in the middle of nowhere, four or five

hours walk from here. Why would we want to stay in this country? (cited in *Libération*, 11 December 2002).

All of these pressures act to heighten the insecurity of those who in many cases have fled to Europe to try and gain a greater degree of security than that they had in their country of origin. Closing down centres like that at Sangatte will not make these people disappear, but will just pass the problem on to other locations. A report a year on from the closure of Sangatte suggests that nothing has been solved by this closure:

> There are still two hundred would-be asylum seekers wandering the streets of Calais, helped only by volunteer associations. Three members of one of these associations have been put on trial for helping foreigners in illegal situations. Outside of Calais migrants have gathered in all the other Channel ports such as Le Havre and Ouistreham. In Paris, since the closure of the camp, dozens of Iraqis and Afghans have appeared and are sleeping rough in the squares, alleyways, and building sites of the 10th Arrondissement. Is this a return to the starting point? In 1999 Sangatte was opened to shelter Kosovar families who were sleeping rough in Calais (*Libération*, 19 November 2003).

Conclusion

The desire to limit inward migration, together with the fact that seeking asylum remains one of the only legal ways for migrants to enter Europe, has led to European governments trying to reduce both the numbers of asylum seekers that enter their country and the number of these asylum seekers who are granted refugee status. In attempting to cut down on the numbers granted refugee status, the French government, like many of its European counterparts, has justified the severity of new policies on asylum by arguing that many of those who come to France to seek asylum are in fact 'false refugees'. However, this emphasis on the need to sort out 'real' and 'false' refugees and to speed up and streamline the processes by which asylum claims are assessed has led to an accentuation of the administrative dimension of the issue, obscuring the real political character of the debate. Rather than a continuing refinement of the procedures for dealing with asylum seekers in order to diminish the number of those who are granted refugee status, what is necessary is a real debate on the bases of the asylum system and the way in which those who are persecuted might be welcomed. The debate over asylum cannot, moreover, be divorced from a more general discussion over immigration, as much of the discourse surrounding the asylum system stems from the way in which immigration has been problematised in recent years. Continuing to roll-back the rights of asylum seekers and to seek ways to deny their claims for refugee status will not make the problem disappear, but is likely to lead to more situations like those presently experienced in Calais and in parts of Paris, with would-be asylum seekers sleeping rough and depending on charitable organisations for food. These types of situations highlight the real crisis that the French asylum system is currently experiencing, a crisis that stems from the fact that France, like other European countries is seeking to protect itself from asylum seekers in place of offering them protection.

Chapter 4

The *Sans-Papiers* Movement: Mobilisation Through Illegality

One of the central features of debates over immigration in many European countries has been the question of illegality and the attempts by many governments to reduce the numbers of 'illegal' immigrants on their territory. This issue has been made even more acute by the configuration of the Schengen Area and the subsequent fears about the insecurity of Europe's external borders as discussed in the previous chapter. In this context illegal immigrants are seen as a central part of the threat to Europe's security, the idea of illegality often being connected in the public imagination, with images of criminal activity, smuggling and trafficking. The reality of illegal immigrants and residents is, however, usually much more complex than these images suggest and is connected to particular national legal and administrative contexts which provide the framework within which migrants become illegalised.

The Contemporary *Sans-Papiers* Movement: Origins and Impacts

One predominant feature of the contemporary debate over immigration in France, has been the presence of the sans-papiers, meaning literally those 'without papers'. Widespread media attention was drawn to the situation of these sans-papiers when the government ordered special police forces to break down the doors of a church in Paris to expel those sans-papiers who had been staging a hunger strike inside. This expulsion and the media coverage it attracted served to mobilise both other immigrants finding themselves in a situation of illegality, and parts of the French population who rallied to the support of the sans-papiers, with a series of demonstrations and public petitions ensuing. This key moment in the recent history of immigration in France symbolised both the determination of the French state to refuse to grant rights to those who were believed to be residing 'illegally' on its territory and also to expel those 'illegal' immigrants wherever possible, and at the same time the political mobilisation both of the immigrant population and their French supporters to resist this categorisation of 'illegality'.

Occupations and hunger strikes are not a new phenomenon of immigrant mobilisation in France. Already in December 1972, nineteen Tunisians faced with expulsion from France occupied a church in Valence and went on a hunger strike. The success of these hunger strikers in bringing their plight to public attention and in eliciting a favourable response from the government – all nineteen were granted legal residence papers – gave rise to similar demonstrations in about twenty other French towns in the following year (Simeant, 1998). Since then there have been a series of sporadic mobilisations of a similar nature. The largest and most sustained movement of sans-papiers, however, began in the mid-1990s as a result of a series of legislation introduced by right-wing governments which had the effect of pushing more and more immigrants into a situation of illegality.

The contemporary sans-papiers movement began on 18 March 1996 when three hundred Africans, originating mainly from Mali and Senegal, began their occupation of the Saint-Ambroise church in the eleventh arrondissement of Paris, an occupation designed to put pressure on the government to regularise their residence situation in France. Four days later the occupation of Saint-Ambroise was ended by the expulsion of the protestors by the police. Mamady Sané, describes this expulsion in his diary recounting the story of the sans-papiers:

> On Friday 22 March, we were woken at five thirty in the morning, by policemen dressed in riot gear with helmets and batons. Touré, the cook, told me how they started hitting some men, those who were on hunger strike. Women and children were screaming, men running to try and escape arrest, chairs flew through the air and broke against the walls of the church. It was complete chaos. Sixty two adults were arrested and the others who had escaped were surrounded by policemen. They told them that they should know that blacks had no place here in France, and asked whether they thought they were in Africa …. (Sané, 1996: 45).

After their expulsion from the church by the police, the demonstrators moved around a variety of locations around Paris, before installing themselves in the Saint Bernard church in the eighteenth arrondissement, on the 28 June. In the interval between the occupation of the two churches, the a college of mediators had been formed on the initiative of the theatre director, Arianne Mnouchkine. This group of mediators, composed of academics, lawyers and other personalities met the government of Alain Juppé on 10 April, but their propositions were rejected. Meanwhile, other occupations and hunger strikes began in various cities and towns around France. Ten of the sans-papiers occupying the Saint Bernard church also began a hunger strike. On the 23 August 1996, over a thousand police and riot police broke down the doors of the church in order to expel the sans-papiers inside. Madjiguène Cissé, a leading spokeswoman for the sans-papiers movements, described the events of that morning:

> At 7.56 huge crashes broke through the back door. The blades of axes appeared through the splintered wood. The door gave way and a crowd of riot police piled in throwing chairs over their heads. Quickly tear gas filled the building … The police started to sort people and to separate the Whites and the Blacks. We were sitting down gripping on to each other. Anyone who resisted received numerous blows (Cissé, 1999: 116).

Ironically, the underlying racist assumptions which motivated the police to separate the occupants of the Church into groups of Black and White – with the White people being allowed to go free whilst the Blacks were arrested – meant that some White sans-papiers were not arrested, whilst many of those Black people who were arrested did actually have legal residence papers, and had been in the Church as a support to their friends and relations (Cissé, 1996). This example illustrates the increasing racialisation of the immigration issue, and the way in which the security of many has been threatened by the presumption that all of the non-White population are potentially 'illegal' immigrants.

The violence of the police intervention at Saint Bernard, together with the widespread media coverage it received provoked a wave of public support and demonstrations in favour of the sans-papiers. A demonstration in Paris the following week brought eleven thousand people on to the street to protest against the government's treatment of these sans-papiers. This massive mobilisation pointed to a further politicisation of the sans-papiers issue, and beyond it, a more general debate on the issues of immigration and citizenship in France. As Terray argues, this issue 'raises problems which are decisive, even vital, for French society' (Terray, 1997: 249).

The movement in support of the sans-papiers gained even greater resonance when at the end of 1996, Alain Juppé's government introduced two new bills relating to illegal residence and work in France. Particular attention was focused on the so-called Debré law, named after the Minister of the Interior, Jean-Louis Debré. This law was adopted at a first reading in the National Assembly in December 1996, with amendments introduced by certain deputies to make it even more stringent. There was little opposition to the adoption of the law from the Left-wing deputies, which attracted great criticism from the extra-parliamentary Left, and from associations defending immigrants' rights. Two articles of this law provoked particular objections from the sans-papiers and their supporters. The first was the decision to end the process of automatic renewal of ten-year residence permits, which meant that even those who had been living in France for at least ten-years could suddenly find themselves without legal residence papers and thus subject to possible deportation. The second measure which aroused vocal criticism was that which stipulated that French nationals who received any non-EU citizens to stay in their houses must inform the local authorities of their arrival and departure. Further to this the local authorities would have the right to check whether any non-EU citizen whose residence permit had expired was still living with this French national. This clause was seen not only as an unacceptable check on the rights of movements of non-EU nationals in France, but also as an infringement of the rights of French individuals and of their liberty to receive visitors of their choice in their private homes. Reaction to this clause was led to a group of film-makers who published a petition in *Le Monde* and *Libération* declaring that they were all themselves guilty of receiving 'illegal' foreign residents in their own houses and calling for a campaign of civil disobedience against this new Debré law (*Le Monde*, *Libération*, 12 February 1997). This petition soon received 120 000 signatures, and a demonstration in Paris against the Debré law on the 22 February 1997 gathered more than 100 000 demonstrators. The Conseil d'Etat also objected to this clause in the law, warning the government that it may be unconstitutional to oblige French citizens to inform on who was staying with them in this way, and so when the final text of the bill was adopted in

April 1997, the clause was re-worded to place the obligation on the immigrant and not their host to inform local authorities of their movements. This partial retreat on one area did not greatly impinge, however, on the major thrust of the law, which showed the government's determination to crack down on illegal immigrants within French territory. This determination has been maintained by successive government, of both the Left and the Right-wing, and despite the limited concessions made by the Left-wing government elected in June 1997, under Lionel Jospin, including the regularisation of a number of sans-papiers under the terms of the Chevènement circular (see chapter 2), a mobilisation by and around the sans-papiers has continued. Indeed, for many, the policies of the Left-wing government on this issue were highly disappointing, failing as they did to repeal the Pasqua-Debré laws and introducing stringent conditions for the promised regularisation of sans-papiers so that eventually only about half of the 160,000 who submitted a request for regularisation did actually receive legal residence papers. And those 79,900 people who were regularised received only temporary one year permits, which still carried with them the insecurity of being unsure whether or not a long-term residence in France could be guaranteed. Balibar argues that the question of the sans-papiers has revealed a new consensus between Left and Right and that:

> The way in which the Jospin government tried to put into force a renewed version of the essential dispositions of the Pasqua and Debré laws, laws against which one of the major mobilisations of the Left in recent years had taken place, and which he himself had promised to abrogate during his election campaign, is very revealing in this sense. All the more so as this was accompanied by an intense production of reactionary rhetoric aimed at stigmatising the 'moral Left' and its 'abstract claims for human rights', in other words the militants who had the weakness to believe – in the light of past experience – that loyalty to engagements which have been undertaken is an essential component of political credibility (Balibar, 1999: 93).

The Jospin government was criticised by the sans-papiers and by those supporting them, for not repealing the previous Pasqua and Debré laws and for not removing many of the repressive aspects of this legislation. Both Jospin and Chevènement declared the necessity to maintain a firm line on immigration and to avoid the danger of a regularisation of sans-papiers becoming an invitation for more immigrants to try and enter France illegally. Although some sans-papiers were regularised under the terms of the Chevènement law and circular, many complained that the policies and legislation in place were ambiguous and left too much room for arbitrary decisions by officials. The Chevènemet circular specified that the situation of certain categories of foreigners in an irregular situation would be re-examined, and thus some were automatically excluded from the process as not being within these certain categories, whatever the particular conditions of their personal situation. In addition, the proofs needed to accompany the dossier requesting regularisation were often impossible to gather, either because of lack of administrative services in a sans-papiers country of origin which did not allow them to have access to birth certificates etc, or as a result of the particular forms of vulnerability that they had encountered whilst they were in France. The obligation to supply eight years worth of pay slips, for example, was difficult to meet for workers who had spent the last eight years working illegally on the black market. As Cissé recounts:

> The arbitrariness which the sans-papiers have constantly denounced is still omnipresent: a dossier which is refused in one prefecture may be accepted by another; a sans-papière receives a response notifying her that her dossier has been refused after her interview at the prefecture, when in reality she has never been asked to come for that interview (Cissé, 1999: 161).

The process of regularisation under the Chevenèment law and circular also led to an anomaly in the situation of those sans-papiers whose requests for regularisation had failed. These roughly 70,000 sans-papiers had registered their dossier at the prefecture and were thus known to the authorities, who also knew that their claim had failed and that they were still 'illegal' residents. These people were now 'official clandestines' whose presence in France was known and registered, and a question arose as to what would happen to them. The government announced that these 'official clandestines' should leave France and that they would be deported from the country if they were stopped and controlled in a public place. However, Jospin said that the authorities would not 'go and look for them in their homes'. Clearly the French administration did not have the political or technical capability to go out and find 70, 000 people and deport them all in one go, but this creation of a set of 'official clandestines' did nothing to clear up the situation, and left many living in a state of great insecurity where they felt scared every time they left their home in case they were stopped by the police.

The Right-wing government elected in 2002, promised to resolve the issue of the sans-papiers once and for all, with a new circular issued by the Minister of the Interior, Nicolas Sarkozy, aiming to clarify procedures for prefectures dealing with claims for residence papers, together with an increased resolve to expel those without papers. Sarkozy announced to prefects that he announced the number of expulsions to double within a year, and he has re-started the use of 'charter' flights to expel illegal immigrants, even reaching an agreement with the Belgian government to run joint 'charters' through Paris and Brussels. This determination to resolve the issue of the sans-papiers has, however, faltered in light of the highly complex nature of the issue particularly in relation to the nature of illegality (see below), and also in the face of continued resistance and mobilisation on the part of the sans-papiers and their supporters. This mobilisation has increasingly centred on the demand for a regularisation of all sans-papiers and not partial regularisations on a case by case basis. In making this demand, the sans-papiers have attempted to contest the government's attempts to divide immigrants into 'good' and 'bad', 'deserving' and 'undeserving' of residence in France, and to highlight the ways in which the attempts to control immigration have led to increasing insecurity for many different individuals and groups.

Since the mid-1990s then, there has been a constant campaign to highlight the position of those who are living in situations of illegality, and a continual succession of occupations of churches and other public buildings, and of hunger strikes by those protesting against their illegal status and resisting attempts by government agents to expel them from French territory. This question of the sans-papiers has occupied a strategic place in the political debate over immigration in France, highlighting as it does the boundaries between nationals and non-nationals, and between citizens of the EU and those from outside of Europe. In addition, it provides an interesting reflection on how those in a position of great insecurity and with few immediately apparent political resources can mobilise to defend themselves against threats posed by the French state.

The Creation of Illegality

The mobilisation of the sans-papiers has brought to the foreground the issue of illegality and of how people come to be 'illegal' residents in France. The issue of illegal or clandestine immigration is not a new one – throughout French history there has been clandestine immigration and sporadic periods of regularisation of these illegal immigrants. Indeed at one point illegal immigration was viewed as completely necessary for functioning of the economy. In the post-War period politicians freely admitted that they could not control all immigration and that to attempt to do so would be to reduce the number of immigrant workers available for French industry, so weakening France's economic performance.

Recently, as anti-immigration discourse has grown stronger, illegal immigration has become a key issue, with politicians trying to create a clear distinction between legal and illegal immigrants, and framing these 'illegal' immigrants as a source of growing insecurity in French society. This focus on illegality has had important impacts across the immigrant population and those of immigrant origin in France, as Marie argues:

> Taken as the principal axis of government thinking and action for ten years, the trilogy of immigration, illegality and insecurity have favoured a manipulation of the notions of legality and legitimacy and have thus perverted the political discourse on the rights of the totality of the populations of immigrant origin and on their place in society (Marie, 1988: 91).

The focus on the legality or illegality of an immigrant's status, and the attempt to draw a strict boundary between the two categories, can be seen to have led the fragilisation of the status and security of all immigrants. As Fassin and Morice argue, even those immigrants who are in a regular situation with legal residence permits find themselves often in a state of 'potential illegitimacy', whereby they become suspect, and feel insecure in their status. This insecurity of even legal residents, is reinforced by political reforms and discourse which has undermined the automatic renewal of ten-year residence permits, thus fragilising the status of those immigrants in possession of one of these cards. This 'potential illegitimacy' even hits the children of immigrants, who have themselves been born in France and who have French nationality, by a continual process of 'ethnicisation' of social relations and of increasing discrimination and stigmatisation of immigrants (Fassin and Morice, 2001).

One of the components of the focus on illegality in immigration control has been to normalise the idea of the security of the French state being breached by foreigners (mainly from Africa and Asia) crossing the borders of France and entering the country without the legal right to do so. The discourse has defined as an 'illegal' immigrant anyone who finds themselves in breach of the regulations controlling the entry and residence of foreigners in France. By so defining illegal immigrants this discourse creates the notion of a homogenous mass of people who are all 'clandestine' and who all pose a threat to the security of the French state. It reduces a complex situation to one of the 'lowest common denominator', depicting all those who find themselves for various reasons without the requisite legal residence papers as criminals who have illegally entered the country. Thus state policies on immigration control can be legitimised by reference to the defence of French national interests against this mass of 'clandestines'. The official discourse on immigration policy has been framed by the idea that there must be a distinction between legal immigrants who should be integrated into French society, and illegal immigrants who must be removed from France. Often the expulsion of illegal immigrants is described as a necessary condition of the integration of legal immigrants. This discourse, however, oversimplifies the nature of illegality and removes the complexities of the situation of many 'illegal' immigrants, and the ambiguous nature of the division between legal and illegal status. Contrary to the attempts to portray illegal immigrants as those who plot to cross the French borders without the necessary papers, many of those who find themselves in a situation of 'illegality', do so not as a result of illegal entry into the country, but as a result of one of a number of other processes. Many of those in the sans-papiers movement have been living in France for many years, since the 1980s or even the 1970s, and have experienced long periods when they had legal residence permits and worked legally. These people have found themselves without legal residence papers due to a number of different circumstances including the non-renewal of residence permits for various reasons.

Ferré attempts to clarify some of these ambiguities and misunderstandings in the discussion of 'illegal' immigrants by describing the different processes involved in leading an immigrant into a situation of illegality (Ferré, 1997). She argues that both the law and its application and particular administrative processes act to create situations of illegality. The terms of the French law on entry and residence in France are complex, but mean that there are many ways in which someone can find themselves in a situation where they may be denied legal residence papers. These include those who have entered the country without the required visa, and those who have outstayed the duration of their visa, but also those whose applications for temporary or long-term residence permits may have been denied for a variety of legal reasons. The parents of French children, for example, should be entitled to receive a legal residence permit whilst that child is living in France. However, the law stipulates that this is only granted on condition that the parent provides adequately for the child's needs and as those who apply on these grounds are foreign nationals with no legal right to work in France, often they are refused on the grounds that they are financially incapable of meeting their childrens' needs. Other sans-papiers recount stories of how, often unknown to them, they have entered into a situation where legal reasons can be found to refuse them residence papers. A sans-papiers on hunger strike in Lyon, for example, explains how despite being resident in France since 1965, he has found himself in a situation of 'illegality':

> I arrived in France from Algeria in 1965 and got married here in 1980. My son, who is French, was born here in 1982. I got a ten-year residence permit valid from 1977 to 1987, but when I went back to Algeria for a holiday and to see my family between July 1986 and January 1987, the French border police refused to let me back into the country because they said that I had stayed abroad for over six months. I came back again in May 1987 and they took away my ten-year residence permit. Since then I've been trying continually to get legal residence papers again, but so far I've had no luck, despite the fact that I've got a wife and child in France (Interview, July 2002).

This type of example shows the ways that the intricacies of the law can create situations of irregularity where people are unable to obtain a legal residence permit despite having strong grounds to justify their claim for such a permit. The complexity of the laws means that there are numerous ways in which people may find themselves in such situations. In addition, the complexity and stringency of these laws are compounded by the administrative practices by which they are applied and particularly the inflexibility of the prefectoral services to whom the responsibility of delivering residence permits is delegated. The practices regarding the delivery of residence permits can vary from one prefecture to the other, but research suggests a general pattern whereby prefectures are sometimes overly strict in their application of the laws, and search for reasons to reject claims for residence permits (Ferré, 1997). In addition, the waiting time for a decision on a person's claim for a residence permit can be extremely long, leaving them without any official papers or status whilst they wait for a decision.

An example of the difficulties posed by the prefectures is the treatment of those sans-papiers claiming a residence permit on the grounds that they have been living in France for at least ten years. Under the terms of a circular issued by Jean-Pierre Chevènement, the Socialist Minister of the Interior, in 1997, all those who can prove residence in France for at least ten years are entitled to a residence permit. However, examples from many prefectures show that the levels of proof demanded of foreigners who make a claim on these grounds may be prohibitive. Many prefectures demand two or three pieces of documentation proving that the person concerned was residing in France for each of the ten years, and some forms of proof are not accepted as not being enough to validate the claim. A sans-papiers from Toulouse recounts his experience when he went to his local prefecture to register his claim for a residence permit:

> I went with all the papers that I could gather together and presented my dossier. But, without even looking at my papers, the woman there began to create obstacles. She said that none of my documents was worth anything, and that I

should just go home. I said that I was willing to find other papers and proofs if she would just tell me what I needed to bring. She finally accepted my dossier but told me there and then that I would not be regularised. Three weeks later I went back with more papers to support my claim. The woman wouldn't even see me, so I just left them at the reception desk. It's now three months since I registered my claim and I have heard nothing (Interview, September 2002).

The government has itself recognised the problems that exist at the level of prefectures, and in December 2002, the Minister of the Interior, Nicolas Sarkozy, issued a circular in which he asked prefectures to make the process of claiming a residence permit smoother and faster, and to make the treatment afforded to those claiming a permit more welcoming. In addition he argued for a homogenisation of procedures across different geographical departments (*Le Figaro*, 9 December 2002). However, there is doubt as to whether the instructions contained in this circular will really improve the processing of claims by prefectures, particularly as the prefects are at the same time under pressure to identify suitable candidates for expulsion. At the same time as Sarkozy was announcing a revision of the procedures at prefectures he was also setting a target of deporting double the number of illegal immigrants as in previous years. This emphasis on the need to find and deport those without legal residence papers will clearly counter any push to make prefectures more 'welcoming' to immigrants seeking residence permits.

In fact, it can be argued that little will be done to improve the situation of these sans-papiers whilst there is a continual process of reinvention of illegality by the policies on immigration (Lochak, 1997). As Fassin and Morice remark:

> For the partner who is refused family reunification following a tightening of the administrative criteria, whilst his/her compatriots have received a favourable decision a few years earlier, for the student whose permits have up to now been automatically renewed and which are now not renewed because of a demand for better results in exams, for the asylum seeker who is refused refugee status on grounds which were not brought forward for relations who came in an earlier and more favourable period for political refugees, for all these foreigners who suffer from evolutions in the law, the production of irregularity is a reality of which they are cruelly aware (Fassin and Morice, 2001: 282).

The insecurities resulting from this constant creation and reinvention of the definitions of illegality are clear, with immigrants unsure as to their status and to whether or not they will be able to obtain a legal residence permit, or to be able to renew their existing residence permits. Such uncertainty with regards to residence status has an impact on their ability to engage in the labour market, their relationships with employers, and their abilities to claim benefits or to receive health care, or education for their children. The Pasqua reforms of 1993, which subordinated the right to claim social benefits to the possession of regular residence status meant that many foreigners living in France were plunged into states of extreme precariousness. Many amongst them had paid social security contributions whilst in possession of legal residence status and legal employment, but were then refused benefits when they lost this legal status.

Fassin recounts the story of a young Chinese couple which illustrates well this insecurity and its effects. The couple arrived in France in 1988, seeking asylum following political persecution in China. They installed themselves in France and found employment (which was allowed for asylum seekers at the time) whilst waiting for a decision on their asylum claim. By the time their claim was finally rejected in 1992 they had been working in France for four years, and had a three year old child. This family situation made them inexpulsable from French territory, but at the same time they could not receive legal residence papers. The insecurities created by such a situation were enormous for the couple. Both were forced to quit their jobs and find 'illegal' employment on the black market. They were unable to pay for hospital treatment when a second child was born to them, or to pay for their older child to receive urgent dental treatment. To this economic insecurity was added the fear of being stopped by the police and arrested for lack of papers. 'Since the morning when, whilst going to buy milk for the baby's bottle, the father was arrested and taken to the prefecture where he was detained all morning without being able to warn his wife, and returned to the flat to find his child terrified and hungry, the couple live in fear of another identity check which will lead to the family being deported, or worse still, to separation from their children. Now they only go out together, they avoid the metro where they are more likely to encounter identity checks, and they panic at the sight of a police uniform' (Fassin, 1997: 110).

This type of example illustrates well the multiple insecurities faced by those who find themselves without papers, and also the fears and insecurities of those with papers but who fear that they may not be renewed. This type of insecurity provided the motivation for the political mobilisation of the sans-papiers movement, but its scale and the support is has received was surprising for many. As Simeant asks, how did a group of foreigners in an illegal situation, a group that might be imagined to be particularly exploited and devoid of any resources, political or otherwise, manage to create such a massive collective action? (Simeant, 1998). The mechanisms of this mobilisation and those of the creation of a collective identity of sans-papiers will be explored in the next section.

Collective Mobilisation and Creation of an Identity

The mobilisation of the sans-papiers of Saint-Bernard in 1996 has led to a vast social movement which has extended from a core of principally African immigrants to involved migrants of all nationalities. As remarked above, the key demand of this mobilisation has been for collective legalisation or regularisation, in other words, the rejection of the idea that the cases of each sans-papier should be examined on a one by one basis. This demand contests the logic of the securitisation of immigration and the portrayal of immigrants as a danger to the French nation, a logic within which each case must be considered carefully by government authorities to see if the individual concerned might enter into the category of 'acceptable' foreigners (Chemillier-Gendreau, 1998).

Although they might be considered to constitute a marginal social category, with no legal status, the sans-papiers have managed to become a central figure in French political debate. They have managed to gain widespread media coverage, divide political parties and provoke a continual mobilisation in their support (Fassin and Morice, 2001). The reasons for the centrality of the issue in political debate are complex, but it can be argued that they return to the major debate on the nature of citizenship in France and also of exclusion from that citizenship. For, in posing illegal immigration as a threat to the security of the French nation, French governments have in turn justified the exclusion of the sans-papiers, these 'illegal' or 'clandestine' immigrants from many citizenship rights. These exclusions affect not only civil rights, but also the economic and welfare rights, and can thus be argued to provoke growing insecurity amongst the populations of sans-papiers. These exclusions and their impacts can also be seen as a source of support for their mobilisations, moving the debate beyond one simply concerning immigration rules, and expanding it to one about the nature of citizenship and inclusion or exclusion.

The collective mobilisation of the sans-papiers in France can be seen as an attempt to overcome some of their insecurity through a creation and re-definition of a collective identity. This process has, of course, not been without many difficulties, and many fissures and disagreements still exist within the movement both regarding the underlying justifications of their struggle, and the tactics to be employed to further their goals. However, it might be argued that despite the many external and internal difficulties experienced by the movement, its very existence has brought about a change in the experience of foreigners living in France without legal residence papers. Rather than existing in an individual state of illegality and insecurity, they have become politically active and have acquired a means of engaging politically with the French authorities.

In addition, the collective mobilisation of these sans-papiers has crystallised support from French nationals for their cause, as demonstrated by the presence of these French nationals amongst the occupants of various churches and at demonstrations on behalf of the sans-papiers, and also the various petitions which were circulated against the Debré laws. The images of immigrants being dragged from a church by riot police were enough to mobilise large numbers of French citizens, many of them not habitually supporters of immigrant rights, in defence of more humanitarian treatment of immigrants. The initial protests were also aimed at a Right-wing government which many believed was too eager to gain the support of the far-Right electorate. The fact that the introduction of the Debré law (see above and chapter 2), coincided with the victory of the Front National in the municipal elections in Vitrolles, only added to the sentiment of many French nationals that the Right and the extreme-Right were progressing together on a xenophobic and anti-immigration platform. Many of those who demonstrated against the Pasqua and Debré laws, and who have continued to demonstrate in support of the sans-papiers, were thus expressing sentiments of rejection towards what they saw as the progress of extreme-Right views on immigration. This mobilisation might be seen to be contributing to the development of a new 'active citizenship' (Balibar, 1999).

Illegal Immigrants and Illegal Workers: The Place of the *Sans-Papiers* in the French Labour Market

The debate over the sans-papiers has often been held concurrently with a debate over illegal work, and indeed the two questions have often been confounded so that all illegal workers are assumed to also be sans-papiers. This assumption which is clearly not correct, mixes up two separate realities, firstly that of workers who are legally resident in France (either French nationals or immigrants with residence and work permits) who may benefit from a salary or income through unemployment or other benefit, but who choose to work on the 'black market' to boost their income; secondly, that of immigrant workers who do not have legal residence or work permits and who are therefore excluded from legal, registered work and from receiving any kind of unemployment benefit or social protection. These second category of workers have no other choice than to work on the 'black market' and are therefore in a singularly weak position when it comes to choice of work and to their relationship with employers. The weakness of their position in relationship to employers poses another cause of great insecurity for these sans-papiers who often work in dangerous and difficult conditions and receive very low wages. Their position within the French economy is not often analysed, and when it is referred to by French politicians it is often as a perceived threat to the security of jobs of French nationals. However, the economic role of the sans-papiers is much more complex than that and it has been suggested that they actually benefit the economy by doing jobs that French nationals would not do, and by working for low salaries which allows certain sectors of the economy to remain competitive, and thus in an indirect way actually creates the conditions in which jobs for French nationals might be maintained. The real place of the sans-papiers in the labour market is rarely examined as governments pursue their policies of restricting illegal immigration and illegal employment.

The very nature of illegal employment makes it almost impossible to make an accurate estimate of the number of people working illegally in France, and of the proportion of these who are in fact sans-papiers. Terray estimates that about 10 per cent of all illegal workers are foreigners without residence papers, but the proportion of sans-papiers is much higher than this in some sectors including building and construction, hotels and restaurants, clothing manufacture, and agriculture (Terray, 1999). In fact, it might be argued that these sectors could not function as they do without employing these sans-papiers. A police officer from the section dealing with illegal employment, for example, told a reporter from *Le Monde* that: 'You can say without exaggeration that the quasi-total of women's clothing made in France comes from hundred of small workshops employing illegal immigrants. What's more the sector is only competitive in these conditions' (*Le Monde*, 16 October 1996). The same can be said of the construction industry where a process of sub-contracting allows employers to cut costs and therefore prices to become more competitive. This sub-contracting process usually entails the employment of workers without legal papers, as they can be employed much more cheaply. A work inspector recounts that: 'Employing a foreigner without a residence or work permit illegally costs less than half of what it would cost to employ a declared worker legally' (*Libération*, 8 October 2003).

The employment of sans-papiers can be seen as part of a more global phenomenon of the re-location of labour, a phenomenon that Terray describes as '*délocalisation sur place*' (on the spot delocalisation) (Terray, 1999: 15). This on the spot delocalisation can be seen as one of the elements of the decentralisation and dispersal of economic and productive activity which have been a part of the global restructuring of production. In general this has led to a greater flexibilisation of labour markets as employers try to reduce costs. Flexibilisation has seen a rise in the occurrence of sub-contracting, temporary and part-time working, self-employment and home working, as employers seek to reduce labour costs, but many of these processes have resulted in greater vulnerability for the workforce. As Sassen argues, forms contemporary economic dispersal entail, 'an organization of the capital-labour relation that tends to maximize the use of low-wage labor and to minimize the effectiveness of mechanisms that empower labor vis-à-vis capital. Thus the term *dispersal*, while suggestive of a geographic aspect, clearly involves a complex political and technical reorganization of production as well' (Sassen, 2001: 26). Sub-contracting in particular has been a favoured strategy of flexbilisation and of reducing the power of labour vis-à-vis capital. The sub-contracting and externalisation of many functions has had the effect of creating long chains of employment within which the employer takes less and less responsibility and it thus becomes more and more difficult to establish that any relation of exploitation exists between employer and worker (Boltanski and Chiappello, 1999).

Migrants have suffered disproportionately from this reorganization and flexibilisation of labour markets both because of their legal status and because of their presence in those employment sectors in which the greatest changes have taken place. Studies have shown that female migrants in particular have been affected by flexibilisation and by a globalisation of domestic work that involves them recuperating the domestic re-productive tasks previously assured by European women or by the State (Scrinzi, 2003) (for a fuller discussion of women and immigration see chapter 6).

Further, those immigrants without legal residence papers are extremely vulnerable in this flexible labour market, as they are without recourse to any kind of legal protection against their employers. In a situation where there has been a dissolution of direct contacts and relationships between employers and workers through various practices of sub-contracting, a laboratory for various practices of evasion of employment rights and new forms of exploitation is created, and these practices very often rest on the employment of migrant workers with no legal status who are hugely vulnerable to exploitation (Marie, 1999).

Empirical evidence points to the fact that the conditions in which many of the sans-papiers are employed create huge insecurities for them. The salaries they receive are minimal, and often they do not get paid, with no means of recourse against their employers. The story of a Chinese sans-papiers working in clothing manufacture is typical. He worked in a small sweatshop with about a dozen other sans-papiers, their boss had not paid them for two weeks. One morning he arrived for work and found the interior of the workshop had been stripped – no more sewing machines, no material. There was nothing the employees could do as they could not call the police for fear of being arrested as illegal immigrants. The man in question eventually found work in another similar workshop where he works from six at night to 9 in the morning, ensuring that the sewing machines continue twenty-four hours a day.

Mamadou a sans-papier from Cameroon has a similar story, having moved from one job to another. 'Of course you take risks', he explains, 'because you can't know if the boss will be honest or dishonest. If he pays me all the better. If not I'm in trouble' (*Libération*, 8 October 2003). Mamadou works in the building trade and earns thirty euros per day.

In addition to direct deception and withholding of pay from workers, employers have found many other means to exploit migrant workers who have no hope of legal recourse against them. Scrinzi recounts the practices of industrial cleaning companies in France who did not give their employees set working hours but instead set them a fixed number of tasks to complete. For example, workers were set a fixed number of hotel rooms to clean on the basis that it should take them seventeen minutes per room. As seventeen minutes proved insufficient time to complete the cleaning of a hotel room the workers found themselves doing many extra hours to complete the allocated number of rooms, but this extra time was not paid and so they found their hourly salary dropped to an even lower level than they imagined. If they did not complete the cleaning of the required number of rooms they were recorded as being absent from work and were not paid at all (Scrinzi, 2003).

The flexibility of migrant workers with no legal status is total, because there is no legal constraint on the relationship between employer and employee. The relationship can be terminated from one day to the next without any warning. Many sans-papiers take work by the day, hanging around in particular locations to see if they will be collected by employers. This complete flexibility is yet another factor in the insecurity of the sans-papiers who will often not know from one day to the next whether they will be able to earn any money to support themselves, and often their family.

Attempts to legislate to resolve the issue of illegal working and in particular of the employment of migrants with no legal status, have had little result. The Barrot law of March 1997 tried to reinforce the liability of employers who used sub-contractors who employed illegal workers. Rather than the prosecutor having to prove that such employers knew about the sub-contractors employing workers illegally, the employer would have to prove that he did not know anything about this practice. However, these articles were rejected by the National Assembly and the Senate, after intensive lobbying by employers' associations, and particularly by the association representing the construction industry. They argued that introducing extra administrative controls and checks on employers would not be an effective way of combating illegal employment (Terray, 1999).

The recent Sarkozy law on the management of immigration also attempts to fight against the employment of migrants with no legal residence status, and contains a clause which will criminalise and penalise immigrants who are found to be working illegally. Originally Sarkozy had intended to impose a 3,750 euro fine on any sans-papiers caught working illegally, together with expulsion from French territory and interdiction from returning. He later dropped the proposal to fine any sans-papiers found working illegally but the law retained the article which will penalise them through expulsion and interdiction from French territory. This new direction in the law has been criticised as likely to increase further the insecurity and exploitation of foreign workers employed illegally in France. Whilst the law previously criminalised employers who illegally employed workers without legal residence papers, the new law will shift the burden of criminality on to the sans-papiers themselves, so that rather than being victims they will be conceived of as profiting from this 'crime'. This is likely to make the sans-papiers even more vulnerable to exploitation by employers.

Terray argues that the failure of governments to deal effectively with the problem of the employment of migrants with no legal status, and indeed the failure to resolve satisfactorily the whole issue of the sans-papiers, is not merely a sign of inefficient government, but rather part of a wider strategy of laissez-faire which has allowed employers to reap the benefits of access to this vulnerable and exploitable section of the workforce. The sans-papiers, he maintains, perform the dual roles of guinea-pigs for new forms of the organisation of labour, and also a shock absorbers, a reserve army of labour for the French economy. For them to fulfil both of these roles it is necessary that at the same time their legal status remains fragile so that they are vulnerable to exploitation, and also that the laws are applied in a flexible manner, so that a large enough body of sans-papiers remains in France at the disposal of employers. As he concludes:

> What we see in reality is a very modulated and selective application of the legislation, which keeps foreigners without any legal status in a state of vulnerability which makes them exploitable, but at the same time permits them to remain in France in sufficient numbers, whatever the individual turnover, to give those employers practising 'on the spot de-localisation', the effectives that they require. The two halves of the equation are scrupulously complementary: without any repressive legislation there would not be any administrative fragility which allowed exploitation; but without a supple application of this legislation, there would be no workers to suffer this exploitation. As for the legislation concerning employers of foreign workers with no legal status ... we cannot even talk about a supple and modulated application of the law, but rather of a matter of fact tolerance: prosecutions are rare, convictions exceptional, and they practically never catch the real employers (Terray, 1999: 22).

Whether or not one accepts the causality in Terray's argument, it is clear that the sans-papiers occupy a particular place in the French labour market, and that their labour is significant in some sectors of the economy. However the conditions within which they are employed are ones of vulnerability and exploitation and this is only exaggerated by the introduction of tighter controls over their legal and political status.

Conclusion

Launching his fight against illegal immigration, Nicolas Sarkozy announced that he believed this phenomenon was not an inevitability. However, attempts to deal with the issue of illegal immigration and with the question of the sans-papiers in particular, have demonstrated that punitive responses do not seem to provide any resolution. Instead a multiplication of legislation to try to control immigration and to deal with the issue of illegal immigration has resulted in an often arbitrary system, and a system within which many former legal immigrants have become 'illegalised'. The paradoxes within this system emerge from an insistence on trying to create a categorical divide between legal and illegal, good and bad immigrants. This attempt at classification ignores the multiplicity of immigrants' trajectories and experiences.

The sans-papiers mobilisation which started in the mid-1990s has not disappeared and has continued to make visible many of the contradictions of French immigration policies. Although a priori a small and exceptional category of residents, the sans-papiers have provided a clear example of processes of exclusion that exist within French society, and of the insecurities with which migrants are faced.

The 'problem' of the sans-papiers in France illustrates well a dilemma faced by most European countries over illegal immigration. Attempts to distinguish between legal and illegal immigration and to 'securitize' the illegal immigration issue have meant a raft of restrictive policies, but the numbers of illegalised immigrants present on French territory means that these policies cannot be effective, and in fact, many of these 'illegalised' immigrants have created a settled family life in France and are playing a role in the French economy. Under these circumstances, perhaps what is needed is not more border controls, more strict measures to deal with 'overstayers', and more internal controls to seek out illegal residents and deport them. These control measures have been seen to have the effect of merely increasing the likelihood of people smuggling and trafficking. What could be suggested instead is a desecuritisation of the issue of illegal immigration, with a facilitation of legal entry and residence that might undercut the need for illegal entry. In addition, this type of approach would allow for the greater legal protection of migrant workers so that the extreme types of exploitation and vulnerability that have been noted might not be able to occur so easily. Those who object to this type of approach, as with those who have criticised any attempt at regularisation of illegal residents, argue that any such measures of regularisation or facilitation of legal entry will act as a beacon for a huge invasion of migrants. Such fears seem largely unfounded, however, if placed in the context of a general history of migration and of its patterns. As Sassen points out, evidence shows that the majority of illegal immigrants are from the same nationality groups as the population of legal migrants, and they typically make up a much smaller percentage of migrants than the legal population. This she suggests, 'signals a measure of boundedness in the process of illegal immigration, and the possibility that it is shaped by similar systemic conditions as the legal population and is thereby similarly limited in its scope and scale' (Sassen, 1999: 143).

Chapter 5

Immigrants' Rights: The Changing Boundaries of Citizenship

The development of immigration and asylum policy in recent years in France has led not only to reinforcement of external controls in order to limit immigration, but also to transformations of the rights of immigrants within France as a form of internal control. For much of this time, twin policies of limiting further immigration (or moving towards 'zero' immigration which has been expounded as a goal by some), and of integrating the immigrants already resident in France, have been proposed. However, the notion of what constitutes 'integration' has often been confused and blurred, and the push towards integration has not always been accompanied by a parallel expansion of the rights that might be deemed necessary to this integration, nor of the conditions for the realisation of these rights. Whilst non-national immigrants' rights do in some respects match those of national citizens, giving support to the idea that some form of postnational citizenship is developing, or has already developed within France, at the same time there has been a process of rolling back the rights of immigrants in some areas. Further, it might be argued that even where formal rights have been granted to immigrants, the conditions for the full realisation of those rights do not exist. Thus, as argued in chapter 1, it might be more accurate to talk about an increasing stratification of rights between different groups, rather than a uniform progression towards postnational citizenship rights for all. This chapter will discuss in greater detail the various debates that have taken place over immigrants' rights, and will argue that the increasing stratification of rights can be seen as a source of insecurity for many immigrants. The chapter starts with an examination of immigrants' political rights, an area which has proved a constant source of disagreement. For some advocates of postnational citizenship, the lack of formal voting rights and the right to be elected is not an important barrier to citizenship, since political citizenship might be provided in the form of participation through associational movements or other alternative forms of participation. It might be argued, however, that on the other hand, the lack of formal political rights provides an insuperable obstacle to immigrants' full citizenship and hampers their full integration into French society. And even for those immigrants who have been naturalised and who therefore have formal political rights, the issue of lack of representation of ethnic minorities in France's National Assembly and in local elected assemblies might be seen as a stumbling block to the realisation of full political rights.

The Debate over Immigrants' Right to Vote

One of the major debates that has taken place over immigrants' political participation and representation has been that over whether or not immigrants should be granted the right to vote in local elections. This debate has been ongoing and may be viewed as a critical factor in the more general discussion of the limits of citizenship for immigrants.

The issue of immigrants' right to vote in local elections was first raised in the mid-1970s by pressure groups and associations such as the FASTI and the Ligue des Droits de l'Homme (Human Rights League). These groups were inspired by the decision taken by Sweden in 1975 to grant the right to vote and to be eligible to foreigners in local elections. These rights were granted on the basis not of nationality but of residence. This call for the right to vote in local elections for those who lived in France but did not possess French nationality was taken up by various groups on the Left, as part of a call for a recognition of diversity – *le droit à la différence* (Favell, 1998). The idea was included as one of the 110 propositions which formed Mitterrand's electoral manifesto for the 1981 presidential elections, proposition number 80 promising to give the vote in municipal elections to those who had been residing legally in France for at least five year. However, this reform was never implemented when the Left came to power, partly due to constitutional obstacles, but for the stronger reason that the Socialist Party leaders decided that it would be an electorally unpopular move, particularly after 1983 when the Front National began to gain ground rapidly in local elections. As outlined in chapter 2, an announcement made by the Minister for Foreign Affairs, Claude Cheysson, in August 1981, stating that the government had resolved to grant voting rights to foreigners met with a storm of opposition despite quick rebuttals by other government ministers. This announcement formed the basis of Right-wing accusation of laxity over immigration which eventually forced the Socialist Party into a retreat on this issue.

Those who cited the Constitution as an obstacle to granting immigrants the right to vote in local elections argued that article 3, which stipulates that national sovereignty belongs to the French people would be breached if non-nationals could be eligible and vote in local elections. This is because local electors would participate indirectly in the election of members of the Senate – Senators being elected by an electoral college composed of mayors and regional and municipal councillors. Several lawyers suggested modifying the Constitution in order to remove this obstacle (Wihtol de Wenden, 1988), but the prevailing political conditions meant that this type of reform was not adopted seriously by any of the major political parties. The difficulty with any such reform was that it would involve a rejection of the link between national citizenship and the right to vote, and for many in France, this link was fundamental to the nature of the Republic and its concept of citizenship. As Philippe Séguin, a leading member of the centre-Right RPR party argued: 'From the moment that immigrants are not French citizens they should not vote, if not the notion of citizenship does not have any meaning' (*Le Quotidien de Paris*, 29 March 1985). And in 1989, the RPR launched a petition in the name of preserving national identity, entitled 'You need to be French to vote' (*Le Monde*, 16 December 1989).

In addition to the Constitutional obstacles posed to the granting of voting rights to immigrants, others put forward arguments based on their incapacity to properly exercise political rights. These arguments can be compared to those used against extending the right to vote to women in the first half of the century (Bouamama, 2001). Some maintained that other forms of political activity, such as community associations or trade union activism, were better suited to the position of immigrants. These types of arguments tended to lose ground, however, as it became clear that they were far from the social reality of the immigrant population. Instead the focus was placed more and more on the issue of national sovereignty, and on the threat to that sovereignty that would be engendered by granting non-nationals voting rights. As Gastaut argues, 'Confounding nationality and citizenship was an easy way to take refuge behind a conservative principle in order to refuse the idea of a right to vote for foreigners' (Gastaut, 2000: 523).

The reluctance to introduce reforms to grant the right to vote to immigrants was also influenced by public opinion which was seemingly hostile to the idea. Several of the Socialist Party leaders declared themselves favourable in principal to giving immigrants voting rights, but argued that in practice the public were not ready for such a development, and that it could do more harm than good to immigrants by stirring up public hostility against them. Opinion polls supported this idea of public hostility. Polls carried out between 1974 and 1994 showed a continuing opposition to the idea of giving foreigners the right to vote in local elections, with the percentage of those against ranging from 55 to 75 per cent (Gastaut, 2000).

Opinion amongst immigrants themselves appeared favourable to having the right to vote in municipal elections, despite the argument from some French politicians that they were not ready to exercise such a right. In a poll carried out in 1990 for *L'Express* magazine, 66 per cent of all those immigrants interviewed said that they would like to have this right to vote, and this figure rose to 73 per cent of all Maghrebin immigrants (*L'Express*, 23 March 1990). For some, however, the right to vote only in municipal elections was too limited a right. Sayad argued that the right to vote only in municipal elections was a right too linked to the colonial period and the notion of 'second-class citizens'. He asked:

> What is an elector worth if they can only elect a mayor: only the mayor and not the president of the Republic? And what is this mayor worth if he is in part elected by citizens who are not like the others? He is not like other mayors; and there will always be someone, in some circumstance, to maliciously and insidiously remind him that he was only elected thanks to the extra votes he got from second-class citizens, citizens who are not necessarily nationals. Do we not run the risk of creating a duality of electoral colleges and of classes of citizens: a college of first class citizens and a college of second class citizens; citizens who vote for all mandates and elect all of their representatives, and citizens who vote for only local mandates and who only elect their mayor. We know only too well this type of system. Colonialism has already made us familiar with this kind of discrimination (Sayad, 1985: 78).

Having been a major issue at the beginning of the 1980s after the election of the first Socialist government of the Fifth Republic, the issue of voting rights for immigrants came to the forefront of political discussion again in 1990 when a ferocious debate led to the issue being buried by the government. Whilst the RPR launched a pre-emptive campaign against voting rights for immigrants (see above), anti-racist and pro-immigrant associations organised a Collective for Citizenship based on Residence, calling for a real integration of foreigners into French political life (*Le Monde*, 9 February 1990). The Socialist Prime Minister, Michel Rocard, who was himself reticent on the issue called a meeting of all parties (excluding the Front National) to try and decide the question once and for all before a parliamentary debate on immigration. In return for the Right-wing opposition's support in this debate, Rocard agreed to drop the idea of giving immigrants the right to vote. This was seen as a sell-out by some in the Socialist Party and led to furious divisions within the Left. The Socialist party's spokesperson in the National Assembly, Jean Le Garrec, made a speech in which he reproached Rocard for his decision and argued that:

> Contrary to you, Prime Minister, I see in granting the right to vote to immigrants not simply the end of a process but a powerful factor for integration. Even if we take into account the difficulties of this way forward, we should not abandon our fundamental values. Immigrants pay taxes, use collective services, share communal life. Why shouldn't they have the chance to express themselves? Why should we not accept that they ought to have an impact on local politics? Giving them the vote has always been one of the objectives of the Socialist Party ... Public opinion may be more reserved on this issue, but the hostility is not as strong as some are pleased to make out (*Le Monde*, 31 May 1990).

The Maastricht Treaty and the European Vote: A Complicating Factor

All of the arguments against granting the right to vote in local elections to immigrants, were challenged by the developments following the Maastricht Treaty, whereby EU citizens were given the right to vote in local elections in any European country in which they were resident, irrespective of their having the nationality of that country or not. This change re-invigorated the campaign for immigrants' right to vote as the granting of this right to EU citizens highlighted the weakness of most of the arguments against this reform. The contradictions that would arise from granting voting rights to EU nationals but not to other resident non-nationals became apparent. As the 2001 municipal elections approached the campaign for immigrant's right to vote gathered greater momentum. However, the idea still met resistance from most of the major political parties. For some politicians it was possible to make a clear distinction between the case of EU citizens having the right to vote in French local elections and other non-national residents not being granted this right. They argued that EU citizens' right to vote was a reciprocal right that was extended to French citizens living elsewhere in the EU, and that this situation was thus judicially different from that of non-EU citizens residing in France. Edouard Balladur, a former Right-wing Prime Minister, argued that:

> The situation of other (non-EU) foreigners who reside on French territory is judicially different because France isn't linked to states other than those of the European Union by a treaty like the Treaty of Maastricht (cited in Bouamama, 2001: 29).

This argument supposes that any rights accorded to non-nationals residing in France should be dependent on reciprocal rights being granted to French nationals living in the former's country of nationality. Any notion that individuals should be granted political rights independent of their possessing a particular nationality is denied, and thus the whole concept of post national citizenship is rejected.

Whilst the Right was firmly against granting voting rights to non-nationals from outside of the EU (and the extreme-Right Front National even argued against granting voting rights to EU nationals, maintaining that only those who were willing to adopt French nationality deserved to have these rights), the Left was more split. In general politicians from the Left declared themselves favourable to the principle of granting voting rights in local elections to non-nationals residing in France, but for many there were still obstacles to this in practice. A constitutional bill proposed by les Verts (the Green Party) in favour of granting non-EU nationals the right to vote in municipal election was passed at a first reading by the National Assembly in April 2000, but although he recalled that he was in principle in favour of the right to vote for immigrants, the then Prime Minister, Lionel Jospin argued that the conditions were not right for the adoption of such a measure at that time.

For some, the French were still 'not ready' to accept this reform, whilst others again cited the constitutional obstacles, or the fact that there was no time to introduce this reform in time for the next municipal elections. Jean-Pierre Chevènement, leader of the Left-wing Mouvement des Citoyens (MDC) was one of those to argue most clearly in favour of granting voting rights to non-nationals, but he was careful to underline that this right should only be granted in particular circumstances and that the link between citizenship and nationality should not be undermined. In an article published in *Le Monde* in December 1999, he argued that there should be no 'ethnic' segregation between EU-nationals and non-EU nationals in terms of voting rights, but that any foreigner with a ten-year resident card should be given the right to vote in municipal elections. This would provide a stepping stone towards the integration of immigrants into French society, and their eventual naturalisation (*Le Monde*, 17 December 1999). Critics pointed to the irony of Chevènement arguing for the right to vote for those in possession of a ten-year residence permit when he had made this permit even harder to secure during his terms as Minister of the Interior. It is also important to note that even this support for granting (limited) voting rights to immigrants came with an emphasis on the need to bolster the link between citizenship and nationality – a further rebuttal to the idea that post national forms of citizenship should be developed in France.

The reluctance of most of the major political parties to lend full support to the proposal to grant voting rights to immigrants meant that only EU citizens had the right to vote in the 2001 municipal elections. Campaigners continued to act, however, to try and prove to politicians that this reform should be undertaken and that it would not be as electorally unpopular as many might fear. In December 2002, several associations organised a 'referendum' on the right to vote for foreigners. This 'citizens' vote' was organised in seventy towns and cities across France and permitted those who supported the idea of extending the right to vote for immigrants to go and vote for this idea in associational headquarters, in markets or in the town hall. One of the organisers from the League for Human Rights argued that this was an important initiative which would serve as petition in favour of extending voting rights to foreigners (*Le Monde*, 11 December 2002). However, such initiatives, although demonstrating some levels of public support for the extension of voting rights to immigrants, have done little to convince politicians that this would be an electorally popular idea. It seems that this right will remain out of the reach of non-EU foreign residents for the foreseeable future.

Other local initiatives have also taken place to try and palliate immigrants' lack of voting rights. In four local communities, Mons-en-Baroeul in 1985, Amiens in 1987, Cerizay in 1989, and Longjumeau in 1990, elections were organised amongst the immigrant population to elect representatives who could participate in the debates in sessions of the municipal council. These initiatives took on some kind of symbolic significance by drawing public attention to the issue of immigrants' participation in local politics, but they were of little real practical significance. The immigrant representatives present in sessions of the municipal councils were not allowed to vote, and in fact, for the session to be legally valid, it had to be suspended every time one of the immigrant representatives spoke, and then reconvened afterwards.

The debate over voting rights for immigrants is just one part of a larger debate over the citizenship status of these immigrants, and the continuing refusal of the major political parties to envisage serious reform on this issue is illustrative of the way in which there is still a perceived need to tie citizenship rights (particularly those concerning political rights) to nationality. Whilst some continue to argue that voting rights must be tied to the acquisition of nationality, others point to the evolution of migratory systems which means that many foreign residents in European countries have not acquired the nationality of those countries. Should not these long-term residents be implicated in the political process, at least at a local level, irrespective of whether or not they have acquired nationality?

The refusal of political parties to envisage granting voting rights to non-EU nationals might also be seen as part of a larger problem relating to the under-representation of ethnic minorities in French political assemblies. This is an issue which will be discussed in the following section.

The Political Representation of Immigrants and Ethnic Minorities

Whilst much of the debate over immigrants' political rights has focused on whether or not immigrants should be granted the right to vote, another issue which has received somewhat less attention is that of the political representation of populations of immigrant origin. It might be argued that full political citizenship cannot be exercised without sufficient representation of a particular group in the elected assemblies of a country, and in France this argument has certainly been made with regard to the under-representation of women in elected bodies. In fact, there has been a recent constitutional revision and legislation to promote parity of representation of men and women in elected assemblies. The mobilisation around the exclusion of women from political representation has not, however stimulated a more general debate about the exclusion of immigrants and ethnic minorities. There are currently no deputies of Maghrebin or Sub-Saharan African in the French National Assembly, nor are there any senators from these two ethnic minority populations. Whilst the arguments over what form of representation is really important in terms of political rights and citizenship, and whilst there are strong arguments against instituting a 'microcosm' variety of representation, it might still be argued that having no representatives of Sub-Saharan African or Maghrebin origin within France's legislature is a real sign of the fact that these communities' experiences and interests are not fully included within the political decision-making process in France. A lack of progress in selecting and electing candidates of immigrant origin to the National Assembly can be seen as a result of the political parties' failure to take seriously the need to have any kind of representation of populations of immigrant origin. The reluctance to talk about or to take action on this issue can be seen to stem, once again, from the insistence on the values of Republican universalism and a rejection of any kind of multiculturalism or communitarianism. The refusal of the French to recognise the existence of any kind of ethnic/racial/religious communities as actors within the public sphere means that it is not possible to have a serious discussion about the possibility of introducing some kind of mechanism to increase the numbers of representatives of such communities in elected bodies.

The lack of representatives of immigrant origin, and particularly of Maghrebin and Sub-Saharan African origin, has however, been a point of contention for these populations. And recently a campaign has been launched by several organisations supporting the rights of populations of immigrant origin in France. Under the slogan 'Donnons-nous des couleurs' (Give Us Colours), the collective is calling for a 'political representation of citizens in their diversity'. Mouloud Aounit of the MRAP, one of the leading anti-racist organisations and part of this collective, explains the need for such a campaign:

> The electoral earthquake of 21 April 2002[1] and the high levels of absenteeism that were noted on that date, showed a rupture between the French people and their

---

[1] The date when Le Pen beat Jospin, to go through to the second round of the presidential elections.

representatives. One of the causes of this rupture is the gap between the composition of the political class and that of the French population. A large proportion of French youth are of immigrant origin. With rare exceptions, this fraction of the population has no access to political responsibilities, either local or national. The weak representation of French people of immigrant origin poses a real problem for our democracy, a problem which can only reinforce the lack of interest of French citizens for politics. This formidable waste of dynamism and of ambition impoverishes public debate and reinforces the discriminations already suffered in numerous domains by this part of French society. Our collective of associations is launching a national campaign for a real political representation of all the varying parts of French society, without discrimination. Political parties must take on their responsibilities and put into practice the principles which they claim to support (*Politis*, 27 November 2003).

Whilst there are no representatives of African origin in the National Assembly, the situation in local and municipal politics is somewhat better. As Oriol remarks, the question of 'how many will they be this time?' has now become almost a ritual with regard to the elected representatives of immigrant origin (Oriol, 2001: 41). In a study of the 2001 municipal elections he found that of the electoral lists analysed, 7.6 per cent of the candidates were of 'foreign origin', of which 4.6 per cent were of Maghrebin origin. All of the parties presented candidates of immigrant origin, even those parties, like the Front National and the Mouvement National Républicain, which fought on overtly anti-immigration platforms. The presence of candidates of immigrant origin on these extreme-Right lists can be used by the parties to demonstrate a cultural pluralism and to support their claims to be non-racist parties. However, despite the presence of candidates of immigrant origin on the lists of all political parties, not all of the parties managed to elect representatives of immigrant origin. Of the representatives elected in the second round of the elections, 5.6 per cent were of immigrant origin, and 3.5 per cent of Maghrebin origin. The majority of these were from Left-wing parties. Oriol points to the special place occupied by the candidates of Maghrebin origin in the landscape of French local politics. Maghrebins have traditionally been reasonably highly visible in local politics, but this visibility might be argued to owe a lot to the fact that their presence relates to a particular social problematic, that of the 'difficult' suburbs. Thus their presence in local politics can be seen as an ambivalent kind of political integration which rests on their identification with a very specific social problem (Oriol, 2001). The general conclusions drawn from this study of the municipal elections are that the major political parties have done little to encourage or facilitate the election of representatives of immigrant origin, despite possessing the political resources to do so if they wished. Instead it is the small and marginal Left-wing parties who have elected proportionally more candidates of immigrant origin because they are closer to 'civil society' and to the cultural diversity of contemporary France (Oriol, 2001).

Thus the political citizenship and political representation of immigrants and of populations of immigrant origins remain in question. Whilst many immigrants who have not acquired French nationality still have no opportunity to vote even at the local level, it is also true that for the population of immigrant origin who do have French nationality, full political citizenship might be said to be far from complete. Although they are French nationals and thus electors and eligible, their presence might be argued to count for little in the French political sphere. Their presence amongst candidates at various elections, and especially national elections, is minimal, and they are even fewer to be elected. This political marginalisation of populations of immigrant origin is an important form of exclusion with which they have to contend.

Immigrant Associations: An Alternative Form of Political Participation?

Whilst a strong case can be made to demonstrate the exclusion of immigrants and those of immigrant origin from political citizenship, it could also be argued that political citizenship is not resumed only by electoral rights and by a presence in elected assemblies. Other forms of political participation and political citizenship must also be considered. In her description of the advances of postnational citizenship, Soysal argues that immigrants' can be incorporated into a polity through indirect political participation – through foreigners' advisory committees, trades unions, work councils in the work place (Soysal, 1994). One of these forms of political incorporation might be seen to be through the associational movement of migrants, which has been discussed in some detail in France. The associational movement of immigrants and populations of immigrant origin was particularly highlighted with the anti-racist marches and demonstrations of the 1980s (see chapter 8), although the associational landscape is far broader and more varied than the few large associations which have received much media attention.

For a long time immigrant associations were subject to a law of 1939 which stipulated that all 'foreign associations' had to be authorised by the Ministry of the Interior and would be subject to discretionary control by the Ministry. This law was not repealed until the Socialist government of 1981 abrogated it, some argued as a substitute for giving immigrants the right to vote in local elections (Abdallah, 2001). As one militant argued:

> One has to ask oneself if granting the right of association allowed an evasion of the debate over the civic rights of foreigners in France. The reform of 1981 was evoked precisely to avoid any reflection on the decoupling of the two notions of citizenship and nationality. It was used as an argument when it was publicly announced that they were renouncing the reform of the right to vote (cited in Abdallah, 2001: 15).

Freeing the right to association for immigrants did not thus indicate an advance towards full political rights. However, whatever the motivations for this reform, the new legal recognition of the rights of foreigners to form associations led to a massive growth in the number of immigrant associations during the 1980s. At first these tended to be local associations, but soon national associations were formed with the goal of promoting equality or combating racism for example (see chapter 8 for a fuller discussion of anti-racist mobilisation). The resulting associational movement was of course extremely diverse, and not all of the associations had a political element, but as Wihtol de Wenden points out the development of this associational movement was accompanied by a qualitative change in immigrants' demands and in their forms of expression:

> To be seen as a collective, even a political, actor; to intervene in the overall structures of society; to create a collective right of recognition for the immigrant presence as a whole, and not just of the immigrant as an individual. A new space thus seemed to have been created by the associative movement within the French political landscape (Wihtol de Wenden, 1998: 366).

Wihtol de Wenden and Leveau point to three types of immigrant associations, defined in terms of a generational dimension, with each succeeding generation inventing new forms of militantism. The first type of association was marked by the perspective of class struggle and the place of the immigrant within the working-class; the second generation of 'beur' associations were led by the second-generation immigrant population and had both opportunistic and oppositional tendencies; and the third generation of associations have encompassed a more social dimension. All of these models overlap and interact with each other (Wihtol de Wenden and Leveau, 2001). The associational movement has certainly had some benefits in terms of the defence of immigrants' rights particularly at a local level, and in terms of the personal trajectories of many of those involved with these associations. However, the movement has also met difficulties with problems of instrumentalisation by the State in a relationship that has been compared to a colonial relationship.

The participation of immigrants in associations is not perceived by the French state as a transition towards full political participation, but as a substitute for full political citizenship (Poinsot, 2001). It is argued that participation in such associations provides a real participation in local affairs and this argument is used to justify the continued refusal to grant immigrants the right to vote (El Yazami, 1993), but associations can never be more than a surrogate political space because of their cultural particularism (Leveau and Wihtol de Wenden, 1991).

Economic and Social Citizenship and Rights

Whilst immigrants and those of immigrant origin might be argued to be far from achieving equal political citizenship with the 'native' French population, through the former's lack of formal rights of voting and eligibility and the latter's exclusion from political representation, what of their social and economic rights? Arguments about the spread of postnational citizenship rights point to social and economic spheres as those in which foreign residents have acquired almost identical rights to national citizens, but it might also be argued that both formal and informal discriminations persist, and that not only are non-nationals excluded from some of these citizenship rights, but also that nationals of immigrant origin may be excluded because of the exercise of informal and illegal forms of discrimination.

Recent changes have in some cases extended the formal rights of foreigners in France. In 1998, for example, the Chevènement law, made it illegal for local authorities to reserve for French or EU nationals any benefits that they might allocate, such as extra child benefit for large families. This law was in response particularly to the policies of 'national preference' adopted by some Front National mayors who had reserved some allowances particularly for European nationals resident in their constituencies. However, in other areas, discriminations between European nationals and foreign residents still persist, and these legal differences in rights are only amplified by the numerous forms of discriminations that exist in housing, employment etc. (see chapter 8 for more details).

One of the persistent forms of legalised discrimination between nationals and non-nationals is in terms of the categories of employment which are closed to non-nationals. Foreigners are excluded in France from all civil service jobs, because the right to become a civil servant is considered as an attribute of national citizenship. The refusal to grant a foreigner a job which will involve him in the exercise of state authority is only a very partial explanation for this exclusion, given that most civil servants carry out tasks which give them very few real prerogatives with regard to the exercise of state power. Instead the explanation can be found in the desire to reserve a domain of employment for nationals, and a refusal to grant to foreigners all the benefits that come with a job as a civil servant.

This discrimination in employment spreads out from the civil service to other forms of public sector employment, with the principal public sector industries being prohibited under the terms of current law, from employing anyone who is not an EU national. There are also a whole variety of jobs in the private sector which are closed to foreigners from outside of the European Union.

The exclusionary effect of closing off many types of employment to non-EU nationals was recognised by the Parisian transport authority, the RATP, who recently opened up employment to foreigners. The director general of the RATP explained in an interview that this measure was taken not because the company was having difficulty in recruiting personnel, but as a measure of inclusion of the different populations who live in Paris, as transport was for them a 'factor of integration in the city' (*Le Monde*, 5 December 2002). However, the decision taken by the RATP was opposed by many of the trades unions representing transport workers, and was signalled as an 'exception' which was unlikely to be copied by other public sector employers.

The economic effects of this legal discrimination in employment on foreign residents are worth noting. A report published in 1999 estimated that the total number of jobs closed to non-EU nationals was between 6.5 and 7.2 million. This represents between 29 and 33 per cent of the total stock of jobs in France (Borrel, 1999) which means that a very large proportion of jobs are closed to foreigners. This exclusion will clearly have an effect on the employment rates of foreigners in France, and contribute to their much higher rates of unemployment (see table 5.1 below). Moreover, the fact that many of the jobs reserved for French and EU nationals are highly valued socially, means that the jobs open to foreigners tend to be those which are less socially valued and this contributes to the production of a negative social representation of the position of foreign workers in

France (GED, 2000). The fact that such legal discriminations exist, and that there is no explicit principle of justification for them, also tends to legitimise informal and indirect discrimination. As Borrel argues: 'So long as such massive and generalised legal discriminations towards foreigners exist, the fight against illegal discrimination is likely to remain in the realms of wishful thinking' (Borrel, 1999: 119).

Table 5.1 below shows that foreigners from outside of the EU living in France are subject to much higher levels of unemployment than French or EU nationals. This over-unemployment of foreigners can be explained by their concentration in the most vulnerable sectors of the economy, which in turn results both from the legal discriminations described above, and illegal discriminations whereby some employers systematically refuse to employ foreigners. These discriminations contribute to creating a great insecurity in employment for many immigrants who occupy jobs which are accorded a low social value and which are easily affected by unemployment.

Table 5.1   Unemployment Rates According to Age, Sex and Nationality (per cent)

Sex and Age		Non EU nationals	EU nationals	French nationals
15 – 24	Men	41.4	20.9	21.1
	Women	55.2	9.5	29.4
	Total	47.2	15.2	24.7
25 – 49	Men	27.4	8.6	8.7
	Women	35.0	10.1	12.6
	Total	30.4	9.2	24.7
50 +	Men	27.2	12.3	6.3
	Women	36.0	11.6	8.6
	Total	29.0	12.0	7.3
Total:	Men	28.3	10.0	9.3
	Women	37.0	10.4	13.2
	Total	**31.4**	**10.2**	**11.1**

Source: INSEE, 1998

Immigration and Welfare: A New Source of Insecurity?

Welfare rights are a particular site of debate in terms of entitlements of different categories of immigrants and foreigners. Those European states such as France which have highly developed welfare systems and an extensive provision of welfare rights have perceived this as a pull factor in attracting immigrants and asylum seekers, and this is one of the reasons advanced for a 'rolling-back' of some of these rights. France, like other European countries, has gradually extended welfare provisions to many categories of immigrants and foreigners, but the welfare state has been a site of both inclusion and exclusion, and the current focus on control and restriction of migration has led to a greater exclusion of some groups. This formal rolling-back of rights, together with the prevalence of racist and xenophobic forms of discrimination can be seen to have resulted in a stratified system of rights and of access to welfare provision. Some have argued that immigration controls coupled with restrictions on access to welfare rights are vital for the maintenance of the welfare state in Europe, because of the limited resources available for the provision of welfare. Freeman, for example, contends that immigration has been a 'disaster' for welfare in Europe and that 'the welfare state required boundaries because it establishes a principle of distributive justice that departs from the distributive principles of the free market' (Freeman, 1986: 52). On the other hand, others have pointed to the problems that discriminatory treatment will engender in terms of lasting marginalisation of some groups and the effects this would have on the state's capacity to maintain 'high standards for wages, work conditions and social benefits' (Brochmann, 1999: 15). This last point would seem to be particularly relevant to migrants with no legal residence status, who, as discussed in the previous chapter, present a particular problem for the French state.

Immigration policy has become, as discussed in previous chapters, a topic at the centre of political debate, and one which is being shaped by political and electoral exigencies. Banting argues that the tension between migration and the welfare state is rooted in the reaction of majorities and outlines three types of majority response to ethnic and racial diversity in relation to welfare provision. Firstly, new immigrant populations might be incorporated into the existing social welfare regime with little challenge to the underlying consensus on social policy; secondly, some sections of the majority population might be driven to 'welfare chauvinism' which supports the welfare state but rejects open immigration policies and the easy access of foreigners to social benefits; and thirdly, a political backlash against immigration and multiculturalism might help fuel a more comprehensive attack on the welfare state (Banting, 2000). Whilst Banting accepts that European countries have revealed signs of welfare chauvinism, he also maintains that such chauvinism has had a limited effect and that 'in the expansive welfare states of Europe, immigrants enjoy formal social rights that differ only at the margin from those of citizens' (Banting, 2000: 22). This argument, which corresponds with those of exponents of the development of postnational citizenship, can, however be interpreted as optimistic with regards to the degree to which welfare rights are enjoyed equally by all. For many, including particularly those with no legal residence status, and asylum seekers, those minimal social rights which they do have are under attack and can be seen to be shrinking (Bloch and Schuster, 2002).

The gradual stratification of rights between different categories of residents (French nationals, EU nationals, foreigners with regular residence status, foreigners without regular residence status), can be seen clearly in the domain of health and social care. The Pasqua laws of 1993 introduced for the first time a criterion of legal residence status before a foreigner had the right to access health and social cover and benefits. A foreigner can no longer be affiliated to the social security system if he or she cannot prove regular residence status. These restrictions meant that anyone who did not have legal residence status could only access medical care through the hospital system, and could no longer get health care from a general practitioner. In addition, if they were prescribed any medication by the hospital they were no longer entitled to financial assistance to pay for this medicine. In creating this legal differentiation between the health and social benefits and care that different groups of residents were entitled to, the Pasqua laws initiated a system that has become more and more stratified. Those without legal residence status were entitled only to emergency medical cover under the *Aide Médicale d'Etat* (State Medical Aid) (AME), whilst those who had been residing legally in France for three years or less were entitled to a lesser level of benefits and treatment than those who had been in France for more than three years (Carde et al., 2002).

More recently, the government has announced its intention of limiting access to the State Medical Aid, a measure which would affect immigrants with no legal residence status in particular. It is estimated that about 160,000 of these foreigners without legal status benefit from the free medical access, but François Fillon, the Minister for Social Affairs, announced in the National Assembly that this right would be restricted and that 'foreigners in an irregular situation cannot expect access to unlimited free rights' (*Libération*, 29 October 2003).

Even for those foreigners with legal residence status, research shows a gulf between them and French nationals in terms of social protection. A study of charitable centres providing free medical treatment showed that a much higher proportion of those accessing this treatment were foreigners than were French nationals. 62.6 per cent of those who sought treatment in a centre run by Médecins sans frontières, and 68.6 per cent of those who sought treatment in a centre run by Médecins du monde were foreign residents (Mizrahi, 2000). These foreign residents who obtained treatment from the centres included both those who had regular residence permits and those who did not. The study showed that even foreigners with regular residence status were far less likely than French nationals to have the benefit of health cover (Mizrahi, 2000).

Limitations of this type on the rights of certain groups of immigrants and foreigners exist in various other domains. Since 1993, for example, governments have instructed universities to check that a potential student has a valid residence permit before registering them for a course and affiliating to the student social security regime. As Slama points out, however, this situation is paradoxical in that a valid registration to a university is a condition for obtaining a residence status for a student (Slama, 1999). A similar situation occurs with regard to students over the age of eighteen who wish to enrol in secondary education, and in certain areas of France the local administration have restricted access to schools for children whose parents do not have a regular residence permit (Slama, 1999).

Thus the idea that foreigners without legal residence status should not benefit from any aspect of the French welfare state is gradually becoming more and more generalised and accepted. This is highly problematic when there is a large group of such residents in France, many of whom are in a situation where they cannot be expelled but neither will they be regularized. In addition, this emphasis on checking the legality of residence status before any welfare benefits are granted, has impacted on immigrants who do have legal residence status in that proof of this is constantly demanded before any social benefits or rights may be exercised.

In addition to the legal discriminations and differentiations between different categories of residents, there are numerous informal and indirect discriminations which occur. One of the most obvious of these is in the allocation of public housing where it is common knowledge that numerous biases in the mechanisms for attributing housing act to penalise foreign and immigrant families. One local council even went so far as to organise a local referendum to ask whether residents believed that the mayor should apply the principle of a 'threshold of tolerance' of foreigners when deciding how to allocate public housing (Slama, 1999).

Conclusion

The combined effects of legal and illegal discriminations results in a situation where 'foreigners are far from having the same rights as French nationals' (Lochak, 1999: 318). Whilst progress has been made in some areas in assuring the same rights for foreigners as for French nationals, the continuing emphasis on the control of immigration, and on restricting rights for certain categories of immigrants has meant that inequalities in rights still exist. And within this context of hostility and suspicion with regard to immigrants it is very difficult for foreigners to fully realise the rights that they do possess and to benefit from full citizenship rights.

Chapter 6

Women Immigrants and Asylum Seekers: Facing a Double Burden of Insecurity

Much of what has been said and written about immigration and citizenship in France is in supposedly gender-neutral language. This claimed gender-neutrality disguises the fact that much of what is said is actually based on the assumption that an immigrant is a man. As argued in previous chapters, the tightening of immigration, asylum and nationality policies has had far-reaching effects on those of immigrant origin resident in France, creating a widening gulf between those with access to the privileges and rights of citizens and those without who are finding themselves in increasingly vulnerable and insecure positions. One factor which has often been ignored in histories of immigration and in analyses of the position of immigrants in France, is that of gender. It is clear, however, that the effects of new immigration laws and policies are experienced differently by male and female immigrants, with women often being placed in a position of double insecurity by the fact of being migrants and being female. This chapter will aim to analyse the way in which immigration policies in France, based as they are on the traditional models of the family, and rearticulating as they do the traditional divisions between public and private, have reinforced racist and sexist discriminations, placing immigrant women in increasingly vulnerable and insecure positions.

The number of migrant women in France, as in other European countries, has increased rapidly as a proportion of the total immigrant communities. Figures for 1990 show that women made up 41 per cent of the Maghrebin and sub-Saharan African and 45 per cent of the Asian population in France (INSEE, 1992). Whilst in 1999 women accounted for 46.9 per cent of the total immigrant population (INSEE, 2000). This increasing 'feminization' of migration, noted as one of the tendencies in contemporary migratory flows, and also specifically as a feature of the 'new migration' in Europe (Castles and Miller, 1998; Koser and Lutz, 1998), has many different causes. One of the reasons that has been cited for the increasing proportion of women in migratory flows into Europe, has been the growing importance of family reunification as one of the only legal means of entry into many European countries. The history and structure of migrations into France mean that women make up a large proportion of those entering the country for family reunification purposes. Immigration in the post-war years was mainly of men coming to work in France, but after the official suspension of immigration in

1974, family reunification became one of the main ways of entering France legally and many women came to join men who had previously immigrated. Successive governments have made the conditions for family reunification increasingly strict in order to try and reduce the flow of immigrants (Prencipe, 1994), but despite these attempts, claims of family reunification still account for a large proportion of immigration into France. Immigration for family reunification remains a largely female phenomenon, between 1990 and 1995 for example, the percentage of women in spousal family reunifications varied between 77.3 per cent and 80.3 per cent (Lebon, 1995 and 1997). Similarly, many of those who benefited from regularisation under the Chevènement circular of 1997 (see chapters 2 and 4), under the principle of family reunification were women. However, although the principle of allowing immigration for family reunification benefits women in that it provides a legal method of entry into France, those who enter by this means are often denied independent legal and economic status because of the ways that immigration laws and policies treat them as dependents of men already resident in France. This leads to increasing problems of dependence and insecurity for many women immigrants, who may find themselves trapped in violent relationships which they cannot leave because of fear of losing their residence status, or who may have been denied the right to work legally as it is assumed that they will be financially dependent on their husband. These gendered causes of insecurity will be discussed more fully further in the chapter.

However, family reunification is not the only reason for the entry of immigrant women into France, and even those women who do enter under the official label of family reunification may have a variety of other motives for immigration (Silberman, 1991). It would be a mistake, therefore, to overlook the other causes for and motivations of female migration. Moreover, the belief that all female immigration is for the purpose of family reunification leads to the misleading representation of women immigrants merely as wives and daughters of male migrants already in France. Women do not migrate merely to join their fathers or husbands, but have a variety of independent migratory projects including migration for study and for work (both documented and undocumented) and migration to seek asylum. The feminization of poverty in their countries of origin is a key factor in these migrations, but there are also specific political and cultural constraints which lead women to seek a different life. A survey of Algerian women immigrants in France revealed, for example, that for many of them the choice to migrate was made in hope of achieving greater personal freedom, and that unlike many Algerian men, their migratory projects did not include the idea of an eventual return to their homeland (Boulahbel-Villac, 1992). Studies of immigration have frequently overlooked the gender differentiated nature of this phenomenon, however. And despite the increased presence of women immigrants, and the variety of women's migratory projects, political representations of immigrants in France have tended to concentrate principally on the image of the male migrant, and have often ignored women's varied migratory projects and trajectories, either rendering women of immigrant origin 'invisible' (which seems particularly to be the case for women of Asian origin) or confining them to the family and representing them principally as wives and mothers (Barison and Catarino, 1997; Bentichou, 1997; Golub, Morokvasic and Quiminal, 1997).

Those political representations that do exist of women of immigrant origin in France have highlighted all of the aspects of women's roles in ethnic processes that are outlined by Yuval-Davis and Anthias in their gendered analysis of nationalism and nation building (Yuval-Davis and Anthias, 1989). Of these four roles assigned to women in immigrant and ethnic minority communities, there has been a particular emphasis placed on women's role in the reproduction of communities of immigrant origin, and the transmission of values to their children. On the one hand, racist stereotyping, typical of extreme-Right discourse, but not by any means the sole preserve of the Front National, highlights women's role in the biological reproduction of ethnic communities in France, creating fears of an 'immigrant invasion' boosted by the supposedly high birth rate amongst communities of immigrant origin. Research carried out amongst Front National supporters reveals their horror at the idea of women of immigrant origin producing numerous children and claiming benefits from the French state to support them. One Front National voter, for example, expresses his feelings of disgust: 'When I see these North African women who have fifteen or twenty children! Who claim benefits of thirty or forty thousand francs … it's abhorrent' (cited in Mossuz-Lavau, 1994: 170). There is a persistent image of women of immigrant origin bearing numerous, illegitimate children and expecting the French state to support them. Those, on the other hand, who maintain a discourse proclaiming the necessity to integrate immigrants, also place their representations of women of immigrant origin within the family. Their role as biological reproducers of the ethnic community is still highlighted, but in this instance, their importance in the transmission of community values, and in particular those values which will aid their children's integration into French society, is stressed. Represented in their role as mothers of families, it is seen to be their duty to ensure the stability of the ethnic minority population and to see to it that their children integrate or assimilate and become 'French'. Women of immigrant origin are thus represented as both the bearers of 'tradition' and agents of 'modernity', responsible both for perpetuating the boundaries of ethnic groups within France and for ensuring that these boundaries are made permeable to French culture. These dominant representations are often both stereotyped and contradictory, and little has been done to moderate them by analysts of immigration or, indeed, by French feminist researchers. One can thus point to a *rendez-vous manqué* between feminisms and anti-racisms in France (Lloyd, 1998a), with both sides tending to prioritize one axis of domination (either sexist or racist) and failing to take full account of the multiple nature of women of immigrant origin's identities, experiences and situations. As Barison and Catarino argue:

> Ignoring, or wishing to ignore that women immigrants are situated in a strategic position at the intersection of the social relations of domination which exist between sexes, classes and ethnic groups, the body of research on migration and feminist research on general themes (work, family, etc.) have respectively, for many years, neglected women and immigrants (Barison and Catarino 1997: 17).

So we can argue that these women face a particular weight of expectation and are under specific pressure from French society. At the same time there are powerful forces acting to exclude these women from this same society, depending on their particular situation. For many first generation women of immigrant origin in particular, adaptation to French society may be difficult. They have broken with systems of solidarity and affiliation in their countries of origin and have to reconstruct their social position in a foreign society. They may find themselves isolated, especially if they have a limited command of the French language. Housing for immigrants is often poor, and one can argue that this has a particular effect on women, who, in many communities of immigrant origin, are almost entirely responsible for the management of the domestic space. In addition, for women of immigrant origin, access to salaried work has been limited both because of domestic and social pressure from within their communities – women of Maghrebin and Turkish origin have the lowest rates of formal employment due in part to the norms in their countries of origin (Hargreaves, 1995) – and because of reluctance by French employers to hire women of immigrant origin, especially those from the ex-colonies. Thus in contrast with many immigrant men who arrived in France to fulfil demands for manual labour, women of immigrant origin have not been able to count on integration through waged employment, particularly in a time of economic recession. Those who do find waged employment are often employed in low-paid service sector jobs, many in temporary and part-time positions with no security. As Quiminal explains, women of immigrant origin may be less prone to overt racist attacks than men, but at the same time, they are expected to occupy a particular place and there is no room in the French imagination for these women to expand their role, take advantage of education and job training opportunities and enter the labour force. French attitudes to women of immigrant origin, particularly from the ex-colonies can be summarized thus:

> They are tolerated as housewives, taking care of the domestic chores, bringing up the children, and taking responsibility for the integration of their family. Immigrant women are assigned to a particular place, and in a time of economic crisis and unemployment, they must not overstep the limits of that place. When they ask for education or training, for example, they are not heard. (Golub, Morokvasic and Quiminal, 1997: 25)

Women, Citizenship and the Law

The position of many immigrant women and women of immigrant origin in France has been made more difficult in recent years by the increasingly restrictive immigration and nationality policies and legislation introduced by successive governments. And, although, as already argued, there may be a case for pointing to the expansion of immigrants' rights in some areas, the effects of many of the new policies and legislation has in fact been to further restrict their access to full citizenship rights and status, and thus to place them in increasingly insecure positions. As discussed in previous chapters, the political representations of immigrants as a threat both to French national identity and to France's social and economic future, have led to a series of policies and laws with the goal of controlling immigration and of restricting the rights of some groups of immigrants already in France. These laws like all others are supposedly gender neutral, but a closer analysis reveals the specific deleterious effects that they have had on women immigrants. The tightening of conditions for family reunification, for example, and the particular conditions placed on 'mixed' marriages, have placed many women in particularly insecure situations. Similarly, the changing of nationality laws has been very hard for immigrant women, and in particular those who have had children in France. As a result of the limitation of access to French nationality and citizenship rights, many women have found themselves in situations with no access to health or social security provision either for themselves of for their children. The reforms introduced by the Left after 1997, which have in general disappointed those who had hoped for a lifting of the restrictive measures imposed by the Right, have had little impact on the insecure situation of many of these women, and indeed measures like the Chevènement circular of 1997, have imposed specific conditions for regularisation which have been harder for women immigrants to fulfil than for many of their male counterparts. Thus even where there has been reform, this has in general not benefited women immigrants as it has not disrupted the underlying gendered implications of immigration policy, as will be discussed further below. As a result the situations of many women of immigrant origin living in France have become increasingly precarious, as may be evidenced by the high profile participation of women in the sans-papiers movement (see chapter 4).

As mentioned previously, these new immigration and nationality laws are, in theory, universal, and thus equally restrictive to men and women of immigrant origin. In practice, however, these laws and policies tend to reinforce women's restriction to a male-defined private sphere, and in conjunction with gendered social and economic conditions mean that men and women are differently affected by the laws concerning immigration and nationality. Immigration laws often operate in ways which deny women independent legal status. If they do enter to join a husband then their right to remain will be dependent on him, and they will not automatically gain the right to work, meaning that they are financially dependent. Equality is further undermined by a gendered division of labour that places the onus for the care of children and family responsibilities on women, whilst sexual discrimination in employment means that those women of immigrant origin who do work generally earn less than men, and many women suffer from unemployment, or exploitation through black-market labour. Immigrant women who do work are often employed in domestic labour, confined again to the private sphere of the home and thus invisible in terms of official recognition of their work. Many immigrant women thus find themselves in a position of double dependence on men, both legal and economic, and this dependence is aggravated by their limited citizenship rights and their experiences of racism in their host society.

Family Reunification, 'Mixed' Marriages and the Reinforcement of Women's Dependence

Dominant representations of women of immigrant origin confine them, as argued above, principally to the context of the family. This is not a coincidence as one of the major concerns of the debate over immigration in France has been that of family reunification. After the government's official suspension of immigration for work in 1974, it was hoped by many that France could put a stop to immigration altogether, but one of the factors preventing this (apart from France's membership of the European Union) was international pressure to allow family reunification (Prencipe, 1994). In practice, however, although the French are obliged under international law to respect families' rights to live together in France, the way in which the laws have been written and the manner in which they are applied make this right of family reunification more and more tenuous for those immigrants coming from outside of the European Union (Rude-Antoine, 1997). The conditions for family reunification have become more and more stringent in an attempt to limit immigration, and this has had a particularly adverse effect on women as they, as detailed above, comprise the bulk of those applying to enter France for reasons of family reunification.

In fact, those wishing to bring their family members to France from countries outside of the European Union, have to satisfy certain conditions, particularly concerning housing and financial resources. Because of the stringency of these conditions, and because it is up to local authorities to decide whether they are fulfilled, there are many occasions when the right to family reunification is denied. The historical patterns of immigration into France where men were encouraged to come alone to work in French industry, mean that although this law is phrased in gender-neutral language, it is more often the case that the family member already resident in France is a man, and those trying to join him are his wife and/or children. Currently about three quarters of those entering France to join a spouse are women (Lesselier, 2003). The difficulties involved in getting these women and children into France legally means that they are often forced to enter the country without the correct papers, usually with a tourist visa which expires after three months, leaving them in a state of perpetual fear of discovery and deportation. Many women, therefore, live in a state of illegality because of these laws, and this reinforces their dependence on the men that they have come to France to join. It means that it is almost impossible for them to find work and if they do it will be on the black market, risking further exploitation. These women are oppressed because in effect their existence is denied. What makes this situation even more difficult is that the law forbids all regularization *sur place* (on site) on conditions of family reunification - the demand for residence papers for those coming to join their family in France must be made when they are still in their country of origin; once they are already in France their case cannot be considered. This added restriction leads to cases such as that described by Quiminal, of a young Moroccan woman who came to study in France. In 1992 during the course of her studies she married a Moroccan man who had residence papers and they had a child. When this woman finished her studies in 1996 her student visa expired and so she applied to renew her papers on the grounds of family reunification. This application was rejected because she was in France and not Morocco at the time she made the request (Quiminal, 1997). This inflexible application of the laws is used to deny many women in similar situations, who have been resident in France for some time, the right to stay and live legally with their families. This situation of illegality and denial of the right of foreign women (and men) to live with their family thus continues, despite promises by the Socialist government to take action in this area. The Chevenèment law of 1998 promised to ensure the right of foreigners to family reunification under the provision for guaranteeing personal and family life, but in fact reports show that this law has had little impact on the practices of local police prefectures and that the right to family reunification remains a tenuous one (*Libération*, 1 February 2002).

Problems also exist for those women of immigrant origin who wish to marry a French man (and vice versa) and to obtain the rights to French residence and citizenship through such a marriage. Although the problem of 'mixed' marriages is one that both men and women of immigrant origin encounter, again the restrictions are more important for women, as women have a higher rate of exogamous marriage than men (Tribalat, 1995). In addition to social and communal pressures against 'mixed' marriages (Lacoste-Dujardin, 2000), there are now greater legal restrictions, which act to discourage such marriages. Under the new immigration laws, mayors are given the power to refuse to marry a French partner to a partner of immigrant origin if they suspect that this marriage is one of convenience, taking place in order for the immigrant partner to gain residence papers to live in France. Moreover, once married, in order for the request for residence papers to be successful, the partner making the request must have entered France and must have been living in France legally and the couple must have been married and living together for at least one year. For many, however, proving that they have entered France legally may involve a return to their country of origin to request a visa, and if they do this the French authorities may hold against them the period of separation from their partner, using this to argue that their marriage is not a genuine one. As Ferré argues, the law does not take into account personal histories and tends to perceive all 'mixed' marriages as suspect, thus problematizing personal relations and denying some couples the right to marry and others the right to live together in France legally (Ferré, 1997). The new law of the management of migration introduced by the current Minister of the Interior, Nicolas Sarkozy, will make marriages between a French national and a foreign partner even more difficult, as under the terms of this law the fact that one partner does not have legal residence papers will be construed as a primary indicator of absence of consent for the marriage. Mayors will be encouraged to reject any marriage of this type because the mere fact that one partner does not have legal residence status will be assumed to cast fundamental doubt on the sincerity of the marriage.

On a more fundamental level, the laws on immigration are geared towards the acceptance of families which not only discriminates against single people and homosexuals[1] – but in fact again discriminates against women by pushing them into marriages that they might not otherwise have accepted, and forcing them to stay in violent or abusive marriages for fear of losing their rights of residence. Immigration laws and policies thus once again force women into the private sphere and the role of wives, making marriage a necessity for many. As Morokvasic argues:

> In order to stay in the host country, immigrants are obliged to marry in a much larger proportion than the native population. The marriage rate amongst immigrants thus appears much higher than it would be if they benefited from the same possibilities as the native population. (Morokvasic, 1997: 27)

And once they are married, there is pressure to stay in a relationship, even though it may be one of oppression or dependence. Divorce or separation could lead to the removal or non-renewal of their residence papers. To this constraint is added that of communal norms, which may view divorce badly or may give the husband greater freedom to divorce than the wife (Lesselier, 1999). Again there is a risk of a double sanction as a husband may use the threat of removing his wife's legal right to residence in France to reinforce communal pressures against separation or divorce. The Réseau pour l'Autonomie des Femmes Immigrées et Refugiées (Network for the autonomy of immigrant and refugee women), a campaigning group set up in 1997 to help immigrant and refugee women in France, is concerned that these women's oppression is worsened by the French law's insistence on the family as a framework for the admittance of immigrants. Their chairwoman, Claudie Lesselier, argues that: 'The attribution of residence permits and eventual regularisation of foreigners in an illegal situation are based, above all, on the family framework. This is especially onerous for women for whom the family is often a site of dependency and constraint' (Lesselier, 1999: 46).

Further, the families which the policies and laws on family reunification seek to promote are those modelled on the 'normal' family – a family composed of father, mother and children. This is a highly normative conception of the family – one that is based on an idealized version of the French family and one that does not take into account variants on this traditional family such as one-parent or polygamous families. The same representations which see women as the key to the successful integration of immigrants into France usually see this happening in the context of such a 'traditional' family, and other types of family living arrangement are therefore rejected as tending to increase instability and decrease chances of integration. For example, in his book *La famille: secret de l'intégration,* Christian Jelen argues that if immigrants have a 'quality' family model, which is coincidentally close to that of the French family, integration and social success will

---

[1] Homosexual couples can now be legally recognised in France, following the introduction of the PACS (Pacte civil de solidarité). However, in terms of immigration, those involved in a PACS have had to wait longer to prove their status and qualify for residence papers than those involved in a traditional marriage. During his 2002 presidential campaign Lionel Jospin promised to review this disparity.

follow (Jelen, 1993). This conception of the family is an archaic one, untouched by feminism, a model which assumes the father as the chief of the family, responsible for providing for his family financially whilst the mother is engaged with bringing up the children and ensuring their proper integration into French society. These representations upon which French law is based not only serve to reinforce the inequality between men and women within families but also justify the discriminatory nature of immigration policies that regard the entry of women as another burden on both immigrant men and on French society. It is not considered that women may go out and work and provide for themselves and their children and families. In fact, this model of the 'traditional' nuclear family is one which is in decline amongst all of the French population, irrespective of their origins, but the multiple variants on the family that now exist in society are not recognized in the laws concerning immigrants into France and this is yet another cause of difficulties for women of immigrant origin.

The Chevènement law of 1998 brought hope of regularisation to many women (and men) without legal residence status, and one of the main reasons that this law stipulates for granting of a residence permit is for foreigners who do not qualify under the terms of family reunification but for whom 'personal and family ties in France are such that a refusal to authorise residence would bring a disproportionate harm to their private and family life.'[2] However, as with the policies and practices governing family reunification and mixed marriages, the prevalent interpretation of this right to 'private and family life' falls within very strict social and moral norms and models. An example of the way the prefectures have applied this rule within this strict moral context is provided by the case of Mina, a Moroccan woman who has been living in France for over ten years with a Tunisian partner who has been married in Tunisia and has not divorced his wife. The fact that her partner is still officially married to another woman was enough to justify the prefecture's rejection of her claim for regularisation on the grounds that the relationship was not stable enough, even though the couple had been living together for many years and had a child together.

Polygamous Marriages

One particular issue that has arisen in connection with the non-traditional family, is that of polygamy, and the situation of the wives of polygamous men living in France. Although this is a problem that is more widespread in the French imagination than it is in reality, there are still a significant number of polygamous families living in France, and this is clearly a model which does not fit the French conception of a 'traditional' family unit. So again women in polygamous families are in a situation where they are doubly oppressed, firstly by the social and economic conditions under which they live, and secondly by the French law. The treatment of polygamy by the French authorities demonstrates the ways in which

---

[2] Article 12b, line 7.

concerns to limit immigration and to be able to deport as many illegal immigrants as possible, have overridden any concerns about guaranteeing the security of foreigners in France.

In fact, the French policy was to tolerate polygamy until it became apparent that the restriction of this practice could provide another means of limiting legal migration and residence of migrants in France. The Pasqua law of 1993 included an instruction to prefects to refuse to grant or renew residence permits for those living in a situation of polygamy. Paradoxically, all the discourse on the restriction of polygamy portrays the new policy of restriction as a defence of women's rights, however, the practical effects on women immigrants have been devastating. As with other laws, the law against polygamy is in theory universal and does not recognize a difference between men and women, in other words it is illegal for a man to have more than one wife and for a woman to have more than one husband, and in both situations these polygamous families will be denied residence permits. In fact, however, it is clear that in the case of populations of immigrant origin where polygamy occurs, it is men who have several wives. Clearly a polygamous marriage is often not an ideal situation for women, especially with the transposition of this type of living arrangement from their country of origin to France where polygamous wives often find themselves living in a small flat with many children. But the repression of polygamy has in fact not defended their rights but worsened their situation by inflicting illegality on them. What the application of the law has done is to create a situation where a man living polygamously is forced to reject all but one of his wives in order to be able to renew his residence permit (and that of the single remaining wife). A circular issued by the Ministry of the Interior in April 2000 positively encouraged polygamous men to reject their 'excess' wives, promising all of those who had come to France before 1993, and who were living polygamously that their residence permits would be renewed without problem if their polygamous status was ended. Thus many men have decided to retain only one of their wives. All other wives find themselves ejected from the family home, often without means of financial support, and without residence papers (Alaux, 2001a). Bissuel reports that in the Paris region where these rejected wives are most numerous, many of them have ended up living in squats with their children (Bissuel, 2002).

Personal Status: The Problems of Islamic Family Codes

Increased insecurity for immigrant women is also caused by the fact that French law considers that in all matters relating to personal status (marriage, divorce, guardianship of children etc.), a foreign person should be subject to the law of their country of origin. This does not cause many problems if these laws are more or less identical to those of France, as would be the case for nationals of other European countries. Where problems may arise, however, is where an immigrant is a national of a state that has vastly different laws relating to personal status to those of France. This is particularly an issue in relation to those originating in states where

Muslim law is applied. Immigrants from Algeria may thus find themselves subject to the Algerian Family Code, and those from Morocco to the Mudawana laws. To be subject to two very different codes of law in matters relating to the family and personal status can create situations of great insecurity as Chammari comments:

> A paradoxical situation thus arises where the institutions of secular Western countries, having adopted egalitarian laws concerning personal status and family relations, must in certain cases apply the charia (Islamic law) as it is codified within the family law of Morocco or Algeria, which thus implies the recognition of polygamy, forced marriage, repudiation and inequality in inheritance. (Chammari, 2000: 8)

Again this is a source of particular insecurity for women, because the laws to which they are subject may be vastly inegalitarian in terms of gender relations. Lesselier points, for example, to the case of Madame S., an elderly Algerian woman, married to another Algerian and living in France in a flat owned by her husband. Without her knowledge, her husband obtained a divorce whilst on a trip to Algeria (Madame S. was not called to the divorce hearing or even informed of its outcome). She only discovered that she had been divorced some two years later when her husband asked her to leave their family home (Lesselier, 2003). In cases like these, the rules of international private law may allow a factor of public order to be invoked when foreign laws are manifestly contrary to French law. However, a woman must be aware of her rights in order to take a case to the French courts and few women have the necessary information. Moreover, as these cases involve a ruling on the priority of one national jurisdiction over another, they are inevitably long and costly, which is another barrier to women being able to obtain a favourable judgement in the French courts. And even where cases are brought before the French courts there is no guarantee of success. Lesselier highlights another case, that of an Egyptian woman living in France whose divorced husband had returned to Egypt. The husband informed his wife that he intended to have their daughter circumcised in that country. The mother took the case to the French courts to try and ensure protection of her daughter, but the French judiciary ruled that they must respect the application of the 'customary laws' of Egypt, and the girl was returned to her father (Lesselier, 2003). This type of judgement seems all the more paradoxical when one considers that the motivation for many women migrating to France from Muslim countries may be to free themselves from such 'customary laws'.

The Issue of Nationality Reform

The various reforms of the nationality codes in France can also be seen to have had gender differentiated impacts. The reforms and attempted reforms of nationality laws were undertaken partly in response to a perception within dominant French representations that foreign women came to give birth in France in order to obtain French nationality for their children, and therefore, ultimately for themselves. The questioning of the right of children born in France to foreign parents resident there to automatically gain French nationality has created particularly insecure conditions for many parents and children, and although women should not be essentialised as solely responsible for their children, in many cases they are the prime carers and so have been primarily affected by these changes. In some cases the changed legal status of their children and the resulting restrictions on access to health care and social security both for them, and for their children.. The fact that children do not obtain French nationality at birth means that many women's legal situation is made precarious. Under the terms of the Debré law, parents not living in a state of polygamy who had children under sixteen residing in France could obtain a residence card for themselves as long as they could prove that they effectively provided for their children's needs. Those in an illegal situation concerning residence at the time they made their request for a residence card often found, however, find that they were refused on the grounds that they were not providing for their children properly. In fact, a vicious circle was created: because of their illegal situation they could not work legally in France and thus it was deemed that they were not providing properly for their children, but they could not get legal residence papers until they proved that they were providing for their children.

Parents of children who do not have French nationality cannot claim any family allowances for them, and are denied access to health and social security cover. A woman *sans-papières* from Toulouse recounts her experience:

> I've lived in France for six years. I came to join my husband who is a craftsman. I have four children of fifteen, twelve, eight and five. The little one was born here. My husband left me and now I live alone with the four children. I became part of the collective of sans-papiers in Toulouse and I was one of the first to be regularized under the terms of Chevènement's circular. But that has hardly changed anything because my children have still not been regularized. It's as if they didn't exist. I don't have the right to any family allowance, I don't have any rights. How am I meant to live?[3]

This problem of their children's nationality is not unique to those women who form part of the *sans-papiers* movement. Benani points to the example of Maghrebi single-mothers who, because of their status as women and immigrants, have children with no nationality:

> Women are in a more fragile position because of their status as women and immigrants, or daughters of immigrants. The phenomenon of Maghrebi single mothers is significant in this regard. Those who have not acquired French citizenship and who are mothers of children born on French territory, are bringing up children who are not recognized by any country. They are not French (and will not become French before the age of sixteen or eighteen) because of the Pasqua laws, and neither are they Moroccan, Algerian or Tunisian, because the family law codes in the Maghreb do not recognize the status of single mothers, and do not accord a legal

---

[3] Interview Toulouse, February 1998.

status to their children . . . From birth, these children live in a position of exclusion. (Benani, 1995b: 217)

Thus women of immigrant origin often find their status as mothers devalued and encounter both legal and material difficulties in bringing up their children in France. Whilst dominant representations portray them first as wives and mothers, responsible for bringing up children who will integrate into French society, the social and legal conditions of this same society make this a sometimes very difficult task.

Women Refugees and Asylum Seekers

The high profile wrangling between France and the UK over the Red Cross camp for asylum seekers at Sangatte, near Calais (see chapter 2 for more details), has highlighted the importance of the refugee/asylum-seeker issue for European government. The images in the French and British media of Sangatte showed young men trying to cross the Channel to enter the UK, and as with other forms of migration the principal representations of asylum seekers are of men. However, there are growing numbers of women refugees and asylum seekers and thus asylum must also be considered as a gendered issue. Of the total number of refugees currently in France, it is estimated that there are 41.4 per cent of women (Chaib, 2001a). The number of women asylum seekers in France is more difficult to ascertain because of the lack of gender disaggregated statistics, and because of the large number of asylum seekers forced into clandestinity by the restrictive policies imposed by governments, but it would seem likely that as with the statistics for those who have obtained refugee status, almost half of asylum seekers are women. As elsewhere in Europe, one of the major problems for women asylum seekers is the lack of recognition of many gendered forms of persecution in assessing claims for refugee status. The current attempts to limit the total number of people to whom refugee status is granted has also had an effect in that women will find it even harder to prove their claims of persecution. And successive governments' attempts to discourage asylum seekers from reaching France have made it even more difficult to even make an asylum claim. A woman asylum seeker from Sierra Leon, for example, was detained at Roissy airport where the police refused to register her claim for asylum and beat her when she refused to get back on the aeroplane, believing that she was a prostitute and not an asylum seeker (Lesselier, 2003). This type of incident seems to be more and more commonplace amongst women attempting to reach France to lodge an asylum claim.

Whilst there is continued debate over whether the category women should be accepted as a social group under the terms of the Geneva Convention of 1951 for the purposes of considering asylum claims (Crawley, 2001; Kofman et al., 2000), campaigners in France have pointed to the limitations that the non-recognition of women as a social group in this context poses for female asylum seekers (Lesselier, 1999). In particular, the Commission des recours de réfugiés (CRR) to which asylum seekers may appeal if their claims are rejected by the

OFPRA, ruled that Algerian women could not be granted asylum on the grounds that they were being persecuted because of their sex in Algeria in being forced to submit to a certain lifestyle and modes of behaviour. The CRR judged that Algerian law which governed the lives of these women was applicable to all women in Algeria, and the fact that certain women contested these laws did not in itself allow them to be considered as a social group under the terms of the Geneva Convention (Créach, 2002). There have been more recent cases where this judgement has been reversed to some extent, and women have been granted refugee status on the grounds that they had suffered persecution because of their sex and their way of life, but in none of these cases was it recognised that women could form a social group for the purposes of the Geneva Convention, thus leaving women's asylum claims of this type to be considered on an individual, case-by-case basis, with no precedent for considering them as part of a social group.

Aside from the issue of whether or not women form a social group for the purposes of considering their asylum claims under the terms of the Geneva Convention, there is the separate but linked issue of what type of persecution is considered relevant as grounds for granting refugee status. Whilst in some cases sexual violence has been recognised by the French authorities as grounds for granting asylum, this is often hard to prove, and the process of interrogations which women have to go through to prove that they have been the victims of sexual violence is often painful and degrading (Bouaoumeur, 2000). As in other cases regarding immigration, one may observe a disjunction between the official discourse and the practice. The experience of refugee women in their treatment by immigration officials demonstrates the lack of regard by the latter for the suffering that these women may have experienced, and although the government has indicated that it will take sexual violence seriously as a grounds for granting asylum, the experiences of women who have to prove their status as victims of such violence before immigration officials and judges shows that this is not always the case. Further, the continuing operation of a public-private division means that many forms of persecution faced by women are not recognised as such in terms of claiming asylum (Crawley, 2000). Issues such as the threat of forced marriage, or of female genital mutilation, for example, are not always considered seriously as grounds for granting of asylum, or may be assigned to 'cultural differences' which are part of the order of things (Lesselier, 2000). On those occasions when the threat of forced marriage or genital mutilation has been accepted as grounds for granting refugee status in France, it has always been the CRR which has finally ruled in a woman's favour, after a primary refusal by the OFPRA. And in these cases, the woman must have provided 'extra' evidence to prove persecution. For example, in the case of a Malian woman, Suzanne K., the CRR granted her refugee status in March 2001 because she was at risk of suffering genital mutilation in Mali, because she had denounced the practice of female genital mutilation on the radio and because of this she was threatened within her country and had not been accorded the support of the Malian authorities. The favourable judgment in this case relied on the accumulation of risks and threats in the particular personal circumstances of this woman – the threat of gential mutilation alone would not have been enough to guarantee her refugee status (Lesselier, 2003). Even outside of those particular procedures for the consideration of asylum claims and the determination of refugee status, women have pointed to a clear lack of concern about the consequences for women, their security and social status in the case of deportation and return to their country of origin.

One aspect of the new asylum law being introduced that has been criticised by feminist groups, is the increase numbers of countries designated as 'safe', and the provision that any person coming from one of these 'safe' countries will not be accorded a provisional residence permit whilst their asylum claim is considered but will have an accelerated hearing within forty eight hours of arrival in France. The criteria for designating 'safe' countries have been criticised on a number of accounts (see chapter 3), but for women there is a particular issue in that gender based discriminations present in these countries are not taken into account in the designation of their status as 'safe'. The inclusion of countries such as Mali, Bangladesh and Ghana, in this new list of 'safe' countries can thus be seen to neglect the significant gender based forms of discrimination and persecution which might occur in these countries, and any claim to refugee status from a woman originating in one of these countries is likely to be rejected despite the gender based persecutions that she may have suffered.

The introduction of the new form of territorial asylum might have been seen as a positive development for women asylum seekers in that it would recognise forms of persecution emanating from civil society and not from the state. This could help to overcome the ongoing structural inequality in the asylum system which gives greater importance in the determining of refugee status to state sponsored persecution whilst the persecution suffered by many women emanates from civil society because of gendered political, economic and social structures. However, even ignoring the fact that territorial asylum is at most a temporary solution, offering only a short-term residence permit and not permanent resident status, it has been a disappointment in that the decisions on this status (taken directly by the Ministry of the Interior and its agents) have been largely negative. In fact 98.3 per cent of the requests made for territorial asylum between the creation of this status in 1998 and the end of 2000, resulted in refusals. This being the case, women's only hope is to rely on the conventional asylum process, which as we have seen, has issues of gender inequality structured within it.

Immigrant Women in the Labour Market

As argued above, the principle representations of women of immigrant origin portray them as wives and mothers, and thus see them as inactive outside the home and absent from the labour market. Despite the fact that statistics show an increasing presence of immigrant women in paid employment, immigration law and policy support these representations and reinforce the public-private divide which relegates immigrant women to the sphere of the home and family. In fact, up until 1984, government policy acted to force women immigrants into illegal work, as Chaib points out:

> Up until 1984, women who entered the country for family reunification would obtain the right to residence but not the right to work. For the public authorities women immigrants were thus meant to be housewives only. It is pointless to spell out that this opened the door to illegal or black market work (Chaib 2001b: 37).

Women who came into France for family reunification officially won the right to work in 1984, but even since then, it has been a struggle for many women to persuade the authorities to issue them with a work permit. Cissé points to the experience of the women *sans-papières* who found that often that if they won their struggle to gain legal residence status, they were given a visitor's card by the police prefecture, which did not entitle them to work and they thus had an added fight to get normal residence cards which would allow them to work legally (Cissé, 2000). Sexist and racist discrimination by employers is thus reinforced by legal structures that do not take into account many immigrant women's desire and need to work, and force them into situations of dependence on men or into undocumented employment where they face the risk of exploitation. In general it can be argued that as in other Western industrial democracies immigrant women represent a cheap and flexible source of labour. They are a group who, as Morokvasic argues:

> Represent a ready made labour supply, which is at once, the most vulnerable, the most flexible and, at least in the beginning, the least demanding work force. They have been incorporated into sexually segregated labour markets at the lowest stratum in high technology industries or at the "cheapest" sectors in those industries which are labour intensive and employ the cheapest labour to remain competitive (Morokvasic, 1984: 886).

Historically it has been difficult for women of immigrant origin to find work in France. Unlike men who came specifically to fill gaps in the French labour market, most women immigrated later when economic conditions were more difficult, and it was not assumed that they would find work. In fact there is an increasing presence in the labour force among women of immigrant origin, but they are also a group who suffer from high rates of unemployment due to numerous exclusionary factors (Chaib, 2001a). Survey data shows that the proportion of immigrants in the total of the active female population has increased from 6.7 per cent in 1990 to 7.7 per cent in 1999, with about 41 per cent of immigrant women being in the labour market (as opposed to 54 per cent of French women) (INSEE, 2001). A breakdown of these figures shows significant differences between immigrant groups however. Portuguese women have levels of activity equal to or higher than those of French women, women from sub-Saharan Africa are considerably less present in the labour market, whilst women of Algerian or Turkish origin have very low rates of labour market participation. These differing rates of labour market participation can be attributed to both the preferences (often racially motivated) of French employers, and to the cultural

traditions of these women's community of origin which may place constraints on their choice of whether or not to take up paid employment outside the home. However, although immigrant women are taking a greater place in the labour market, there is still a differentiation between the type of employment that they are involved in, and that undertaken by French women. INSEE statistics show that immigrant women are more likely to be employed in a part-time or temporary job than French women, and if they are in a temporary job it is likely to be of a shorter duration than that of a temporary job taken by a French woman (INSEE, 2001). Half of the immigrant women who do work are employed in the sector labelled by INSEE as 'direct services to individuals' i.e. personal and domestic work and work in hotels and restaurants (INSEE, 2001). The statistics thus seem to illustrate a tendency to a greater rate of labour market participation amongst immigrant women, but a participation usually in the lower sectors of the labour market, with immigrant women doing the less well-paid and more precarious jobs. Further, these statistics include only immigrant women living and working in France legally, and do not take account of the large numbers of undocumented migrant workers who are working in even harder and more precarious conditions. The number of women working illegally is hard to estimate, but, as explained below, estimates have put the figure at a high level. Finally, it must be noted that even as immigrant women are entering more and more into employment, they are also a group who have a high risk of unemployment. In 1990, 38.4 per cent of all women of immigrant origin in France who came from outside of the European Union were unemployed (INSEE, 1992). The groups worst affected by unemployment are those women who originate from Algeria and Tunisia. A study in 1996 revealed that 46 per cent of the active female population of Algerian and Tunisian origin were unemployed (Thave, 1997). Women of immigrant origin can thus be seen to be the victims of both racial and gendered discrimination in their access to the labour market. Compounding this with the stricter immigration controls which denies many the right to a legal work permit, means that for many immigrant women, paid employment is a realm of insecurity and exploitation.

Growing areas of employment for immigrant women in France are, as elsewhere in Europe, in domestic labour or in prostitution and sex work. As the statistics above reveal, many immigrant women in France are legally employed in domestic service, and to this we should add a high number of immigrant women working illegally in this sector. Lutz estimates that there are at least one million undocumented female migrant domestic workers currently working in the European Union (Lutz, 1997). France, unlike some other EU countries, has made some attempt to regulate domestic work, but these attempts have proved to be complex, and have had little effect in terms of improving the conditions for migrant domestic workers (Anderson, 2000). Any attempt to regulate or improve the conditions for migrant domestic workers are made much more complex by the fact that many of the women who undertake this kind of employment are undocumented immigrants. Much of the domestic work takes place in private households but there are also many women working for companies providing domestic services who have been victims of constant insecurity and discrimination.

In 2002, for example, women of immigrant origin working for a national cleaning group went on strike to complain about their conditions of employment. These women, originating mainly from Senegal and Mali, were being paid half the salary of their French colleagues, and because of their uncertain legal status, were subjected to highly insecure and degrading working conditions – women interviewed described, for example, the way that they were forced to hide in toilets to take a break or to eat their lunch.[4] The women working for individuals are also liable to exploitation, especially if they are undocumented migrants for whom their illegal status creates a dependency on the employer. Studies carried out at the time of the regularisation of illegal immigrants in 1981 showed that of all the women regularised, 62 per cent had been employed by private employers for domestic work (Marie, 1984). Anderson lists some of the problems faced by such domestic workers: 'excessive working hours, working with animals, working for no extra money in the homes of employers' families, having to provide free "trial" labour (and often not employed at the end of it), sexual harassment and false accusations of stealing' (Anderson, 2000: 76). And being without legal residence papers as many of these women are merely intensifies their problems and their dependence on their employers:

> If their rights are abused they have no recourse to authority, since they are likely to end up in prison. As women they face particular problems with pregnancy, often losing their job in consequence, and with no rights to state health care during their pregnancy and birth. When born their children often have no rights to health or education. Being undocumented does not mean that workers are independent of their employers; indeed it gives the employers a direct hold over the workers: if they are dissatisfied with them they may simply report and deport them, or may even do so to avoid paying their wages (Anderson, 2000: 179).

Another growing area of employment for migrant women is in sex work. Some of these women who engage in sex work may have been smuggled into the country specifically for this purpose. France, as other countries in Europe (Lim, 1997) has seen as recent rise in the incidence of trafficking of women for sex work, and estimates suggest that over four thousand 'trafficked' women are working in Paris alone (*AFP*, 31 January 2001). The legal system seems powerless faced with this phenomenon, and there have even been reports of women being recruited into sex work and prostitution by networks who frequent immigration tribunals in an attempt to conscript new workers with both police and judges turning a blind eye (*Libération*, 31 October 2001). Migrant sex workers have become a prime target for the new government's attempts to restore internal security – but the aim of these policies is clearly not to provide added security for those engaged in sex work. The new internal security bill, which was presented to the Council of Ministers by the Minister of the Interior, Nicolas Sarkozy on 10 July 2002, and received its first reading in the National Assembly on 17 July 2002, brought together the two issues of prostitution and immigration, with a clause stating that

---

[4] Interview Paris, August 2002.

'Those responsible for actively or passively soliciting will be liable to systematic removal from French territory and to a definitive withdrawal of all rights of residence when they are of a foreign nationality' (cited in *Le Monde,* 7 August 2002). As a result of the government's determination to reduce prostitution and their linking of this issue specifically to immigration, prostitution support networks have reported increasingly frequent police raids which target immigrant sex workers. Cabiria, an organisation which promotes community health amongst prostitutes in Lyon, kept a 'diary' of the violence experienced by migrant sex workers in the city at the hands of the police. Their report highlights the ways in which these women are being pushed into greater and greater insecurity because of the way that they are targeted by the police under orders from both the Ministry of the Interior, and the Mayor of Lyon. Although these actions are portrayed as part of a drive against prostitution in general, one of the police commissioners of Lyon, apologised to a French prostitute for having taken away her car, explaining that the police had through that it belonged to an African woman, and that French women were not being targeted by the police (Cabiria, 2002). Another prostitute, one of those clients is a policeman reported that:

> He had warned her that there would be a growing repression of prostitutes and that this time all of the immigrants would be expelled, and that even those women who had French nationality but were of immigrant origin would suffer repression. The 'traditional' prostitues [ie white French women] would be offered places in retraining workshops (Cabiria, 2002: 6).

At the same time as migrant sex workers are being targeted by police in all major French cities and threatened with deportation, little is being done to fight against one of the major causes of insecurity for these women, that is the organized traffickers and smugglers who are often responsible for having recruited them into prostitution, and who take a large proportion of their earnings. Those who have been brought into France by traffickers or smugglers are in a situation of illegality with regard to their entry and residence in the country, and thus have no legal recourse to help them to escape from exploitation. In January 2002 the National Assembly passed a bill, 'reinforcing the fight against different forms of slavery'.[5] Article two of this bill stipulated that those victims of trafficking who were prepared to lodge a complaint and testify against the trafficker should obtain a one year residence permit in France. However, this bill was never passed by the Senate, and has since been superseded by the new law on internal security discussed above. In addition, even if this bill entered into law, its provisions were criticised as inadequate by associations campaigning on behalf of trafficked women who point to the fact that the measures envisioned by the bill were below those contained in certain international conventions on trafficking.[6] They argued that trafficked

---

[5] Proposition de loi, number 3522.
[6] In particular the Additional Protocol to the Convention on Transnational Organized Crime, Vienna 2000 (chapter II), and the Resolution of 15 August 2001 of the UN Committee on Human Rights.

women should be able to obtain more than a temporary one-year residence permit
which carries no guarantee of renewal, and that their being granted a residence
permit should not, in any case, be dependent on the fact that they had to lodge a
complaint and testify against a trafficker, because to do so might frequently
involve the threat of reprisals against them or their families in their country of
origin. In fact, however, even the minimal protection which would have been
offered by this law has not been realised, and instead the new laws which are being
introduced will only add to the insecurity of migrant sex workers, whether
trafficked or in France through their own volition, by criminalising them and
making them liable to instant deportation.

In addition to an increase in the numbers of migrant sex workers in
France, there has also been a perceived rise in the number of young 'second
generation' immigrants (particularly from North Africa) who have become
engaged in prostitution. In a report on this phenomenon, Bouamama notes that this
increase in prostitution amongst the 'second generation' Maghrebin immigrants is
firstly the result of the social condition of families of Maghrebin origin in France.
These families are more profoundly affected by unemployment and poverty than
others, and also have difficulties relating to social identity, difficulties which are
not fully understood by the social structures designed to help them (Bouamama
1998).

The French treatment of both immigrant women sex workers and
domestic workers seems to rest not only on assumptions about the nature of
women's work, but on racialized views of immigrant women as fit only for certain
types of employment. This view is also reflected in the policy and political
discourses on skilled immigrant workers which although couched in gender neutral
terms have had a much more favourable impact on male immigrants due to existing
socio-economic conditions and ideological presuppositions. The Chevènement law
on immigration of May 1998 is an example of how socio-economic and legal
conditions can contribute to discriminate doubly against women. This new law
makes it easier for certain categories of foreigner to receive residence cards in
France. This includes those whose professional qualifications may be seen to
benefit France: scientists, those with artistic and cultural professions, and anyone
else whose residence is considered to be advantageous for France. Again, although
this law is not gender specific, in reality it is clear that these categories will
probably benefit men much more than women given the unequal access of women
to education in their countries of origin (Cissé, 1999). Those skills which are
valued under this law are not necessarily ones which women will easily have
acquired. Those skills which women do possess and which are equally necessary to
France (and exploited by French employers) are not always recognised as such,
and so women will benefit less under this new law and will continue to be
frequently relegated to the arena of private, and undocumented employment.

So those women who do want to work in France often have to do so
illegally and this means that they are dependent on employers who will give them
work on the black market. They have no employment rights, and are often isolated
and exposed to the risks of sexual harassment and sexual violence (Lesselier,

1999). This black market employment also militates against the possibilities of women of immigrant origin having access to legal residence cards in the future. The Chevènement law allows for the 'regularization' of those who have been living in France for at least ten years, even if they have been doing so illegally. This clause, however, which gave hope to many *sans-papiers* has in fact delivered far less than it promised. For many women who have been living in secrecy and working on the black market, it may be impossible to convince the local authorities of their length of residence in France. *Le Monde* recounts the case of a young Haitian woman, living in Paris since 1989 and working as a black market cleaner. Her requests for residence papers have been rejected by the authorities because she does not have adequate proof of her length of residence in France, nor of the fact that she earns a living, as none of her employers will testify that she has been working for them because it is illegal to employ someone without declaring it. A voluntary worker trying to help in this case has persuaded her employers to sign letters acknowledging that they have known the woman in question for several years but she comments: 'The prefectoral offices know very well that this type of declaration is really an implicit recognition of work that has not been declared. But I have the impression that they do not want to regularize them because they are single women' (*Le Monde,* 14 November 1999).

Conclusion: Women's Associations – A Recourse Against Discrimination

Throughout this chapter, it has been argued that women of immigrant origin face a double discrimination within French society, and are often in a situation of double dependency on men. It is important, however, not to paint a picture of these women as helpless victims who are unable to defend themselves against these oppressions. One important manifestation of women's agency and of their desire to fight the discriminations of which they are victims is the formation of women's associations to provide solidarity and self-help for women of immigrant origin. A well-known example of a women's association is that of the Nanas Beurs (now known as the Meufs Rebeus or Voix d'Elles Rebelles) an association for young Maghrebi women. One of the founding members describes how she and other young women from the North African immigrant community set up this association to defend their interests as: 'Women's concerns were often overlooked in the ideological battle for equal opportunities for immigrants. None of the slogans or campaigns showed how young women of North African origin were the victims of discrimination or oppression' (Benani 1995a: 79).

Their association provides help for women having trouble with their residence or nationality papers, refugees, unmarried mothers and battered wives amongst others. They also stage debates and public meetings on topics of concern to women of immigrant origin and act as a point of liaison between women of immigrant origin and the French authorities in the forms of social and welfare workers, courts and police. And the *Nanas Beurs* is not the only such organization of women of immigrant origin, there are numerous other associations of women of different immigrant origins (Quiminal, 2000), providing self-help in negotiating a path towards an easier life in France. Women have also been active in the *sans-papiers* movement, and in fact have ensured the movement's survival and success (Cissé, 2000).

In addition, although French feminists and women's organizations may have been slow to realize the problems facing women of immigrant origin, and to organize to help them (Barison and Catarino, 1997; Lloyd, 1998a), a campaigning network, RAJFIRE, has now been set up whose goal is to defend the rights of women of immigrant origin, to fight for the right of asylum for women who are victims of sexist persecution and violence, and to achieve the introduction of an autonomous legal status for women of immigrant origin. Until women of immigrant origin achieve such an autonomous status, they argue, they will be prevented from accessing the rights they should have as individuals. It seems that until the problems of women of immigrant origin in regard to nationality and citizenship are considered specifically and apart from general issues relating to these subjects, women will continue to be the victims of particular exclusions. Despite the efforts of women of immigrant origin to organize and struggle against these exclusions, there is still a long way to go before they overcome their double source of oppression and achieve equal citizenship status in France.

Chapter 7

The *Affaire des Foulards*: Islam, Integration and Secularism

One of the major issues that has arisen in the debate over immigration in France is the perceived 'problem' of integrating a large number of Muslim immigrants into French society. There have been many ways in which this supposed 'problem' has been brought to public attention, but one which has received a particularly large amount of attention from politicians, media and public, is that of the *foulard islamique,* or rather the headscarf which some Muslim girls have chosen to wear to school. This debate over whether Muslim girls should or should not be allowed to wear their headscarves in the secular schools so dear to the heart of French Republicans, has exposed one of the fundamental difficulties that the French conceptions of nationhood and citizenship pose for immigrants, namely the residual assimilationism which demands some kind of cultural uniformity as part of its project of integration. As Brubaker comments: 'While French nationhood is constituted by political unity, it is centrally expressed in the striving for cultural unity. Political inclusion has entailed cultural assimilation, for regional cultural minorities and immigrants alike' (Brubaker, 1992: 1). The reactions to the girls wearing headscarves to school were particular to France in that secularism plays a key part in the definition of French Republican identity, especially as a principle in the French education system. However, the way in which the affair played out must also be placed in an international context of post-colonial relations. France's ambivalent relationship to her ex-colonies, particularly Algeria[1], and her fear of the spread of Islamic fundamentalism or *intégrisme,* has created tensions within French society, with immigrants of Islamic origin at risk of being stereotyped as 'fundamentalists' or 'terrorists'. The global political context even before the terrorist attacks of 11 September 2001 gave support to those who saw Islam as a threat to the security of Western countries, with events such as the Gulf War, and the rise of fundamentalisms in Iran, Algeria and elsewhere only adding to the fears

---

[1] The long and bloody decolonisation of Algeria has had a continuing effect on France's relationship with its ex-colony. The Algerian War itself split France, and was the principal cause of the collapse of the Fourth Republic. Debates over the War have continued and at the same time the relationship between France and Algeria has been further strained by France's intervention to attempt to block the election victory of an Islamic Party in the Algerian elections in 1992. This intervention was in turn a cause of terrorist attacks by Algerian Islamic groups in France. The continuing unrest in Algeria and the perceived threat of terrorist action by Algerian Islamic organisations has had an important impact on the ways in which France's Muslim community is perceived.

of the French concerning the dangers that Islam posed to their country (Venel, 1999). Indeed, the girls at the centre of the *affaire des foulards* were often represented by the French media as tools of Islamic organisations aiming to infiltrate France. The 11 September attacks have only added to this tendency to make a link between Islam and terrorism, and the recent recurrence of the debate over the *foulard* has occurred within this context. This chapter will examine the debates over the *affaire des foulards* in the context of the more general issue of the position of Muslim immigrants and ethnic minorities within French society, arguing that the emphasis placed on integration, and the pressure to maintain Republican values, such as secularism, place a huge burden on Muslims in particular. In addition it will examine the way in which the affair has highlighted the gendered nature of discourses on immigration and integration, causing splits amongst French feminist groups, and drawing attention to a disjuncture between feminist and anti-racist movements in France. The chapter begins, though with an examination of the position of Muslims in French society, and of the ways in which French attitudes towards Islam have impacted on many of the population of immigrant origin.

Islam in France

The Muslim population in France grew rapidly after the Second World War, as the process of decolonization[2] began and more and more immigrants began to arrive from France's colonies and ex-colonies in Africa and Asia, and particularly from the countries of the Maghreb: Algeria, Morocco and Tunisia, as well as sub-Saharan countries such as Senegal and Mali. As noted in chapter 1, many in France expressed a preference for immigrants from other European countries, but shortages of labour meant that recruitment was actually carried out widely in North Africa. Algeria in particular which had been heavily colonized by France and was regarded as an integral part of France itself, was a prime site for the recruitment of workers. The legal status of Algeria established in 1947 allowed for free movement of population between there and France. Even the protracted and bloodthirsty war of independence did not stop the flow of immigrants from Algeria to France, and indeed added to it when with the arrival of Algerian independence in 1962, the *harkis*, those Algerians who had fought on the side of the French, were forced to flee to France. Following the official suspension of labour migration in 1974, families of these Maghrebi workers arrived, and the population became more feminised and settled in France. This settlement was not what had been expected by the French authorities, who had assumed that the workers who came to France would then return to their countries of origin. The creation of a large Muslim population has posed some particular questions, particularly with the production of a second and third (and even fourth generation) who have forged their own

---

[2] The process of decolonization began with the independence of France's colonies in South East Asia. The independence of Morocco and Tunisia followed in 1958 and that of Algeria in 1962.

identities as French Muslims. In 1999 it was estimated that more than 30 per cent of the Muslim population in France was second-generation (Esposito, 1999), and this figure is growing rapidly. The emergence of these younger generations of Muslims poses particular issues for French society, and especially issues to do with education, of which the headscarf affair is a prime example.

It is estimated that there are currently between four and five million Muslims in France, although it is impossible to arrive at an exact figure because census data does not include any information on religion. These Muslims are of course a diverse population, with different national and ethnic origins and differing levels of religious observance and practice. As El Hamel comments: 'We may think of Islam in France, often even more than in the countries of origin, as constituting something of a spectrum, a continuum of diverse practices and levels of commitment extending from religious to rejection or mere absence' (El Hamel, 2002: 295). But although the Muslim population in France is far from homogeneous, the dominant French representations have often tended to treat Islam and Muslims in a reductionist and essentialist fashion, failing to note the important variations and cleavages amongst the Muslim community. A significant essentialism present in dominant French representations, and one to which we will return later in this chapter, is that concerning the oppression of women by men within Muslim culture. In this situation, Muslims, even those who were born in France and have French nationality, are often reminded of their foreign origins through discrimination and racism (see chapter 8), and many describe themselves as 'second class citizens'. So whilst statistically Islam is the second religion in France, 'socially it is practiced by a group of people that is dominated, underprivileged and reduced to political silence' (Etienne, 1989: 203). In these circumstances Islam becomes for some a manner of self-affirmation and resistance to the outside world (Venel, 1999). This may be the case particularly for the younger generations for whom religious practices are often seen as a form of self-identification rather than a sign of real religiosity. The studies carried out by INED, for example, show that there are similar levels of disaffection towards religion amongst children born in France to Algerian parents, as there are amongst children of native French origin. 'The proportion of non-believers or of non-practising young people is very similar to that found in the totality of young people of the same age living in France' (Tribalat, 1995: 97). There was however evidence that this disaffection with religion was less likely to affect the observance of Ramadan, and of dietary restrictions. These declarations by young Muslims that they were likely to observe Ramadan and dietary practices owed more to a loyalty to their origins than to an interest for religion as such, indicating the need to affirm their identity in respect of their origins. The creation of these new identities by young French Muslims are clearly highly influenced by their experiences of economic and social exclusion (Khosrokhavar, 1998) and must thus be understood as part of the social, cultural and economic landscape of French society. For many young women of Muslim origin the wearing of an Islamic headscarf can be seen as part of this assertion of identity as discussed below.

In the current context of limited tolerance towards immigrants, and the emphasis on the integration of immigrants that are in France, one of the key issues that has arisen has been the creation of a Muslim community in France and the perceived difficulties in 'integrating' this community into French society. In conjunction with the growing tendency to perceive Islamic fundamentalism as a threat to the security of European countries, the fear of Islam has blossomed, as Venel comments: 'The questions posed by the practice of Islam in France create a wave of disturbance in French society closely linked to the unfavourable perception of this religion (due to colonial imagery), but also to current international events which are not likely to calm the spirits' (Venel, 1999: 17). An opinion poll carried out in 1989 found that respondents characterised Islam by women's submission, fanaticism, anti-modernism and violence (*Le Monde*, 30 November 1989). This linking of Islam with religious fundamentalism and terrorism has only worsened since 11 September 2001. For example, the General Secretary of the MRAP, one of the major anti-racist organisations described how he had learned of a leading French management company which had issued a confidential internal memo stating that in order to contribute to the fight against terrorism they would not be recruiting any employees of Arab or Muslim origin (*Libération*, 30 October 2003). Such examples illustrate the ways in which fears about terrorism and security have created difficulties for Muslims in France, as elsewhere in Europe.

The ways in which Islam is perceived and treated in France are unlike those in other European nations, however, because of the particularities of the French Republican tradition within which secularism is a key principle in the management of public institutions (Khosrokhavar, 1998). Islam in this context is understood as a menace to the Republic and to its forms of socialisation and integration. As Etienne argues, the obstacle that Islam is seen to represent to integration is as much political as religious because Islam refuses secularism, one of the principles at the heart of French Republicanism (Etienne, 1989). The following section will discuss the issue of secularism and its importance for the French Republican tradition.

The Secular Republic

It is difficult to understand the importance that the seemingly minor event of Muslim girls wearing headscarves to school carried for French society without realising the importance of secularism in French national identity and without understanding the ways in which immigration, particularly from France's ex-colonies has brought this national identity into question.

Laïcité or secularism has a long history in France, and a key place in French national identity. It is a principle which is closely connected with Republican universalism and with the doctrine of *liberté, égalité, fraternité* elaborated at the time of the French Revolution. It is perhaps no coincidence that the *affaire des foulards* exploded as France was celebrating the bicentenary of the Revolution and the principles it expounded. In effect, the founding project of the French Republic was the disappearance of difference through the assimilation of all to one 'legitimate' culture. Republican ideology seeks to overcome all types of specific identities and belongings and create equality through sameness. Secularism seeks to enforce this equality in the public sector with regard to religion: by removing all religious observance from public institutions the private religious divides that exist in society should be overcome. It is a principle which has been a key part of the French state education system since the end of the Nineteenth Century when a series of laws known as the *lois laïques* decreed the secular nature of French schools. This secularism in education was reinforced by the formal separation of church and state in 1905 (Chadwick, 1997). The French Republican idea of nation places education at the heart of a project of integration into universal French citizenship: through a uniform, secular education children are brought up to be equal citizens. School has always been conceived as the prime site of integration. State schools have always played a role as both instrument and expression of a politics of national identity which aims to detach individuals from their particular community or group of belonging and to assimilate them to the vast collective community which is the French nation. Indeed it may be argued that in the late nineteenth and early twentieth centuries, schoolteachers provided a critical service in reinforcing a particular idea of the French nation. As Brubaker argues: 'The political, assimilationist understanding of nationhood in France was reinforced in the late nineteenth century by the internal *mission civilisatrice* carried out by the Third Republic's army of schoolteachers – the instituteurs, whose mission was to *institute* the nation' (Brubaker, 1992: 11). It is impossible to understand the importance of the *affaire des foulards* without grasping the importance of this Republican conception of national identity and the place that secular education is seen to have in preserving this identity even today.

This principle of secularism has been challenged, however, particularly within the French education system by the growing religious diversity of the French population due to an increasingly settled immigrant population. As argued above, one of the fundamental obstacles perceived in the integration of Muslim immigrants in France is that of the clash between Islam and the secular values of the Republic. The anxieties about the preservation of national identity and of Republican values in the face of the new multi-racial France have been played out through an often polemical debate over the right of Muslim girls to wear a headscarf in French secular schools.

The *Affaire des Foulards*

Although *affaire des foulards* is often referred to in the singular, it is actually constituted by a series of different 'affairs' and perhaps should be categorised more accurately as an ongoing political debate. The question of the *foulard* or *voile* (the Islamic headscarf)[3] first hit the headlines in France in October 1989 when Ernest

---

[3] The terms *foulard* or *voile* are those widely used in dominant French discourse to describe all the different types of headscarf worn by Muslim women. The refusal of the French to use the Arabic terms such as *hijab* can be seen as another indication of their opposition to multiculturalism in France.

Chenière[4], a headmaster in Creil, a suburb of Paris, refused to allow three Maghrebi girls to come to school wearing their headscarves on the grounds that this would contravene the Republican principle of secularism. Creil, where the issue of Islamic headscarves first hit the headlines, is like many other suburbs a town built in the post-war economic boom to house migrants from rural areas and immigrant workers from France's ex-colonies. Its school was founded to educate the children of these new housing estates or *cités*. In 1989 when the *affaire des foulards* began it had almost nine hundred pupils of twenty-five different nationalities and five hundred of these pupils came from Muslim families. Chenière's action in excluding the three girls for wearing their headscarf could thus be seen as an act of racist provocation[5] against the Muslim community served by his school, although for many in France he was seen rather as a hero taking a stand to defend the secularism of a French school against the rising tide of a multi-racial society. The affair was first reported in the daily newspaper *Libération* under the headline 'The secularism of Creil's school comes up against the Islamic headsarf' (*Libération*, 4 October 1989), and the story was quickly taken up by other newspapers. The majority of the reports focused on the affair as a challenge to secularism in the French education system and a sign of the failure to integrate immigrants into the system. The dispute in Creil was seemingly resolved within a week when a compromise was agreed whereby the girls were allowed to wear their headscarves in the school playground and corridors but would let them drop around their shoulders in the classrooms, but this compromise did not last, and the girls were again excluded from school, provoking further debate in the media. The affair refused to die down, and the debates surrounding it widened to include not only the rights and wrongs of excluding these girls from school, but also the position of Islam and Muslims in French society. As Beski remarks: 'The majority of journalists drew attention to the fact that this affair far surpassed the simple story of "three veiled young women in Creil", and presented itself as revelatory of serious questions and anxieties amongst the French concerning the subject of the integration of Muslim immigrants into French society' (Beski, 1997: 44).

The importance of this subject for French national identity was testified to by the violent reactions it provoked. An article by five Left-wing intellectuals in the *Nouvel Observateur* magazine likened the acceptance of the headscarf in schools to the appeasement of Hitler in the 1930s and argued that the end of a strict secularism in schools could signal the downfall of the Republic itself:

> The future will tell whether the bicentenary of the Revolution will have seen the Munich of the Republican school … The French model of democracy is a Republic. It is not a mosaic of ghettos where personal freedom can be used to disguise the law of the strongest. Devoted to free enquiry, linked to the expansion of knowledge and confidently relying on the natural light of human reason, the Republic's foundation is in schools. That is why the destruction of the school system means the destruction of the Republic itself (*Le Nouvel Observateur*, 2 November 1989).

---

[4] Chenière was later elected to the National Assembly as a deputy for the centre-Right RPR.
[5] It is interesting to note that at the time of the affair, some in the media argued that Ernest Chenière could not be accused of racism since he himself was of French West Indian origin.

In response to this type of condemnation of the *foulard*, others pointed to the 'secular fanaticism' involved in excluding girls from school merely because of the way that they were dressed. They pointed to the underlying xenophobia of those who wished to ban the headscarf, and the impossibility of integrating young Muslims if they were to be excluded from school. Alain Touraine discussed the true role of French public schools in another article in the *Nouvel Observateur* and argued that this role should be to 'understand that one of the greatest problems of our time, a problem that will not cease to grow, is to integrate the new arrivals who have come from cultures further and further removed from ours' (*Le Nouvel Observateur*, 16 November 1989).

Whilst the reaction to the affair in the press was rapid, political parties were divided and took longer to make any comments on the issue. The only party who had a clear line on this question was the Front National for whom the fact that Muslim girls wishes to wear a headscarf to school was a clear sign of an Islamic 'invasion' of France. Their spokesman, Bruno Mégret announced that:

> A Muslim civilisation has arrived in France. After its installation on French soil, it is now implanting itself symbolically by the wearing of the headscarf in schools. We must ask ourselves the question: Should France adapt her principles to those of immigrants, or should immigrants adapt their customs to the laws of our country? You can imagine our reply (*Le Quotidien de Paris*, 18 October 1989).

It is clear that the sentiments voiced by the Front National were not without echo in public opinion, an opinion poll published in *Le Monde* in November 1989 showed that 75 per cent of those questioned were hostile to the idea that girls should be allowed to wear a headscarf in school (*Le Monde*, 20 November 1989). This tide of opinion against the *foulard* was reflected in numerous other polls, and opinion seemed to become even more strongly against the girls' right to wear a headscarf as the political debate progressed (Gastaut, 2000). Other political parties and movements were more divided, however, over the issue. The Socialist Party was particularly divided, torn as they were between their long-standing loyalty to the Republican principle of secularism and their desire to pursue a policy that was more favourable to immigrants in France. About half of the party leadership were not hostile to the wearing of headscarves in schools, whilst others announced that they were against it. The moderate-Right also showed some divisions. Finally, in an attempt to put an end to the debate, the Socialist Minister for Education, Lionel Jospin, turned to the Conseil d'Etat who ruled that wearing a religious sign to school was not in itself sufficient reason for exclusion from school, and overturned the decisions that had been taken to exclude Muslim girls who were wearing a headscarf. Although this decision brought a temporary end to the affair, before its re-emergence in 1994 (see below), the effects on political debates on immigration and integration were more far-reaching. Opinion polls showed that in the aftermath of the affair, immigration had risen rapidly up the issues ranked as important by voters, coming from eighth place in September before the affair erupted, to second place, beaten as an issue of concern only by unemployment (Mayer, 1991). The polemics over the *foulard*, and the rising electoral importance of the immigration issue, can be argued to have contributed to President Mitterrand's announcement on television in December 1989, that France had reached a 'threshold of tolerance' as far as the number of immigrants was concerned (Fysh and Wolfreys, 1998). Meanwhile, the Front National continued to exploit the question of the headscarf. In a parliamentary by-election in the town of Dreux in November, the National Front candidate Marie-France Stirbois ran with a slogan of 'No to the headscarf in schools, no to mosques', and won a sensational victory gaining 61 per cent of the vote in the second round of the election.

The debate over the issue of girls wearing headscarves to school died down for several years after 1989, submerged in the larger debates over immigration. However, the affair was rekindled in 1994 when François Bayrou, the Minister for Education in a Right-Wing government, responding to growing fears about the influence of Islam in French schools, published a circular affirming that 'ostentatious' religious symbols should not be allowed in schools. Although he did not name the *foulard* as such, it was clear that this was the 'ostentatious' symbol he was referring to as he specifically excluded the wearing of a crucifix or a Jewish kippa which he declared were 'unostentatious'. It is significant to note the timing of this ruling by the Minister, made as the political situation in Algeria was deteriorating and the Front Islamique de Salut (FIS), an Islamic fundamentalist organisation, was gaining more power. Fears about the place of Islam in French society and the threat that fundamentalist Islam posed were growing in this context, as signalled by newspaper headlines such as, 'Fundamentalism attacks schools' (*Le Point*, 10 September 1994), and 'Headscarves, the plot: How Islamists are infiltrating us?' (*L'Express*, 17 November 1994).

Bayrou had been one of the Right-wing politicians who had supported the right of Muslim girls to wear a headscarf when the affair first erupted in 1989, but he explained his change of attitude by reference to the fact that he now fully understood the threat posed by Islamic fundamentalism. In an interview he explained that:

> My first reaction at the time (in 1989), was one of understanding. I thought that wearing a headscarf was a personal form of religious expression. But since then there has been so much evidence that we can no longer afford to ignore the real meaning of the headscarf for fundamentalists … There are some movements faced with which it is impossible to be naïve: we all know where that can lead. That is why, even if it is difficult, it seemed to me that it was time to say no (*Le Nouvel Observateur*, 3 November 1994).

Bayrou was not the only one to have changed his mind about the headscarf. SOS-Racisme, the anti-racist organisation which had fully supported the girls excluded from school in 1989, now changed its allegiance and supported the government's stance. The leaders of the organisation explained this stance by the fact that they believed that the growth of Islamic fundamentalism was a real danger in some of the suburbs with large immigrant populations (*Le Monde*, 27 October 1994). For many, however, this change of attitude represented a sign of the co-option of the anti-racist movement by mainstream politics resulting in a failure to represent the real interests of many immigrants (see chapter 8). The conversion of many to the view that the headscarf should be banned may also be seen as evidence of the final disappearance of the movement in favour of *le droit à la différence* (the right to be different), and of the re-assertion of the primacy of French Republicanism over any form of multiculturalism. As Gastaut argues: 'The question of the headscarf in schools caused opinion, in the name of Republican cohesion, to turn against tolerance and the right to difference and to choose between a categorical and rigid assimilation, and rejection' (Gastaut, 2000: 594).

Again, the *foulard* affair of 1994 was linked to the wider debate over immigration and in particular to the issue of nationality. The Right-wing government's attempts to reform the nationality laws had clear implications for issues of integration and citizenship. In a speech justifying his reforms, the Minister of the Interior, Charles Pasqua clearly linked the issue of nationality, and particularly the acquisition of French nationality, to the idea that in order to become French an immigrant must reject any kind of 'religious fundamentalism'. This reference to 'religious fundamentalism' was clearly meant to refer to Islamic fundamentalism as he then went on to condemn the wearing of headscarves by Muslim girls as a danger for the French Republic, and also as a potential cause of racism.

> The willingness to become French has no meaning if it is accompanied by a total submission to religious fundamentalism which is foreign to all French traditions, contrary to the principle of secularism, incompatible of our understanding of society, irreconcilable with our notions of men and women, incompatible with our citizenship ... There is no place in our Republican and secular schools for the Islamic *foulard*. That is the truth of French cultural and sociological reality. That is the truth of Republican philosophy. Forcing the acceptance of the *foulard* would do nothing but incite exasperation, which as I have already said is very dangerous. (Speech to UNESCO, 14 October 1993).

This argument of Pasqua's that the girls who wear headscarves to school are liable to incite racist and xenophobic feelings is one that has been used often. According to this point of view, the security of immigrants in terms of their protection from racist attack, can only be guaranteed by their assimilation and integration into French society. Further, the presence of immigrants who present visible signs of difference such as wearing a *foulard*, presents a danger to the stability and security of French society itself. This idea of the girls wearing a headscarf as a threat to France and its Republican tradition may seem somewhat overstated if the number of girls actually wearing headscarves is considered. In 1994, the Ministry of the Interior estimated that about 15,000 girls were wearing headscarves to school, but even if this figure were correct (and it seems likely that it is an estimate which errs on the high side of reality), that would constitute only a small proportion of the 350,000 or so Muslim girls who were attending public schools (Hargreaves, 1995).

Since Bayrou's rekindling of the *affaire des foulards* with his 1994 circular, the debate has rumbled on, with regular incidents of exclusion of girls from schools for wearing headscarves and industrial action by teachers in schools where girls are allowed to attend wearing their headscarf. The Conseil d'Etat ruled in 1995 that the Bayrou circular did not have the force of law, and that it was up to each individual head-teacher to consider the particular circumstances of a case before making a decision to exclude a girl wearing a headscarf. This ruling meant that many localised disputes and debates erupted over girls wearing headscarves in school, and that the practices of exclusion varied from one school to another. The continuing debate over this issue is symbolic of the difficulties that France has had coming to terms with the presence of a large Muslim community, and with the need felt by some to constantly reaffirm a commitment to the Republican principles, of which secularism is held up as a key part.

Most recently, the Right-wing government elected in 2002 has declared its intention of introducing new legislation which would 'solve' the problem of the *foulard* by making it illegal to wear any kind of religious insignia on school premises. The Stasi Commission, appointed by President Chirac to examine the question of secularism in France, is due to report by the end of 2003, and it is anticipated that this report will be strongly in favour of such a law. As Chirac explained in justifying his intention to legislate in this area:

> We cannot accept that some people are hiding behind a aberrant conception of religious freedom in order to defy the laws of the Republic and to put into question some of the fundamental principles of a modern society, namely sexual equality and women's dignity (*Libération*, 6 November 2003).

Alain Juppé, the former Prime Minister, and president of the UMP, the largest Right-wing party, also argued in support of a law banning the wearing of headscarves and any other religious signs. He stated clearly that he believed that girls who wore headscarves were not demonstrating religious piety or modesty but were instead undertaking 'a militant act which is supported by real fundamentalist propaganda' (*Libération*, 6 November 2003). Although the Socialist Party has been more moderate in its arguments, it has also lent support to the proposed new law. François Hollande, the General Secretary of the PS, argued that the Socialists were committed to 'fighting for secularism' and that they would be firm and clear in support of this principle (*Libération*, 13 November 2003). Again, public opinion seems to support the idea of a new law to outlaw religious signs in schools. In a survey carried out by CSA for *Le Figaro*, 55 per cent of respondents said that they were favourable to such a law, with the figure rising to 62 per cent of Right-wing voters. Interestingly, although arguments against the *foulard* are often made on the grounds of defending women's rights, fewer women (53 per cent) than men (58 per cent) were favourable to the introduction of the law (*Le Figaro*, 8 November 2003).

If this proposed new legislation is introduced as expected and passed by the National Assembly and Senate, then it will be illegal for Muslim girls to wear headscarves to school, and head-teachers who choose to exclude these girls will have the backing of the law. Those who argue for the law maintain that this will bring to an end years of dispute over the issue and that the secularism of the French education system will be protected and guaranteed. However it seems unlikely that the dispute over the *foulard* will end, as the underlying issues of how immigrants, and in particular Muslim immigrants, should be treated has not gone away. What is more likely is that such a law will only reinforce the exclusion felt by many young Muslims in France today, an exclusion based not only on the non-recognition of their religion and culture but also on social and economic inequalities. As one newspaper article commented:

> Is it a few dozen girls wearing headscarves in schools who are threatening the Republican pact? Or is it the inequalities, discrimination, ghettos and unemployment, that are so often ignored when it comes to reform? (*Le Monde Diplomatique*, June 2002).

Roman echoes this point when he argues that the main challenge facing the Republican school system is not a few Muslim girls wearing headscarves, but rather the fact that the education system seems to be massively failing children from poorer areas, most of them of children of immigrant origin (Roman, 1999).

The *Foulard* as a Gendered Issue

One striking feature of reactions to the *affaire des foulards* and its aftermath has been the lack of media attention on the gendered element of the question, and the way in which few women were called upon to express their opinions. As one woman writing about the affair remarks:

> These debates were also monopolized by men, notwithstanding their apparent concern with the question of women's rights in Islam. French men, Muslim men, male intellectuals and politicians, male personalities gave their opinion ad nauseam over the wearing of the scarves and its socio-political and cultural consequences. Women, on the other hand, whether Muslim, Maghrebi or French, were hardly heard (Bloul, 1996: 259).

The young women who chose to wear headscarves to school were represented by many media reports as mere passive agents: either victims of dominating fathers who insisted on them wearing headscarves, or unwitting tools of Islamic organisations who manipulated them for their own purposes. Those who opposed the wearing of headscarves argued that they were protecting Muslim girls from a patriarchal order which restricted their freedom. Even those who supported these girls' right to attend school wearing headscarves argued that the French school system would help integrate them into French society and 'liberate' them from Islamic pressure within their families and communities, implying a superiority of French society over patriarchal Islamic society whilst ignoring the presence of male domination within their own social order. As Balibar remarks, the argument that the headscarf demonstrates the institutionalised oppression of women is one which Western societies (themselves male dominated) have used to try and prove their superiority over Muslim societies (*Libération*, 3 November

1989). This type of response is typical of a post-colonial discourse which divides women of Muslim (mainly North African) origin into two types: those that have assimilated into French society and adopted French modes of dress, behaviour etc. and those that remain faithful to their traditional, Islamic cultures. This binary categorisation is a crude and oversimplistic representation of Muslim/Maghrebi women in France whose lives bear witness to a much more complex series of social positionings. As Beski points out: 'The stereotyped images of women immigrants of Maghrebi origin which categorise them according to certain traits either as "traditional women", "women as objects", or as "Westernized women", "women as subjects", prevent the understanding of the diversity and the complexity of the reality lived by these women' (Beski, 1997: 46).

It is also interesting to note that those who opposed Muslim girls' right to wear a headscarf in school on the grounds that this was an oppression against women, had little to say about the fact that the girls' mothers also wore a headscarf. It seems that for many, the problem lay not in the patriarchal domination of women signified by the wearing of a headscarf as such, but in the decision by young, supposedly 'integrated' and 'Westernized' women to don a *foulard*. As Dayan-Herzbrun comments, it is the conjunction between the headscarf and modernity which seems unbearable to many French citizens (Dayan-Herzbrun, 2000), a sign of the failure of French Republican system to fully assimilate second and third generation immigrants into French society, or a challenge by these second and third generation immigrants to the integrity of French national identity.

This type of confusion over the problem of the Islamic headscarf has also characterised feminist responses to the affair. In fact, many feminists have adopted the position that the headscarf is a symbol of male domination and should, therefore, be execrated. This type of knee-jerk response, taken without listening to the voices of the girls involved, only served to further distance feminists from anti-racists. Gisèle Halimi, for example, a leading feminist lawyer and former deputy, resigned from SOS-Racisme when this organisation first defended the girls excluded from school in Creil in 1989. She argued that: 'There cannot be integration without respect for the laws of the receiving country. There cannot be a change in mentalities without women's dignity equalling that of men' (*Le Quotidien de Paris*, 2 November 1989). Yvette Roudy, a former Minister of Women's Rights, took a similar standpoint, claiming that accepting the wearing of Islamic headscarves would be: 'Equivalent to saying yes to the inequality of women in French Muslim society' (*Le Quotidien de Paris*, 6 November 1989). Well-known feminist academics such as Dominique Schnapper and Elisabeth Badinter also came out in support of secularism in schools and argued for the exclusion of girls wearing headscarves (*Libération*, 24 November 1989). They argued that secular education would have an emancipatory effect on these girls and that a ban on headscarves would help young Muslim women to escape from the confines of patriarchal power.

On the ground, many of the teachers who fired the conflict by excluding girls wearing headscarves from their classes or by taking industrial action and striking in protest at the girls being allowed to wear headscarves, did so out of supposedly feminist sensibilities. Elizabeth Altschull, a teacher who has published a book recounting her experience in a school hit by the *affaire des foulards* and arguing strongly against the wearing of the headscarf, recalls how she asked one of her pupils, a thirteen year old girl named Aïcha, to take off her headscarf because she felt it her duty to do so as a feminist. She recounts that her reaction to the headscarf was: 'More feminist than secular to tell the truth: a thirteen year old girl wearing a headscarf seemed evidently unacceptable to me' (Altschull, 1995: 11).

Whilst these type of feminist reactions are 'well-meaning' in that they believe themselves to be fighting against the oppression of women, they also demonstrate a failure to comprehend the situations of Muslim women in France, and the complex reasons why women choose to wear headscarves. This failure of comprehension leads to easy condemnation of the Muslim religion and Islamic societies as patriarchal, a condemnation which does nothing for the cause of anti-racism, and indeed plays into the hands of racists. The Front National and their supporters are only too happy to see Muslim immigrants being described as patriarchal oppressors. This feminist condemnation of the *foulard* as an oppression of women also assumes a homogeneity within the Islamic community, with all Muslim women being similarly positioned. In fact, there are vast differences of opinion amongst Muslim women themselves concerning the headscarf: those who wear a headscarf do so for various reasons, others oppose the wearing of a headscarf.

Amongst those Muslim women who do oppose the headscarf were those belonging to an organisation called Expressions Maghrébiennes au Féminin (EMAF) who organised a demonstration at the time of the original *affaire des foulards* in 1989. These women opposed the exclusion of Muslim girls from school but at the same time planned to tear up a headscarf in public to demonstrate their belief that this was an oppression of women and counter to individual liberties. Similarly, Saoud Benani, a founder member of the Nanas Beurs, an association of young Maghrebi women, argued that: 'To legitimise the wearing of the headscarf is to put under pressure all those who are fighting for their emancipation and their liberty' (Benani, 1995b: 216). These voices of Muslim women were seized upon by French feminists wishing to justify their position. They are, however, only the voices of a section of Muslim women in France. For others, the wearing of the headscarf is an autonomous decision, a key part of their identity. One of the few feminists who took the time to listen to Muslim women before passing judgement on the *affaire des foulards* was Françoise Gaspard, a former Socialist deputy, and keen anti-racist, who had previously fought against the Front National in the town of Dreux. Together with the sociologist Farhad Khosrokhavar, she undertook a series of interviews with Muslim women to discover what meaning the *foulard* had for them. Their findings contradict the dominant representations in the French media which portrayed the girls at the centre of the *affaire des foulards* as lacking the capacity to make their own choices, to decide to wear headscarves as an expression of their own particular identity, and not as a result of pressure from a patriarchal social order. In fact they report that for many young Muslim women, often those most 'integrated' into French society, the choice to wear a headscarf was an autonomous one taken not for militant religious or political reasons, but as an affirmation of identity, an attempt to open up a new space where French and

Islamic identity could be combined without conflict:

> It is not a question of conquering society (nor even the Islamic community in
> France), but of opening up a personal space. In the great majority of cases, there is
> no such thing as "veiled militancy", but rather a tendency to reconcile the multiple
> demands of an identity which feels a need to distinguish itself with respect to the
> outside' (Gaspard and Khosrokhavar, 1995: 51).

As Leila Ahmed has argued, all of the discourse and narrative surrounding
the Islamic headscarf are caught within the context of Western colonial discourse.
Both the narrative of the headscarf as an oppression, and the counter-narrative of
the headscarf as a form of resistance have their roots in the misperceptions of this
colonial discourse (Ahmed, 1992). Within these two opposing narratives, the
multiple meanings and reasons for young women to wear a headscarf are often
ignored. It can be argued that the headscarf has been the object of much
unwarranted attention in France, serving to hide many of the real issue to do with
inequalities of gender, class and race that actually exist in French society. It seems,
however, that feminists who argue for a ban on the headscarf in the name of the
liberation of Muslim women, may be in fact contributing to the further exclusion of
these young women by denying them equal access to the public education system.

Conclusion

The continuing debate over the *foulard* is a symbol of the difficulties that France is
experiencing in coming to terms with the presence of a large, settled Muslim
community, and of the perceived threat of this Muslim community to French
national identity. But, as Silverman argues, 'those elements deemed to be alien to
the French tradition only appeared in that light due to a mythologised
reconstruction of the development of the French nation' (Silverman, 1992: 111).
This construction of national identity constructed a dichotomy between the
universalist/assimilationist traditions of France and the differentialist traditions of
other countries. An education system within which a strict secularism reigned was
placed at the heart of this universalist/assimilationist Republican tradition. The
dispute over the girls wearing headscarves at school was painted as a battle
analogous to that between the secular Republic and the Catholic Church at the
beginning of the century, and it was argued that as in this first battle, any
concession on the part of the secular Republic could lead to its downfall, a
downfall into a society of different communities living in separate ghettos. In the
words of historian Michel Winock:

> Two scenarios can be imagined. Either we are disposed to allow the formation –
> contrary to our tradition – of religious communities living according to their own
> rules, constituting different ghettos in society, a state within a state, with its own
> specific laws, customs, tribunals; and then we enter into the logic of segregation in
> the name of 'difference'. Or, faithful to our history, we believe that Muslims can,
> if they want, become French citizens, in which case their religion – a minority

religion in a pluralist society – will accept the concessions which Catholicism was obliged to make in the past (*L'Evénement du Jeudi*, 9 November 1989).

Within this discursive framework, even many of those who argued against the exclusion of the Muslim girls wearing headscarves from school did so because they believed that entering the secular Republican school system would be the best way of 'emancipating' the girls from their Muslim beliefs and traditions and thus better integrating them into French society. Many have argued that this framework makes it very difficult for the Left and for anti-racist movements in French society, and although these anti-racist movements did originally make a stand against the exclusion of girls from schools, as the affair has progressed the number of those arguing for the girls right to wear a headscarf as part of their right to adhere to their own particular cultural and religious values has decreased. The way in which the proposed new legislation to ban the *foulard* (as well as any other visible signs of religious belonging) is being supported by both Right and Left in terms of defending clearly the values of the Republic, shows perhaps a final defeat for the advocates of the *droit à la différence* (the right to difference). In these circumstances the position of those wishing to continue to uphold their Muslim traditions within the public sphere of this secular French state becomes very difficult. The rejection of the foulard can be seen as a profound refusal to accept the reality of Maghrebin and Muslim immigration, and as a readiness for exclusion of these populations. Paradoxically, whilst arguing for greater integration, the government seems to be creating the conditions for greater exclusion of some immigrant and ethnic minority populations in France.

Chapter 8

Racism and Discrimination: A Failure of Anti-Racism in France?

As the previous chapters have shown, issues of religion, race and ethnic belonging are at the centre of the debate over immigration in France. The electoral success of the Front National has focalised worries over the rise of racism in France, but as some commentators suggest, the Front is not solely responsible for the production of racism but merely for profiting from institutional and 'ambient' racism already present in French society (Bataille, 1997). The current variety of racism in France has been described by some as a new racism[1] differentiated from its predecessors by its insistence on cultural rather than biological difference. Whilst the extent of the originality of this form of racism might be contested by pointing out its links to previous incarnations of racism such as anti-semitism and colonial domination, it is evident that France has proved fertile ground for the propagation of racism based on cultural differentialism (Bataille, 1997; Wieviorka, 1998). This cultural racism promotes the idea of the inassimilable nature of ethnic minority communities, and poses this impossibility of integration as a danger to the French nation. Taguieff, who labels this 'new' form of racism which has developed since the beginning of the 1980s as 'heterophobia', describes a dual process of stigmatisation and exclusion:

> Which consists of presenting populations of immigrants, or of immigrant origin, in ethno-cultural, or more precisely ethno-religious terms, of dividing them into distinctive and exclusionary categories: 'Arabs', 'Maghrebins', 'Muslims' ... It is on the basis of such a categorisations that the schema of a 'struggle between the races' is re-invested, in the semantically more acceptable form of a conflict or 'clash' of civilisations. Anti-immigrant xenophobia can thus be reformulated as the legitimate defence of a civilisation threatened by other civilisations which are incompatible with it, with its values, its norms and its beliefs (Taguieff, 1997: 96).

As Wieviorka comments, tackling this type of racism provides particular difficulties in a country such as France where the Republican tradition is hostile to any form of recognition of cultural difference (Wieviorka, 1998). This chapter will discuss the manifestations of racism in France in public opinion, in the discourse of the extreme-Right, and in a particular form of 'institutional racism'. It will then go on to examine responses to racism, both through anti-discrimination policies and

---

[1] The concept of 'new racism' is drawn from the work of Martin Barker who first explored the concept in his book *The New Racism*, London: Junction Books, 1981.

legislation and through grass-roots mobilisation against racism. It will argue that through lack of an effective anti-racist policy or mobilisation, racism remains a key source of insecurity for immigrants and for members of ethnic minorities in France today.

The Front National: Legitimisting Racism

One of the clearest arguments in support of the thesis that there has been a re-emergence of racism in France in recent years has been the growing success of the Front National (for more detail on the electoral rise of the FN see chapter 2).

Taguieff argues that the Front National represents most visibly the 'Republican dilemma' mentioned above. Le Pen, he points out, never ceases to affirm that the Front National is neither racist nor xenophobic, and that he believes that all of the French are deserving of equal rights and dignity. On the other hand, all of the anti-immigration measures which the party advocates are based on the presupposition that populations of immigrant origin are, by nature, inassimilable, and that they thus present a danger for French society (Taguieff, 1997). This notion of the inassimilable nature of populations of immigrant origin is central to the FN's doctrine, reflecting a change in the extreme-Right's rhetoric from a focus on biological/racial difference to a focus on cultural/ethnic difference.[2] This change in emphasis is part of a strategy to make the Front's views more acceptable to the French electorate, and it has also made it harder for anti-racists to combat the party's discourse other than through a very strongly universalist/assimilationist standpoint. This was made clear when the Front adopted and adapted the discourse of the *droit à la difference* (the right to difference) which was put forward by sections of the Left and the anti-racist movement in the 1980s. The discourse was turned around by the FN to suggest that it was the 'native' French population who needed to have their right to difference i.e. their right to preserve their own national identity, protected. But the very fact that the FN could adapt this standpoint made it difficult for those on the Left who had championed the notion to continue to defend it.

The concept of the inassimilability of culturally diverse communities is of course closely linked to the Front National's anti-immigration policies, and to its key doctrine of 'national preference'. The idea of national preference is that in matters of employment, housing, education, and other state benefits, French and other EU nationals should be given preference over others. This policy was justified by Le Pen by his famous explanation that he prefers his daughters to his cousins, his cousins to his neighbours, his neighbours to people he doesn't know,

---

[2] Although behind this rhetoric of cultural difference there is clearly still a belief in racial difference as revealed by some of Le Pen's remarks. In 1996, for example, he referred to the notion of racial equality as 'absurd', citing the Olympic Games as a prime example of the obvious inequality between 'black' and 'white' races (Fysh and Wolfreys, 1998).

and people he doesn't know to his enemies[3]. His statement expresses the idea of hierarchisation which can be applied not only to family but in a larger sense to different national and ethnic groups. This policy of national preference has proved 'politically, morally and philosophically difficult' for opponents of the Front National (Balibar, 1996: 197), as it is in some ways merely an extension of other policies already in place. Employment in public services, for example, is open only to EU citizens. The principle of hierarchisation of the rights of different groups according to national origin is therefore not completely absent from mainstream political discourse and practice, and as pointed out in chapter 1, successive governments' policies on immigration and nationality have had the effect of increasing stratification and hierarchisation of the rights of different groups of foreigners and ethnic minorities in France. Thus when the National Front mayor of Vitrolles decided to award a subsidy to parents of children born in the commune, according to the principle of 'European preference', she merely adapted for her own purposes the legally acceptable distinction between EU citizens and others. As Jean Daniel argued in an editorial in the *Nouvel Observateur*, the danger of the policy of national preference is that it seems seductively simple and reasonable: 'It has a mask of good sense and is, moreover, apparently neither aggressive nor really racist. It seems to be a "protective" policy' (*Le Nouvel Observateur*, 15 June 1995). The racist logic of absolute and natural difference is thus displaced and remodelled in the euphemistic discourse of national preference (Taguieff and Tribalat, 1998).

Dominique Schnapper points to the way in which the doctrine of national preference makes an 'abusive assimilation between nations and people' (Schnapper, 1995: 201). The French nation is imagined as a huge family founded on ties of blood. This understanding of national preference reveals that behind the FN's attempt to appear moderate and reasonable, lies an obviously racist and racialising agenda. Whilst Le Pen constantly denies that he or his party is racist, their anti-immigration platform and attempts to create a hierarchy of different national and ethnic groups are clearly linked to a differentialist racism. The Front argues that not only are different cultural and ethnic groups inassimilable into French society, but also that these groups present a real danger for the French nation and for French national identity. The racialisation of difference is clear in the Front's arguments that not all French citizens are true citizens. Thus although the Front believe that preference should be given to French nationals, they also hold that those of Maghrebin or sub-Saharan African origin who have acquired French nationality, or children born to parents of foreign origin who are French nationals, do not really deserve the same treatment as real 'native' French nationals. As one of the architects of FN policy, Le Gallou, argued:

> A young North African born in France and having, in theory, lived here continuously between the ages of thirteen and eighteen, automatically acquires French nationality at the age of eighteen, but does not feel any more French, and is not thought of as any more French by his community (Le Gallou, 1985: 20).

---

[3] Le Pen first made this now (in)famous statement when he appeared on the television programme *L'Heure de vérité* on 13 February 1984.

This refusal to accept that second and third generation immigrants, of North African of Sub-Saharan African origin, who have French nationality are actually French is linked to the Front National's rejection of all immigration and refusal to accept any difference between legal and illegal immigration. For the party, any immigrant presence is a threat to the French nation because of the different cultures of immigrant and ethnic minority communities and because of the supposed links between crime, unemployment, insecurity and the presence of immigrants in France. To quote Le Gallou again:

> There is no evidence to show that legal immigration is less disturbing than illegal immigration. Denouncing the criminality of illegal immigrants is more to do with a precautionary language than an objective analysis. The few statistics that exist on crime and the prison population show that foreigners, especially those from the Maghreb, are over-represented. But these statistics do not distinguish between illegal immigrants and legally established residents in provoking the rise in insecurity. Moreover, the large majority of immigrants in France entered illegally before being 'regularised' (Le Gallou, 1985: 20).

The Production of Institutional Racism

The progression and even banalisation of the racist ideas of the Front National could not have taken place in a vacuum, and some commentators point to the racism inherent in France's institutional structures as the context within which the overt racism of the extreme-Right can manifest itself. As Wieviorka argues, the progress and institutionalisation of the Front National in French politics has been made possible because:

> Racism, outside of the vector constituted by the Front National, has for a certain time found a greater and greater place within French institutions, whilst these are meant to ensure the opposite, namely equality and fraternity. We can point to discrimination in access to housing which, although not studied in France, is clearly an important reality; to the mechanisms of segregation which are in action, often on a huge scale, in access to employment; to the education system which tends not only to produce, but also to reproduce inequalities of which children of immigrants are the principal victims. We can also recall that racism at the counter is a distinct reality in numerous public services, a reality which is amplified by what goes on behind the counters in the very functioning of the administration where 'native' French or even just those of 'European' origin are treated very differently from those who look like immigrants or who have a 'foreign' name... We could also point out in passing the French practice of closing off employment in the public services to non-European foreigners, a legal extension to Europeans of the theme dear to the Front National of national preference (Wieviorka, 1998: 8).

This institutional racism can thus be seen as the acceptance and normalisation, not of racist intentions, but of the banality of racist actions. And it can be argued that the French state has made the fight against such institutional racism more difficult by its insistence on Republican values of integration and assimilation and its refusal to recognise cultural difference. Thus employees within different institutions are faced with the reality of cultural and ethnic differences in their everyday work and practice, but there is no accepted or recognised framework for dealing with or contextualising these differences. Further the insistence on the integration of populations of immigrant origin can itself be seen as a form of institutional racism, as individuals are defined by their distance from the norm of Frenchness, the difference between what is French and what is not becomes a vital measure.

Lapeyronnie points also to the growing spatial segregation which accompanies the increase in practices of discrimination. This spatial segregation is a result of long-term processes of discrimination in housing, and other discriminations which have led to a lack of social or geographical mobility. As a result some peripheral urban areas have populations which are largely composed of immigrant or ethnic minority communities, and some of these areas have acquired such bad reputations that it is better to avoid mentioning your address when you go for a job interview or even to try and get into a nightclub (Lapeyronnie, 1998).

The existence of racism and discrimination within public institutions is attested to by the perceptions of immigrants and ethnic minorities about their experiences in French society. Whilst there are few studies which provide detail about discrimination because of the reluctance of French authorities to collect data which reveals individuals national or ethnic origins, one study carried out in 1992 provides interesting information about the ways in which discrimination is experienced by different national and ethnic groups. Table 8.1 below shows the perception of discrimination in different institutional settings of populations of different national origin.

Table 8.1   Perception of discrimination in different institutional settings according to national origin (in per cent)

	Algeria	Morocco	Portugal	Spain	SE Asia	Turkey	Sub-Saharan Africa
Post Office	16 (5)	11 (4)	5 (3)	10 (2)	9 (3)	11 (7)	15 (4)
Bank	10 (7)	7 (5)	3 (2)	7 (3)	8 (3)	9 (7)	16 (7)
Hospital	12 (5)	10 (4)	5 (4)	6 (5)	8 (6)	11 (6)	12 (7)
School	15 (12)	13 (9)	9 (5)	10 (5)	9 (7)	12 (10)	18 (14)
Public Housing	30 (16)	27 (16)	8 (23)	7 (21)	15 (19)	29 (17)	35 (19)
Police	31 (19)	25 (18)	11 (16)	11 (14)	18 (15)	20 (25)	37 (19)
Judicial System	20 (26)	17 (26)	6 (24)	8 (19)	10 (25)	12 (32)	21 (30)

Note: The figures in brackets indicate the number of respondents (in per cent) who did not express an opinion.
Source: MGIS, 1992

The table demonstrates the widespread perception that discrimination does exist within institutional structures and settings, although clearly the perception of discrimination varies according to the national origin of the respondents. This corresponds to the racialised categorisation of immigrants whereby those of European origin are accorded far more respect and are seen as less of a 'threat' than those of non-European origin.[4] This type of categorisation of 'good' and 'bad' immigrants according to national origin, goes back to the type of schemas established at the beginning of the Twentieth Century and in the years following the Second World War, when France was trying to encourage immigrants of nationalities which were seen as culturally and religiously compatible with France.

A second part of the study showed a further differentiation in perceptions of racism according to the age of the respondent, the age at which they had come to France, and whether or not they had French nationality. The results of this part of the study, shown in table 8.2 below, demonstrate a higher level of perception of discrimination amongst young people of immigrant origin. Generally, those under forty years of age have a much stronger perception of having experienced discrimination in institutional settings. As Simon points out, this reflects not only the fact that this generation may have been more exposed to discriminatory behaviour, but also to their different expectations regarding French society and their place within it (Simon, 1998). Those young people who have been brought up in France do not consider themselves as 'immigrants' and find it difficult to accept that French people should regard them in this way and that they should receive any kind of unequal treatment. This explanation is reinforced by the fact that those who arrived in France before the age of sixteen have much higher levels of perceptions of discrimination. Similarly, those people of immigrant origin who have obtained French nationality feel discrimination more keenly than those who still have foreign nationality. Again this can be explained by a difference in expectations and also by a gulf in the reality of the rights afforded to French nationals and the ability or inability to fully realise those rights because of discriminatory practices and behaviour. Thus the acquisition of French nationality can in no way be seen as a barrier against discrimination and racism. These critical perceptions of the institutions of education, police and justice, by those who have undergone a naturalisation process and become French, shows the difficulties with Republican ideals of integration of which naturalisation is the ultimate step. If the institutions at the heart of the French nation continue to treat as unequal those who have expressed a desire to become French through naturalisation, then the whole structure of Republican citizenship comes under question.

---

[4] The definition of European here is of those from inside of the European Union, i.e. Spanish and Portuguese in this survey. The fact that Turkish immigrants perceive themselves as victims of reasonably high levels of discrimination can be linked to the fact that many of them are Muslim and are thus associated with other Muslim populations of African origin.

Table 8.2 Perceptions of Discrimination in Different Institutional Settings According to National Origin, Age, Age of Arrival in France, and Nationality (in per cent)

		Algeria	*Morocco*	*SE Asia*	*Turkey*	*Sub-Saharan Africa*
School	Under 40	22 (7)	18 (4)		16 (8)	
	Over 40	12 (14)	12 (13)		9 (11)	
	Arrival before age 16	26 (4)	26 (3)	13 (3)	23 (5)	22 (5)
	Arrival after age 16	13 (15)	12 (10)	7 (8)	11 (11)	18 (15)
	French nationality	22 (6)	23 (6)	10 (4)	10 (3)	22 (7)
	Foreign nationality	15 (12)	14 (9)	7 (8)	14 (10)	17 (16)
Public Housing	Under 40	34 (15)	32 (16)		33 (16)	
	Over 40	28 (16)	23 (17)		24 (19)	
	Arrival before age 16	37 (13)	37 (10)	16 (21)	38 (13)	20 (26)
	Arrival after age 16	28 (17)	25 (18)	14 (18)	27 (18)	37 (19)
	French nationality	30 (18)	28 (19)	13 (21)	15 (26)	32 (22)
	Foreign nationality	31 (16)	28 (15)	17 (16)	31 (16)	35 (20)
Police	Under 40	39 (18)	32 (17)		27 (23)	
	Over 40	29 (19)	22 (18)		15 (25)	
	Arrival before age 16	46 (15)	42 (11)	21 (19)	36 (18)	43 (16)
	Arrival after age 16	27 (20)	23 (19)	16 (15)	18 (26)	38 (19)
	French nationality	43 (15)	40 (11)	16 (15)	23 (16)	42 (16)
	Foreign nationality	31 (19)	25 (19)	18 (18)	22 (24)	38 (19)
Justice	Under 40	22 (28)	20 (25)		16 (32)	
	Over 40	20 (25)	16 (25)		9 (30)	
	Arrival before age 16	28 (24)	27 (18)	9 (28)	22 (29)	28 (23)
	Arrival after age 16	18 (27)	16 (27)	9 (26)	11 (32)	22 (31)
	French nationality	29 (20)	25 (13)	7 (24)	2 (23)	22 (24)
	Foreign nationality	20 (27)	17 (27)	10 (31)	14 (32)	23 (32)

Note: The figures in brackets indicate the number of respondents (in per cent) who did not express an opinion.
Source: MGIS, 1992

Attitudes to Racism and Discrimination: A 'Lepenisation' of French Ideas?

The progress of seemingly 'racist' attitudes in France has often been attributed to a 'lepenisation' of French opinion. By 'lepenisation' is meant not a full acceptance of the Front National as a party and of Le Pen as a leader, but a general acceptance and legitimising of the Front's policies and ideologies. As Soudais points out, the Front National remains the most detested party in France, but gradually opinion polls have demonstrated a greater and greater adhesion to the ideas put forward by Le Pen (Soudais, 1996).

Evidence about French perceptions of the existence of racism and about the different groups against which racism is targeted is provided by reports published by the Commission Nationale Consultative des Droits de l'Homme (National Consultative Commission on Human Rights) (CNCDH). The results of surveys carried out for these reports, shown in tables 8.3 and 8.4 below, demonstrate that the French believe that racism is still common in France, and that the major targets of racism are Maghrebins, or immigrants from North Africa. In the survey carried out in 2000, for example, 91 per cent of respondents felt that racism was common in France, and 75 per cent believed that the principal targets of this racism were North Africans.

A new response was added to the question about the principal targets of racism in 1997, with the category of 'native' French being included. A relatively substantial percentage of the respondents chose this category, demonstrating the way in which the French have begun to think of themselves as targets of racism. This echoes the discourse of the National Front who have argued that the real targets of racism in France are the 'native' French whose culture is under attack and who are discriminated against in access to jobs, housing etc.

Table 8.3 Perceptions of the level of racism that exists in France (in per cent)

Q: Would you say that at this moment racism in France is very common, rather common, rather rare or very rare?

	1990	1991	1992	1993	1994	1995	1996	1997	1998	1999	2000
Very common	38	38	36	35	34	39	41	35	32	30	29
Rather common	56	52	53	55	55	54	53	56	60	62	62
Rather rare	5	7	9	7	8	6	4	6	6	6	7
Very rare	-	2	1	1	1	-	1	1	1	1	1
Total	100	100	100	100	100	100	100	100	100	100	100

Source: CNCDH, 2001

Table 8.4 Perceptions of principal targets of racism and xenophobia in France (in per cent)

Q: In your opinion, who are the principal targets of racism, xenophobia and discrimination in France?

	1990	1991	1992	1993	1994	1995	1996	1997	1998	1999	2000
Maghrebis	85	83	83	79	77	77	83	75	76	77	75
Beurs	59	57	65	61	67	67	71	63	65	57	55
Black Africans	35	37	38	37	35	33	43	42	41	41	44
Travelling People	31	24	29	33	30	28	36	37	38	28	41
Jews	24	20	23	19	16	16	16	19	20	14	19
Native French	-	-	-	-	-	-	-	14	13	7	10
Antilleans	7	7	6	8	6	7	8	7	8	7	10
Mediterranean People	6	4	5	5	4	4	4	5	5	5	8
Eastern Europeans	-	-	-	-	-	-	7	12	12	6	7
Asians	7	7	7	6	8	5	6	5	7	6	6
Others	5	4	6	7	5	8	4	2	1	1	1

Source: CNDH, 2001

Another poll carried out in 2000 showed similarly high levels of racism in French public opinion. 69 per cent of respondents classified themselves as very, quite or a bit racist, whilst only 29 per cent said that they were not at all racist. This number of people admitting to some degree of racist sentiments would seem to demonstrate the way in which racism has become normalised and accepted in French society. The same poll found that these racist views were closely linked to negative views on immigration: 61 per cent of respondents felt that there were too many foreigners in France, and 63 per cent that there were too many Arabs. Moreover, the feelings of resentment against foreigners and insecurity were clear in that 72 per cent said they believed that foreigners received favourable treatment in access to social services and benefits (*Libération*, 16 March 2000).

The organisation which carried out the poll, Louis Harris, grouped the respondents into four types according to their responses, those who felt besieged by foreigners, those who were worried about the number of foreigners in France, those who felt that foreigners were not well enough integrated into French society, and those who showed clear antiracist beliefs. The four categories and the percentage of respondents falling into each category are shown below in table 8.5.

Table 8.5 Typology of Respondents According to Views on Racism and
**   Immigration**

Besieged	19 %
Worried	32 %
Integrationists	28 %
Antiracists	21 %

Sociological data collected alongside the poll showed very clear divisions of age, educational level and rural or urban location between the different categories. Whilst anti-racists were likely to be young, highly educated and live in large urban centres, those who fell into the 'besieged' category were on the contrary likely to be elderly, have a low level of educational achievement, and live in rural areas. This categorisation also demonstrates that racism is not unitary in its forms. The reasons for which people feel racist and anti-immigrant sentiment vary from those who feel frightened and under siege, who may feel that they have lost their place in society, to those who are scared of the insecurity they feel that immigrants cause, or those who feel that communities of immigrant origin do not make enough effort to integrate into French society.

What all of these polls seem to demonstrate is that there is a significant anti-immigrant sentiment and fear of foreigners in France, and that many French people admit to racist sentiments. These results indicate that racism still poses a significant threat to the security of immigrants and ethnic minorities within France.

Legislation Against Discrimination: A Slow Reaction

Whilst successive French governments have been keen to introduce policies and legislation to combat the insecurities supposedly provoked by uncontrolled immigration, there has been less enthusiasm, until very recently, for legislation to combat the insecurities created for immigrant and ethnic minority communities by the existence of racism and discrimination. Despite a campaign for some form of anti-discrimination legislation from the end of the Second World War, the first piece of legislation on the subject was not passed until 1972. Further, this legislation was not particularly effective and it was not until the end of the 1990s that real substance was given to the legal structures which aimed to combat racism and discrimination.

The constitution of the French Fifth Republic affirms inalienable rights for all humans irrespective of race, but until 1972 there was no legal bar to discrimination on the grounds of race. The lack of any such legislation was a point of contention for anti-racist movements and associations who pointed to the insecurity this may cause for many immigrant and ethnic minority residents. In a famous case in 1963, black clients were refused service in a bar near the Gare du Nord in Paris, but could not bring a case against the owner of the bar or the waiter on grounds of discrimination. Instead a case was brought on the basis of an old law

which was designed to prevent goods being sold on the black market and which made it illegal to 'refuse to satisfy the demands of purchasers or of those wishing to pay for a service if these demands do not present any abnormal features' (cited in Bleich, 2003). The outcome of the case was a fine for the owner, manager and waiter of the bar, but anti-racist associations pointed to the fact that this case would have been much clearer if a specific law existed to condemn racial discrimination.

Although there was support for anti-discrimination or anti-racist legislation from several of the major political parties, with the Communist Party and others submitting parliamentary bills on the issue, the government maintained throughout the 1960s and early 1970s that France did not need any laws against racism, because racism was not that widespread in France for legislation on the subject to be necessary. This opinion prevailed until the government's about turn of 1972 when legislation was quickly introduced and passed. The reasons for this change of opinion can be traced back not to any single event, but more to a constant pressure from anti-racist organisations, and to the more liberal stance of the government following the events of May 1968. Whilst the events of 1968 'opened up a new sense of the possible in politics' (Lloyd, 1998b: 168), pressure for a change grew as anti-racist organisations mobilised around the focus of the UN Year against Racism and Discrimination in 1970. Support for a law against racism and discrimination was also provided by the evidence of a growth in racist attacks, and particularly a group of racially motivated murders in 1971 and 1972 which involved both older immigrant workers, and children of the 'second-generation'. These killings underlined the need for urgent action to tackle racism (Lloyd, 1998b). The law against discrimination and racism was finally passed by the Assembly National and the Senate in July 1972 with little or not opposition (Freeman, 1979), leading some to comment that in fact the lack of opposition indicated that it was a law which did not mean very much anyway (Bleich, 2003).

The anti-discrimination law passed in 1972 made any discrimination on the basis of race, ethnic belonging, national origin, or religion, illegal. However, the law was criticised by being of more symbolic than real value. For a prosecution to take place under the law, the victims of any discrimination on the basis of the four categories outlined above, had to provide substantial proof that they had been discriminated against. In fact, because of the difficulties of providing such proof, very few convictions were ever made under the law. The law permitted anti-racist organisations to bring cases on behalf of victims, and these organisations did bring forward a large number of cases. However, as there was no publicly funded organisation that was set up to combat racism and discrimination, the organisations that existed lacked funds and resources to initiate major campaigns on the issue. Thus although the 1972 law was theoretically strong, in practice it was limited in its effects by the small number of cases actually brought to court, and by the lack of a public body which could have led the fight against discrimination at a national level (Bleich, 2003).

The situation remained more or less the same, with no really effective legislation or co-ordination against racism and discrimination, until the end of the 1990s. The reasons for the change at this time can be traced to several sources, one of which is the process of putting in place a European policy on discrimination.

The French government adopted the EU Directives of June 2000, based on the Treaty of Amsterdam, which deal with direct and indirect discrimination in the workplace and in provision of public services. The acceptance of this European legislation, which originated from concepts of ethnic relations that would seem to be more founded in the 'race relations' traditions of other European countries such as the UK or the Netherlands, may be seen as signalling a shift in French policy and an acknowledgement that more direct political intervention was needed to combat racism and discrimination.

At the same time as external pressure from the EU forced a re-think on anti-discrimination policies, pressure was also building for a change from within France, where a growing number of actors began to mobilise on the issue. The Haut Conseil à l'Intégration (HCI) published a report in 1998 which dealt directly with the problem of discrimination and made a number of recommendations for changes in the way that the problem was tackled institutionally. In response to this, Martine Aubry, the Minister for Employment and Solidarity in the Socialist government of the time, commissioned a special report to take a more in-depth look at the issues. The report Belorgey (named after the member of the Conseil d'Etat by who it was written) which was published in March 1999, recommended the establishment of a new administrative body which could deal specifically with the problem of discrimination. Although such a body was not established directly, it became clear that the government saw the fight against racism as a priority. A group for studying the causes of discrimination, the *Groupe d'Etudes sur les Discriminations* (GED), was established by the government at the end of 1998, and in 2000 this became the group for studying and fighting against discrimination, *Groupe d'Etudes et de Lutte Contre les Discriminations* (GELD). The aim of this group was to study the causes of discrimination and to diffuse knowledge and good practice on how best it should be tackled. In addition, departmental commissions on access to citizenship, *Commissions départementales d'accès à la citoyenneté* (CODAC), were set up to coordinate debates and action within each department, and a telephone number was established through which citizens could report complaints about discrimination. In the first two years of its existence, between 2000 and 2002, this telephone service received almost 40, 000 calls, and of these more than 10, 000 cases were reported to the CODAC for further action to be taken.

The establishment of such bodies to try and tackle discrimination would not be effective, however, without an accompanying change in the law. In 2001, the law of 1972 on discrimination was revised to make it easier to bring claims for discrimination. Instead of authorising only criminal procedures to deal with discrimination, the new law allowed complaints of discrimination to be brought before civil tribunals. Moreover, the burden of proof was reversed, so that rather than the complainant having to prove discrimination, it is now the person accused who has to prove that they did not discriminate on the basis of race, ethnic or national origins or religion. The new law also gave greater powers to work inspectors and committees to investigate charges of discrimination.

These changes in the law, together with a new focus on trying to tackle racism and discrimination, particularly in the workplace, constitute a major move forward for the French state, which until recently had few institutional structures in place to deal with these problems. However, whilst the change of emphasis, and the recognition that there is a need for policies, laws and institutions to combat discrimination is clearly welcome, there is a consensus amongst many specialists that this reform has not gone far enough. Some have accused the French government of 'half-measures' in this area, arguing that whilst the new law and new institutional structures are a step forward, they do not go nearly far enough towards creating an anti-discrimination policy that will have tangible and far-reaching results (Hargreaves, 2000). One of the barriers to a really effective anti-discrimination policy is the lack of information in this area. This results from the refusal to collect data based on race or ethnic identity, because this is contrary to the Republican ideal of universalism. This means that in employment terms, for example, the ethnic identity of candidates is not noted, and it is therefore not possible to compare the racial/ethnic profile of those who are offered jobs with those who are not successful in gaining employment. The lack of data in this area prevents the state from having any accurate idea about the scale of discrimination which exists, and this makes the problem of tackling discrimination more difficult. It is evident that discrimination exists but it is impossible to quantify it (Simon, 1998).

In addition, the continuing lack of one national body for co-ordinating anti-discrimination efforts is still an obstacle to an effective policy. There are a proliferation of organisations that have in their remit to tackle racism and discrimination, both NGOs and bodies set up by the government (such as GELD or the CODAC). However, there is no clear direction as to which organisation will be responsible for which area, nor of who might coordinate the actions of the various organisations involved. In some instances the different organisations also fight against each other, both for resources, and on issues of principle (Bleich, 2003).

There are now legal and institutional structures to tackle racism and discrimination in France, but how far these will go in reducing the insecurities of foreigners and those of immigrant origin due to racism remains to be seen. What seems clear is that the effectiveness of any of these policies, laws or institutions will be compromised if French politicians continue to make reference to concepts such as a 'threshold of tolerance' for immigrants, and to talk about immigration as a threat to French security. These type of pronouncements do nothing to reduce the racist and xenophobic atmosphere within which discrimination thrives.

Anti-Racist Mobilisation

France has a long-tradition of organised anti-racist groups. Foremost amongst these have been the Ligue des Droits de l'Homme (Human Rights League) formed in 1989, the Ligue Contre l'Antisémitisme et le Racisme (League Against Antisemitism and Racism) formed in 1928, and the Mouvement Contre le Racisme et pour l'Amitié des Peuples (Movement Against Racism and for Friendship between Peoples) formed in 1949.[5] These organisations associate themselves with the tradition of the enlightenment and the revolution and the ideals of equality and fraternity espoused by these. They have been effective in putting pressure on governments to adopt anti-racist and anti-discrimination legislation as discussed above, and continue to campaign on issue of racism and discrimination. In recent years these long-standing anti-racist organisations have been joined by newer associations often formed by young 'second-generation' immigrants protesting at their treatment by French society. However, despite the long history of anti-racist organisations in France and the creation of new youth organisations in recent years, for many there has still been a 'failure' of French anti-racist mobilisation (Lloyd, 1998). This section will discuss the new mobilisations around the issue of anti-racism from the 1980s onwards, before asking whether French anti-racist mobilisations can really be described as 'failing' and if so, why?

A new form of mobilisation against racism could be seen from the 1980s onwards, a mobilisation it has been argued is based on the alienation of young people of immigrant origin from a French society which seems to offer them little opportunity and within which they face racism and discrimination both from institutions and individuals. Faced with the apparent failure of the French State to take any effective action to tackle racism, and with the rise of the Front National with its anti-immigrant and xenophobic discourse, young people felt that they had to show their opposition to racism through their own mobilisation. The fact that the mainstream political parties showed little inclination to resist the influence of the Front National as they became a force in French politics during the 1980s confirmed to many that these politicians were not willing to sacrifice electoral popularity to defend the rights of immigrants or ethnic minorities against racism. As de Rudder argues, the failure of the Socialist Party to honour their election promise to give immigrants the right to vote in local elections, together with the mainstream parties willingness to enter into the 'numbers game' over immigration and to talk about 'thresholds of tolerance' and immigration quotas, were all taken as evidence that these political parties could not be relied upon to combat racism (de Rudder, 1980; Lloyd, 1998b). Young people of immigrant or ethnic minority origin felt this failure of the political parties profoundly, particularly as it was combined with their day-to-day experiences of racism and discrimination in education, housing, employment and faced with the police and justice systems. Anti-racist mobilisation by these young people was thus derived, 'not from a sense of ethnic community but from a burning sense of injustice ignited by a shared experience of racism and exclusion and the internalisation of the dominant French value system based on equality of all citizens before the law' (Fysh and Wolfreys, 1998: 145). This sense of injustice and of the failure of institutions and mainstream political parties to deal with injustices, discrimination and racism, meant that the activists involved in these mobilisations insisted on their autonomy from the established political system, as well as from already established immigrant associations. As Jazouli remarks in his study of these young people's mobilisation:

---

[5] For a more detailed account of the operation and discourses of these anti-racist movements see C. Lloyd (1998), *Discourses of Antiracism in France*, Aldershot: Ashgate.

The anger which encourages them to act and react collectively, together with the fact that their desires are continually thwarted by the suffering that they encounter, makes the issue of autonomy even more fundamental to them ... Young activists of North African origin insist on respect for their autonomy of ideas, decisions, and organisation, which they view as a precondition to any partnership. They are suspicious of any attempt to manage of institutionalise their action which in part explains their ambiguous relationship with the political system (Jazouli, 1986: 42).

Mobilisation against racism at the start of the 1980s was triggered by protest against racist violence. In 1980 an organisation called *Rock against police* (RAP) was founded, and organised free concerts in the suburbs of Paris, Lyon and Marseille. The idea of free rock concerts was borrowed from the UK example of Rock against Racism, which had taken place a couple of years previously. But the more combative title signalled the frustration of the young people organising the events, not just with racist violence, but with the attitudes of the French police, who often failed to investigate incidents of racism and who routinely harassed immigrant and ethnic minorities for minor offences. One of the young people interviewed by Jazouli, expressed his views about the police thus:

> The policeman arrests you and then sometimes he insults you, sometimes he smashes your head in, and then after that you end up in front of a judge who finishes the job by sending you for a rest behind bars. I think that all of them are working hand-in-hand to repress us more and more, to smother us (Jazouli, 1986: 55).

The continuing violence and perceived police indifference or repression led to a string of local mobilisations, and the emergence of the *Beurs* as a new force in the political arena. The word *beur* was used to refer to young French people of North African origin, those whose parents had immigrated to France from Algeria, Morocco or Tunisia. The term, which came from a slang version of the French word *Arabe* (Arab), was adopted by these young people as a way of expressing their identity. As Bouamama explains, the word indicates something different from the identity of their parents, the first generation of immigrants, whilst at the same time affirming their Arab origins: 'it expresses the emergence of a new aspect of French identity: the existence of *French* Arabs. Up until then, France had known only Arabs *in France*' (Bouamama, 1994: 69). A key point of this *Beur* identity was that these young people had French nationality and should therefore have enjoyed the same rights as other young French people, however, the continuing discrimination that they experienced because of their ethnic and religious origins, meant that they could not exercise their rights in the same way as others. The need to express a French Arab identity stems in part from these feelings of exclusion and alienation from French society.

The success of the Front National in the local elections of 1983 added fuel to the mobilisations of the Beurs, and in October of that year a 'March for Equality and Racism' was organised. Ten young Maghrebis marched from Marseille to Paris, being supported along the way by thousands of demonstrators and sympathisers. When the march arrived in Paris in December it was met by a demonstration of about 100,000 people in solidarity with the marchers, and they were received by President Mitterrand. Mitterrand promised, in response to the demands of the marchers, to reform the 1972 anti-discrimination law and to introduce a new law punishing racist violence more severely. However, as noted in the discussion of anti-discrimination policy above, no new legislation on discrimination and racism was introduced until 2001. The march of 1983 was followed by a similar initiative in 1984 called *Convergences*. This involved five marches of young people of different ethnic origins converging on Paris from five French cities. The idea behind this was to stress the multi-ethnic and multicultural nature of the protest, and to challenge the assimilationist tendencies of French Republicanism which refuses to recognise different ethnic communities as legitimate political actors.

These marches fitted a social movement paradigm of 'anti-authority, anti-institutional grass-roots activity, articulating broad, universalist demands and protesting against the social exclusion of young people from immigrant families in the call for equality' (Lloyd, 2002: 68). This laid the foundation for the emergence of two anti-racist organisations France-Plus and SOS-Racisme. These two organisations had differing agendas and became open rivals, but both were criticised for moving away from the grass-roots radicalism of the previous youth mobilisations and being co-opted by mainstream political parties and movements for their own ends. France-Plus is an organisation which has focused on mobilising young Maghrebis as a force in electoral politics to exercise fully their citizenship rights. In 1989, for example, it commissioned opinion polls to convince local politicians that they ought to offer Maghrebis places on their lists for the forthcoming local elections. This exercise proved relatively successful, with about one thousand Maghrebi candidates appearing on electoral lists and several hundred winning seats on town councils (Hargreaves, 1995). However, the strategy and operation of France-Plus has been criticised for favouring upwardly-mobile middle-class Maghrebis and ignoring the grass-roots who continue to suffer from exclusion and alienation. Further, the organisation was criticised as a mere tool of one faction of the Socialist Party to be used in a battle with another faction who were supposed to support its rival organisation SOS-Racisme (Bouamama, 1994). This other anti-racist group, SOS-Racisme, was founded at the same time as France-Plus. The president of the group, Harlem Désir, writes about the way that the organisation came into existence after a group of friends became outraged at a racist incident suffered by a black friend, and realised that they had all been the victims of racism and should do something about it. As Désir explains in his account of the movement:

> In fact we felt targeted, directly threatened. Insidiously, without us raising our defences, racist 'affairs' had become more and more common ... Enough is enough. The time for scorn was over. We had to respond ... We had to do something to end the indifference, to make sure that racism was opposed by more than a whingeing resignation (Désir, 1985:25).

Other accounts reject this story of spontaneity amongst friends and explain the movement as a manoeuvre of some members of the Socialist Party (Weil, 1995). As Fysh and Wolfreys argue:

> Although in 1995 visitors so the SOS national office were still being regaled with the myth of the 'apolitical' founding pals, it had long since been known that the association owed its meteoric rise to help from the Socialist establishment, astutely aware of their need to widen their bases of support ahead of Mitterrand's campaign for re-election (Fysh and Wolfreys, 1998: 164).

SOS-Racisme certainly had a huge success in terms of highly visible organisation and mobilisation, organising massive free concerts, recruiting supporters amongst well-known French celebrities and politicians, and appearing widely in the media. Their slogan 'Touche pas à mon pôte' (Don't touch my mate) was ubiquitous in France during the second half of the 1980s. However, as with France-Plus, the organisation was accused of betraying its grass-roots origins and supporters. Jazouli points to the gulf between the organisations like SOS-Racisme and France-Plus which have been incorporated into policy-making structures, and the broader grass-roots social movements which protested about racism and discrimination (Jazouli, 1992). This gulf still seems to exist, and the problems about which the young *Beurs* mobilised in the early 1980s are still very much present. Ethnic minorities still suffer from higher unemployment levels, lower educational attainment, poor housing, and racist violence has not disappeared. One issue which might be seen as symbolising this dichotomy between anti-racist organisations and the ethnic minority communities that they supposedly represent, is the *affaire des foulards*, discussed in the previous chapter. When the *affaire* first emerged in 1989, SOS-Racisme indicated its support for the girls excluded from school and for their right to wear a headscarf. By 1994, however, the organisation had changed its opinion and argued that all forms of religious dress should be banned from schools. They justified this position by pointing to the supposed growth of Islamic fundamentalism in France (*Le Monde*, 27 October 1994), but this position is clearly an indicator of their adherence to the Left's Republican tradition and values, and can be seen as distancing from the attitudes and problems of young Muslims who challenge these Republican values of assimilation.

Conclusion: A Failure of Anti-Racism?

The discussions of varying manifestations of racism in this chapter have shown that this is not a phenomenon which can be reduced to support or voting for the Front National. Racist sentiments and fear of foreigners and immigrants are widespread in public opinion, and racist attitudes and practices have been normalised within institutional settings. Within this context various explanations have been given for the 'failure' of anti-racism in France, and varying strategies have been suggested to counter this racism and discrimination within French society.

Taguieff, for example, has argued that anti-racism in France has been unsuccessful because anti-racists have failed to define racism correctly (Taguieff, 1993). Anti-racists, he maintains, need to respond to 'the displacement of biological inequality in favour of the absolutisation of cultural difference' (quoted in Lloyd, 1998: 10). Certainly it is important for anti-racists to understand the ways in which the extreme-Right have taken up the theme of cultural difference and used it to suggest the inassimilable nature of immigrant and ethnic minority populations in France. But the difficulty lies in how to respond to this privileging of cultural difference. One answer has been to deny difference and to reinforce the Republican values of universalism and assimilation. This can be seen to have happened in France with the gradual disappearance of the lobby for the *droit à la différence* and the resurgence of neo-republican and neo-universalist discourse (Brubaker, 2001). Evidence of this change in perspective can be seen in the across the board support for new legislation banning the Islamic headscarf (along with all other visible signs of religious belonging) in French public schools (see chapter 7). This investment in the values of Republican universalism has been supported as a way of combating differentialist racism, and many in France have argued for the superiority of this Republican universalist system over the 'Anglo-Saxon' models of multiculturalism. However, this French Republican version of equality also has its limitations, and the emphasis on the need to assimilate or integrate immigrants in order to negate the difference which give rise to racism, ignores the fact that for many immigrants and ethnic minorities these differences are a valuable part of their identities and culture. The emphasis on integration means that many institutions have no recognised way of dealing with difference and thus an institutional racism becomes entrenched (Bataille, 1997; Wieviorka, 1998). Alongside this focus on integration, the continuing construction of the 'problem' of immigration and the threat that it poses to the French nation acts to further institutionalise racist discourses and practices. Thus to really combat racism and discrimination the French state must move beyond its insistence on integration and assimilation. To do so would bring into question some of the foundations of French Republicanism, but as some would argue, without a thorough examination of the interconnections of racism and the nation state, it is impossible to understand racism properly. Indeed some would contend that the connections between racism and discrimination on the one hand and nationalism on the other hand have not been properly understood by anti-racists (Balibar, 1992; Galissot, 1985).

The arguments put forward throughout this book point to a failure of French Republicanism to deal adequately with issues of immigration, asylum, racism and discrimination. For some it is because these Republican values have not been pushed hard enough in the face of new-Right emphasis on difference. It would seem, however, that this points to a need to re-evaluate the values of French Republicanism that lie at the heart of the French nation state. Perhaps, as Balibar argues, anti-racism will only become genuinely political when it moves beyond the confines of the nation state and becomes a truly transnational movement, organising its efforts at the level of Europe (Balibar, 1992).

Bibliography

Abdallah, M. (2001), 'La longue marche du mouvement associatif pour transcender les frontières politiques de la citoyenneté', *Hommes et Migrations*, 1229, pp. 10-20.

Ahmed, L. (1992), *Women and Gender in Islam*. New Haven: Yale University Press.

Alaux, J-P. (2001a), 'A la rue sous prétexte de polygamie', *Plein Droit*, 51, pp. 5-12.

Alaux, J-P. (2001b), 'Loi Chevènement: Beaucoup de bruit pour rien', *Plein Droit*, 47-48, pp. 2-25.

Altschull, E. (1995), *Le voile contre l'école*. Paris: Seuil.

Anderson, B. (2000), *Doing the Dirty Work? The Global Politics of Domestic Labour*. London: Zed Books.

Balibar, E. and Wallerstein, I. (1988), *Race, nation, classe. Les identités ambiguës*. Paris: La Découverte.

Balibar, E. (1992), *Les frontières de la démocratie*. Paris: La Découverte.

Balibar, E. (1996), 'De la preference nationale à l'invention de la politique: comment lutter contre le néofascisme', in J. Viard (ed), *Aux sources du populisme nationaliste*. Paris: L'Aube.

Balibar, E. (1999), 'Le droit de cité ou l'apartheid?', in E. Balibar, M. Chemillier-Gendreau, J. Costa-Lascoux and E. Terray (eds), *Sans-papiers: l'archaïsme fatal*. Paris: La Découverte.

Banting, K. G. (2000), 'Looking in three directions. Migration and the European welfare state in comparative perspective', in M. Bommes and A. Geddes (eds), *Immigration and Welfare: Challenging the Borders of the Welfare State*. London: Routledge.

Banton, M. (2001), 'National integration in France and Britain', *Journal of Ethnic and Migration Studies*, 27, 1, pp. 151-168.

Barison, N. and Catarino, C. (1997), 'Les femmes immigrées en France et en Europe', *Migrations Société*, 9, 52, pp. 17-19.

Barker, M. (1981), *The New Racism*. London: Junction Books.

Barou, J. and Le, H. K. (1993), *L'immigration entre loi et vie quotidienne*. Paris: L'Harmattan.

Bataille, P. (1997), *Le Racisme au travail*. Paris: La Découverte.

Bataille, P. (1999), 'Racisme institutionnel, racisme culturel et discriminations', in P. Dewitte (ed), *Immigration et intégration: l'état des savoirs*. Paris: La Découverte.

Benani, S. (1995a), 'Les Nanas Beurs', in *Immigrant women and integration*. Brussels: Council of Europe Publications.

Benani, S. (1995b), 'Le voile et la citoyenneté', in M. Riot-Sarcey (ed), *Démocratie et représentation*. Paris: Kimé.

Bencheikh, S. (1998), *Marianne et le Prophète. L'Islam dans la France laïque*. Paris: Grasset.

Bentaieb, M. (1991), 'Les femmes étrangères en France', *Hommes et migrations*, 1141, pp. 4-12.

Bentichou, N. (ed) (1997), *Les femmes de l'immigration au quotidien*, Paris: L'Harmattan.

Bertaux, S. (2000), '"Processus" et "population" dans l'analyse démographiques de l'immigration en France (1932-1996)', in H. Le Bras (ed) *L'invention des populations*. Paris: Odile Jacob.

Beski, C. (1997a), 'Les difficultés spécifiques aux jeunes filles issues de l'immigration Maghrébine', in N. Bentichou (ed), *Les femmes de l'immigration au quotidien,* Paris: L'Harmattan.

Beski, C. (1997b), 'Les femmes immigrées maghrébines: Objet ou sujet?', *Migrations Société,* 9, 52, pp.37-46.

Bigo, D. (1991), 'Menace du Sud: images et réalités', *Cultures et Conflits,* 2, pp. 7-29.

Bigo, D. (1998), 'Sécurité et immigration: vers une gouvernementalité par l'inquiétude?', *Cultures et Conflits,* 30, 13-39.

Bissuel, B. (2002), 'Divorcer ou vivre sans-papiers', *Le Monde,* 10 February 2002.

Bleich, E. (2003), 'Histoire des politiques françaises antidiscrimination: du déni à la lutte', *Hommes et Migrations,* 1245, pp. 6-18.

Bloch, A. and Schuster, L. (2002), 'Asylum and welfare: contemporary debates', *Critical Social Policy,* 22, 3, pp. 393-414.

Bloul, R. (1996), 'Victims or Offenders? "Other" Women in French Sexual Politics', *European Journal of Women's Studies,* 3, 3, pp. 251-268.

Boltanski, L. and Chiappello, E. (1999), *Le nouvel esprit du capitalisme.* Paris: Gallimard.

Bommes, M. and Geddes, A. (eds) (2000), *Immigration and Welfare: Challenging the Borders of the Welfare State.* London: Routledge.

Bonnafous, S. (1991), *L'immigration prise aux mots.* Paris: Kimé.

Bonnafous, S. (1992), 'Mots et paroles de l'immigration', *Revue française des affaires socials,* 39, 3: 5-15.

Borrel, C. (1999), *Immigration, Emploi et Chômage: Un état des lieux empirique et théorique.* Paris: CERC.

Bouamama, S. (1994), *Dix ans de Marche des Beurs: Chronique d'un movement avorté.* Paris: Desclée de Brouwer.

Bouamama, S. (1998), *Trajectoires prostitutionnelles et processus migratoires.* Report for the Mouvement du Nid. Paris.

Bouamama, S. (2001), 'Droit de vote pour tous. Les contours d'un débat', *Hommes et Migrations,* 1229, pp. 21-33.

Bouamama, S., Cordeiro, A. and Roux, M. (1992), *La citoyenneté dans tous ses états.* Paris: L'Harmattan.

Bouaoumeur, L. (2000), 'Témoignage d'une demandeuse d'asile', *Femmes étrangères et immigrées en France.* Paris: Comité de suivi des lois sur l'immigration.

Boulahbel-Villac, Y. (1992), 'Les femmes algériennes en France', *Revue française des affaires sociales,* 46, 2, pp. 105-123.

Bouteillet-Paquet, D. (2001), *L'Europe et le droit d'asile.* Paris: L'Harmattan.

Brachet, O. (2002), 'La condition du réfugié dans la tourmente de la politique d'asile', *Hommes et Migrations,* 1238, pp. 45-58.

Brah, A. (1993), 'Difference, Diversity, Differentiation: Processes of Racialisation and Gender', in J. Wrench and J. Solomos (eds), *Racism and Migration in Western Europe.* Oxford: Berg.

Brochmann, G. (1999), 'Controlling Immigration in Europe', in G. Brochmann and T. Hammar (eds) *Mechanisms of Immigration* Control. Oxford: Berg.

Brochmann, G. and Hammar, T. (eds) (1999), *Mechanisms of Immigration Control.* Oxford: Berg.

Brubaker, R. (1992), *Citizenship and Nationhood in France and Germany.* Cambridge, MA: Harvard University Press.

Brubaker, R. (2001), 'The return of assimilation? Changing perspectives on immigration and its sequels in France, Germany and the United States', *Ethnic and Racial Studies,* 24, 4, pp. 531-548.

Cabiria (2002), *Journal de repression. Violences faites aux prostituées à Lyon.* Lyon: Cabiria.

Carde, E., Fassin, D., Ferré, N. and Musso-Dimitrijevic, S. (2002), 'Un traitement inégal. Les discriminations dans l'accès aux soins', *Migrations Etudes*, 106, pp. 1-10.

Carrère, V. (2002), 'Sangatte: un toit pour des fantômes', *Hommes et Migrations*, 1238, pp. 13-22.

Castles, S. and Davidson, A. (2000), *Citizenship and Migration.* Basingstoke: Macmillan.

Castles, S. and Miller, M. (1998), *The Age of Migration.* Basingstoke: Palgrave.

Chadwick, K. (1997), 'Education in secular France: (re)defining laïcité', *Modern and Contemporary France*, 5, 1, pp. 47-60.

Chaib, S. (2001a), *Facteurs d'insertion et d'exclusion des femmes immigrantes dans le marché du travail en France.* Paris: CFDT.

Chaib, S. (2001b), 'Femmes d'ailleurs, vies d'ici', *CFDT Magazine*, 271, pp. 15-40.

Chemillier-Gendreau, M. (1998), *L'injustifiable: Les politiques françaises de l'immigration.* Paris: Bayard.

Cissé, M. (1996), 'Sans-papiers: les premiers enseignements', *Politique la revue*, 2, pp. 9-14.

Cissé, M. (1999), *Parole de sans-papiers!* Paris: La Dispute.

Cissé, M. (2000), 'The sans-papières', in J. Freedman and C. Tarr (eds) *Women, Immigration and Identities in France.* Oxford: Berg.

Collinson, S. (1993), *Europe and International Migration.* London: Pinter.

Cordeiro, A. (1984), *L'immigration.* Paris: La Découverte.

Cordeiro, A. (2001), 'Pour une citoyenneté attachée à la personne', *Hommes et Migrations*, 1229, pp. 34-40.

Costa-Lascoux, J. (1995), 'Immigrant women: out of the shadows and on to the stage', in *Immigrant women and integration*, Council of Europe Publications.

Crawley, H. (2000), 'Gender, persecution and the concept of politics in the asylum process', *Forced Migration Review*, 9, pp. 17-21.

Crawley, H. (2001), *Refugees and Gender: Law and Process.* Bristol: Jordan.

Créach, X. (2002), 'Les évolutions dans l'interprétation du terme réfugié', *Hommes et Migrations*, 1238, pp. 65-75.

Dale, G. and Cole, M. (eds) (1999), *The European Union and Migrant Labour.* Oxford: Berg.

Dayan-Herzbrun, S. (2000), 'Le voile islamique et ses enjeux', in J. Freedman and C. Tarr (eds), *Women and Ethnicities in Contemporary France*, Oxford: Berg.

De Courson, C. et Léonard, G. (1996), *Les fraudes et les pratiques abusives.* Rapport au Premier Ministre. Paris: La Documentation Française.

De Rudder, V. (1980), 'La tolerance s'arrête au seuil', *Pluriel*, 21, pp. 3-13.

De Witte, P. (ed) (1999), *Immigration et intégration: l'état des savoirs.* Paris: La Découverte.

Désir, H. (1985), *Touche pas à mon pote.* Paris: Grasset.

Diop, A. (1997), *Dans la peau d'un sans-papiers.* Paris: Seuil.

Eatwell, R. (1998), 'The Dynamics of Right-Wing Electoral Breakthrough', *Patterns of Prejudice*, 32, 3, pp. 26-43.

El Hamel, C. (2002), 'Muslim Diasporas in Western Europe: The Islamic Headscarf (*Hijab*), the Media and Muslims' Integration in France', *Citizenship Studies*, 6, 3, pp. 293-308.

El Yazami, D. (1993), 'Associations de l'immigration et pouvoirs publics: éléments pour un bilan', *Migrations société*, 28-29, pp. 21-30.

Esposito, J. (ed) (1999), *The Oxford History of Islam.* Oxford: Oxford University Press.

Etienne, B. (1989), *La France et l'Islam.* Paris: Hachette.

Fassin, D. (1996), *L'Espace politique de la santé*. Paris: Presses universitaires de France.

Fassin, D. (1997), 'La santé en souffrance', in D. Fassin, A. Morice and C. Quiminal (eds), *Les lois de l'inhospitalité: les politiques de l'immigration à l'épreuve des sans-papiers*. Paris: La Découverte.

Fassin, D. and Morice. A. (2001), 'Les épreuves de l'irregularité: les sans-papiers entre déni d'existence et reconquête d'un statut', in D. Schnapper (ed), *Exclusions au coeur de la Cité*. Paris: Economica.

Fassin, D., Morice, A. and Quiminal, C. (eds) (1997), *Les lois de l'inhospitalité: les politiques de l'immigration à l'épreuve des sans-papiers*. Paris: La Découverte.

Favell, A. (1998), *Philosophies of Integration: Immigration and the Idea of Citizenship in France and Britain*. Basingstoke: Macmillan.

Ferré, N. (1997), 'La production de l'irregularité', in D. Fassin, A. Morice and C. Quiminal (eds) *Les lois de l'inhospitalité: les politiques de l'immigration à l'épreuve des sans-papiers*. Paris: La Découverte.

Fraisse, G. (1995), *Muse de la raison: Démocratie et exclusion des femmes en France*. Paris: Gallimard.

Freedman, J. (2000), 'Immigrant and ethnic minority women', in A. Tidd and A. Gregory (eds) *Women in Contemporary France*. Oxford: Berg.

Freedman, J. (2001), 'The affaire des foulards: defining a feminist anti-racist strategy in French schools', in K. Blee and F. Twine (eds) *Feminism and Anti-Racism: International Struggles for Justice*. New York: New York University Press.

Freedman, J. (ed) (2003), *Gender and Insecurity: Migrant Women in Europe*. Aldershot: Ashgate.

Freedman, J. and Tarr, C. (eds) (2000), *Women, immigration and identities in France*. Oxford: Berg.

Freeman, G. (1979), *Immigrant Labour and Racial Conflict in Industrial Societies*. Princeton: Princeton University Press.

Freeman, G. (1986), 'Migration and the Political Economy of the Welfare State', *Annals of the American Academy of Political and Social Science*, 485, pp. 51-63.

Freeman, G. (1995), Modes of immigration politics in liberal democratic states, *International Migration Review*, 29, 4, pp. 881-902.

Freeman, G. (1998), 'The decline of sovereignty? Politics and immigration restriction in liberal states', in C. Joppke (ed), *Challenge to the nation-state: Immigration in Western Europe and the United States*. Oxford: Oxford University Press.

Fysh, P. and Wolfreys, J. (1998), *The Politics of Racism in France*. Basingstoke: Macmillan.

Gallissot, R. (1985), *Misère de l'anti-racisme*. Paris: Arcantère.

Gaspard, F. and Khosrokhavar, F. (1994), 'Sur le problématique de l'exclusion: de la relation des garçons et des filles de culture musulmane dans les quartiers défavorisés', *Revue française des affaires sociales*, 2, pp. 4-15.

Gaspard, F. and Khosrokhavar, F. (1995), *Le foulard et la République*. Paris: La Découverte.

Gastaut, Y. (2000), *L'immigration and l'opinion en France sous la Ve République*. Paris: Seuil.

GED (2000), *Une forme méconnue de discrimination: les employs fermés aux étrangers*. Paris: GED.

Geddes, A. (2000), *Immigration and European Integration: Towards Fortress Europe?* Manchester: Manchester University Press.

Geddes, A. (2001), 'International Migration and State Sovereignty in an Integrating Europe', *International Migration*, 39, 6, pp. 22-42.

Geddes, A. (2003), *The Politics of Migration and Immigration in Europe*. London: Sage.

Golub, A., Morokvasic, M. and Quiminal, C. (1997), 'Evolution de la production des connaissances sur les femmes immigrées en France et en Europe', *Migrations Société*, 9, 52, pp. 17-36.

Grioterray, A. (1984), *Les immigrés: Le choc*. Paris: Plon.

Guillaumin, C. (1992), *Sexe, Race et Pratique du pouvoir*. Paris: Côté-femmes.

Hainsworth, P. and Mitchell, P. (2000), 'France: The Front National from Crossroads to Crossroads?', *Parliamentary Affairs*, 53, pp. 443 -456.

Hansen, R. (1999), 'Migration, citizenship and race in Europe: Between incorporation and exclusion', *European Journal of Political Research*, 35, pp. 415–444.

Hargreaves, A. (1995), *Immigration, 'race' and ethnicity in Contemporary France*. London: Routledge.

Hargreaves, A. (2000), 'Half-measures: antidiscrimination policy in France', *French Politics, Culture and Society*, 18, pp. 83-101.

Haut Conseil à l'intégration (1997), *Affaiblissement du lien social, enfermement dans les particularismes et integration dans la cite*. Paris: La Documentation Française.

Hollifield, J. (1992), *Immigrants, Markets and States: The Political Economy of Postwar Europe*. Cambridge, MA: Harvard University Press.

Hollifield, J. (1999), 'Ideas, Institutions, and Civil Society: On the Limits of Immigration Control in France', in G. Brochmann et T. Hammar (eds) *Mechanisms of Immigration Control*. Oxford: Berg.

INSEE (1997), *Les immigrés en France*. Paris: INSEE.

INSEE (2000), 'La proportion d'immigrés est stable depuis 25 ans', *Insée Première* No. 748. Paris: INSEE.

INSEE (2001), 'De plus en plus de femmes immigrées sur le marché du travail', *Insée Première* No. 791. Paris: INSEE.

IOM (2000), *World Migration Report*. Geneva: IOM.

Ireland, P. (1994), *The Policy Challenge of Ethnic Diversity. Immigrant Politics in France and Switzerland*. Cambridge MA: Harvard University Press.

Jazouli, A. (1986), *L'action collective des jeunes maghrébins de France*. Paris: L'Harmattan.

Jazouli, A. (1992), *Les années banlieues*. Paris: Seuil.

Jelen, C. (1991), *Ils feront de bons Français: enquête sur l'assimilation des Maghrébins*. Paris: Robert Laffont.

Jelen, C. (1993), *La famille: Secret de l'intégration*. Paris: Robert Laffont.

Jennings, J. (2000), 'Citizenship, Republicanism and Multiculturalism in Contemporary France', *British Journal of Political Studies*, 30, pp. 575-598.

Joppke, C. (1997), 'Asylum and state sovereignty: a comparison of the United States, Germany and Britain', *Comparative Political Studies*, 30, 3, pp. 259-298.

Joppke, C. (ed) (1998), *Challenge to the Nation State: Immigration in Western Europe and the United States*. Oxford: Oxford University Press.

Kepel, G. (2000), *Jihad, expansion et decline de l'islamisme*. Paris: Gallimard.

Khellil, M. (1991), *L'intégration des Maghrébins en France*. Paris: PUF.

Khosrokhavar, F. (1998), 'L'Islam des nouvelles generations', *Hommes et Migrations*, 1211, pp. 83-91.

Kofman, E., Phizacklea, A., Raghuram, P. and Sales, R. (eds) (2000), *Gender and International Migration in Europe*. London: Routledge.

Koser, K. (2001), 'New approaches to asylum?', *International Migration*, 39, 6, pp. 85-100.

Koser, K. and Lutz, H. (eds) (1998), *The New Migration in Europe*. Basingstoke: Macmillan.

Kostakopoulou, T. (2001), *Citizenship, Identity and Immigration in the European Union*. Manchester: Manchester University Press.

Laacher, S. (2002), *Des étrangers en situation de « transit » au Centre d'Hébergement et d'Accueil d'Urgence Humanitaire de Sangatte.* Paris: CNRS-EHESS.

Lacoste-Dujardin, C. (1992), *Yasmina et les autres de Nanterre et d'ailleurs: Filles de parents maghrébins en France.* Paris: La Découverte.

Lacoste-Dujardin, C. (2000) 'Maghrebi families in France', in J. Freedman and C. Tarr (eds) *Women, Immigration and Identities in France.* Oxford: Berg.

Lapeyronnie, D. (1993), *L'individu et les minorités.* Paris: PUF.

Lapeyronnie, D. (1998), 'L'ordre de l'informe. La construction sociale et politique du racisme dans la société française', *Hommes et Migrations*, 1211, pp. 68-82.

Lavenex, S. (2000), 'France: international norms, European integration and state discretion', in J. van Selm (ed) *Kosovo's Refugees in the European Union.* London: Pinter.

Lebon, A. (1995), *Migrations et nationalités en France en 1994.* Paris: La Documentation Française.

Lebon, A. (1997), *Immigration et présence étrangère en France 1995/1996.* Paris: La Documentation Française.

Lebon, A. (2000), *Immigraiton et présence étrangère en France en 1999.* Paris: La Documentation Française.

Le Bras, H. (1991), *Marianne et les lapins. L'obsession démographique.* Paris: Orban.

Le Bras, H. (1998), *Le Démon des origines: Démographie et extrême droite.* Paris: Editions de l'Aube.

Le Gallou, Y. (1985), *La préférence nationale: Réponse à l'immigration.* Paris: Albin Michel.

Legoux, L. (1995), *La Crise de l'asile politique en France.* Paris: Ceped.

Legoux, L. (1996), 'Crise de l'asile, crise de valeurs', *Hommes et Migrations*, 1198 -1199, pp. 69-86.

Lelièvre, F. (1997), 'Quelques repères à propos des femmes migrantes', in N. Bentichou (ed), *Les femmes de l'immigration au quotidien.* Paris: L'Harmattan.

Leonetti, J. (2003), *Rapport sur le projet de loi (No. 810) modifiant la loi No. 52-893 du 25 juillet 1952 relative au droit d'asile.* Paris: Assemblée Nationale.

Lesselier, C. (1999), 'La législation sur l'entrée et le séjour des personnes étrangères en France: pour une analyse féministe'. Paris: RAJFIRE.

Lesselier, C. (2000), 'Sans-papières et droit au séjour', *Femmes étrangères et immigrées en France.* Paris: Comité de suivi des lois sur l'immigration.

Lesselier, C. (2003), 'Women Migrants and Asylum Seekers in France', in J. Freedman (ed), *Gender and Insecurity: Migrant Women in Europe.* Aldershot: Ashgate.

Leveau, R. and Wihtol de Wenden, C. (eds), *Modes d'insertion des populations de culture islamique dans le système politique français.* Paris: Mire.

Lim, L. (1997), *Flexible Labour Markets in a Globalizing World: The Implications of International Female Migrants.* Geneva: ILO.

Lister, R. (1997), *Citizenship: Feminist Perspectives.* Basingstoke: Macmillan.

Lloyd, C. (1998a), 'Rendez-vous manqués: feminisms and anti-racisms in France', *Modern and Contemporary France*, 6, 1, pp. 61-74.

Lloyd, C. (1998b), *Discourses of Antiracism in France.* Aldershot: Ashgate.

Lloyd, C. (2002), 'Anti-racism, social movements and civil society', in F. Anthias and C. Lloyd (eds), *Rethinking Anti-racisms: From theory to practice.* London: Routledge.

Lochak, D. (1985), *Etrangers: de quel droit?* Paris: PUF.

Lochak, D. (1997), 'Les politiques de l'immigration au prisme de la législation sur les étrangers', in D. Fassin, A. Morice and C. Quiminal (eds) *Les lois de l'inhospitalité: les politiques de l'immigration à l'épreuve des sans-papiers.* Paris: La Découverte.

Lochak, D. (1999), 'Les droits des étrangers, entre égalité et discriminations', in P. Dewitte (ed), *Immigration et integration: l'état des savoirs*. Paris: La Découverte.

Lockwood, D. (1996), 'Civic integration and class formation', *British Journal of Sociology*, 47, 3: 531-550.

Long, M. (1988), *Etre français aujourd'hui et demain*. Paris: La Documentation Française.

Lutz, H. (1997), 'The limits of European-ness: immigrant women in Fortress Europe', *Feminist Review* 57, pp. 93-111.

MacEwen, M. (1995), *Tackling Racism in Europe*. Oxford: Berg.

Marcus, J. (1995), *The National Front and French Politics: The Resistible Rise of Jean-Marie Le Pen*. Basingstoke: Macmillan.

Marie, C-V. (1984), 'De la clandestinité à l'insertion professionnelle régulière', *Travail et Emploi*, 22, pp. 21-19.

Marie, C-V. (1988), 'Entre économie et politique: le "clandestin", une figure sociale à géométrie variable', *Pouvoirs*, 47, pp. 75-92.

Marie, C-V. (1999), 'Emploi des étrangers sans-titre, travail illegal, regularisation: des débats en trompe-l'oeil', in P. Dewitte (ed), *Immigration et integration: L'état des savoirs*. Paris: La Découverte.

Massenet, M. (1994), *Sauvage immigration*. Paris: Editions du Rocher.

Mauco, G. (1932), *Les étrangers en France, leur rôle dans l'activité économique*. Paris: Armand Colin.

Mayer, N. (1991), 'Le Front National', in D. Chagnollaud (ed), *Bilan politique de la France 1991*. Paris: Hachette.

Mayer, N. and Perrineau, P. (eds) (1989), *Le Front National à découvert*. Paris: Presses de la fondation nationale des sciences politiques.

Merckling, O. (1998), *Immigration et marché du travail. Le développement de la flexibilité en France*. Paris: L'Harmattan.

Messina, A. (1996), 'The not so silent revolution: Postwar migration to Western Europe', *World Politics*, 49, 1, pp. 130 – 154.

Miller, G. (1992), 'Le clandestine ou l'immigré des immigrés', *Hommes et Migrations*, 1153, pp. 15-23.

Mizrahi, A. (2000), 'Les étrangers dans les consultations des centres de soins gratuits', *Hommes et Migrations*, 1225, pp. 95-100.

Mohseni, C. (2002), 'L'accueil des demandeurs d'asile en France: le cas des Kurdes de l'East Sea', *Hommes et Migrations*, 1238, pp. 59-64.

Money, J. (1999), *Fences and Neighbours: The Political Geography of Immigration Control*. Ithaca: Cornell University Press.

Morris, L. (2002), 'Britain's asylum and immigration regime: the shifting contours of rights', *Journal of Ethnic and Migration Studies*, 28, 3: 409-425.

Naïr, S., Etcherelli, C. and Lanzmann, C. (eds) (1985), *L'immigration Maghrébine en France*. Paris: Denoël.

Nicollet, A. (1993), *Femmes d'Afrique noire en France*. Paris: L'Harmattan.

Noiriel, G. (1988), *Le Creuset français. Histoire de l'immigration XIXe-XXe siècles*. Paris: Seuil.

Noiriel, G. (1991), *La Tyrannie du national. Le droit d'asile en Europe (1793-1993)*. Paris: Calmann-Lévy.

Oriol, P. (2001), 'Les Français d'"origine étrangère" aux elections municipals de 2001', *Migrations Société*, 13, 77, pp. 41-54.

Perrineau, P. (1997), *Le symptôme Le Pen. Radiographie des électeurs du Front National*. Paris: Fayard.

Phizacklea, A. (1996), 'Women, Migration and the State', in S. Rai and G. Lievesley (eds) *Women and the State*. London: Taylor and Francis.

Poinsot, M. (2001), 'Le movement associatif, un instrument au service des politiques publiques d'intégration?', *Hommes et Migrations*, 1229, pp. 65-75.

Prencipe, L. (1994), 'Famille-Migrations-Europe: Quelles relations possibles?', *Migrations Société*, 6, 35, pp. 27-42.

ProAsile (1999), *L'accueil des demandeurs d'asile en Europe*. Paris: France Terre d'Asile.

Quiminal, C. (2000), 'The associative movement of African women and new forms of citizenship', in J. Freedman and C. Tarr (eds) *Women, immigration and identities in France*. Oxford: Berg.

Rea, A. (ed) (1998), *Immigration et racisme en Europe*. Brussels: Complexe.

Roman, J. (1999), 'La laïcité française à l'épreuve de la diversité', in P. Dewitte (ed), *Immigration et integration: l'état des savoirs*. Paris: La Découverte.

Rude-Antoine, E. (1997), *Des vies et des familles: les immigrées, la loi et la coutume*. Paris: Odile Jacob.

Sané, M. (1996), *Sorti de l'Ombre. Journal d'un Sans-papiers*. Paris: Le Temps des Cerises.

Sassen, S. (1999), *Guests and Aliens*. New York: The New Press.

Sassen, S. (2001), *The Global City*. Princeton: Princeton University Press.

Sayad, A. (1991), *L'immigration ou les paradoxes de l'alterité*. Brussels: De Boek.

Schnapper, D. (1991), *La France de l'intégration. Sociologie de la nation en 1990*. Paris: Gallimard.

Schnapper, D. (1992), *L'Europe des immigrés. Essai sur les politiques d'immigration*. Paris: François Bourin.

Schnapper, D. (1995), 'Penser la préférence nationale', in D. Martin-Castelnau (ed), *Combattre le Front National*. Paris: Vinci.

Schnapper, D. (1998), *La relation à l'autre. Au Coeur de la pensée sociologique*. Paris: Gallimard.

Scrinzi, F. (2003), 'The globalisation of domestic work: women migrants and neo-domesticity', in J. Freedman (ed), *Gender and Insecurity: Migrant Women in Europe*. Aldershot: Ashgate.

Silberman, R, (1991), 'Regroupement familial: ce que disent les statistiques', *Hommes et Migrations*, 114, pp. 13-17.

Silverman, M. (1992), *Deconstructing the Nation: Immigration, Racism and Citizenship in Modern France*. London: Routledge.

Simeant, J. (1998), *La cause des sans-papiers*. Paris: Presses de la fondation nationale des sciences politiques.

Simon, P. (1998), 'La discrimination: contexte institutionnel et perception par les immigrés', *Hommes et Migrations*, 1211, pp. 49-67.

Simon-Barouh, I. and De Rudder, V. (eds) (1997), *Migrations internationals et relations interethniques*. Paris: L'Harmattan.

Slama, S. (1999), 'Un service pas "tout public"', *Plein Droit*, 41-42, pp. 23-30.

Soudais, M. (1996), *Le Front National en face*. Paris: Flammarion.

Soysal, Y. (1994), *Limits of Citizenship. Migrants and Postnational Membership in Europe*. Chicago: Chicago University Press.

Spire, A. (1999), 'De l'étranger à l'immigré', *Actes de la Recherche en Sciences Sociales*, 129, pp. 50-57.

Taguieff, P-A. (1988), *La force du prejugé*. Paris: La Découverte.

Taguieff, P-A. (1993), 'L'antiracisme en crise: Eléments d'une critique réformiste', in M. Wieviorka (ed), *Racisme et modernité*. Paris: La Découverte.

Taguieff, P-A. (1996), *La République menace*. Paris: Textuel.

Taguieff, P-A. (1997), 'Universalisme et racisme évolutionniste: Le dilemma republican hérité de la France coloniale', *Hommes et Migrations*, 1207, pp. 90-97.

Taguieff, P-A. and Tribalat, M. (1998), *Face au Front National. Arguments pour une contre-offensive*. Paris: La Découverte.

Terray, E. (1997), 'La lutte des sans-papiers, la démocratie et l'Etat de droit', in D. Fassin, A. Morice and C. Quiminal (eds), *Les lois de l'inhospitalité: Les politiques de l'immigration à l'épreuve des sans-papiers*. Paris: La Découverte.

Terray, E. (1999), 'Le travail des étrangers en situation irrégulière ou la delocalisation sur place', in E. Balibar, M. Chemillier-Gendreau, J. Costa-Lascoux and E. Terray, *Sans-papiers: l'archaïsme fatal*. Paris: La Découverte.

Thave, S (1997), 'Emploi des femmes immigrées: des chiffres qui parlent', *Informations Sociales*, 63, pp. 3-5.

Tiberghien, F. (1998), *La protection des réfugiés en France*. Paris: Economica.

Todd, E. (1994), *Le destin des immigrés. Assimilation et ségrégation dans les démocraties occidentales*. Paris: Seuil.

Tribalat, M. (1991), *Cent ans d'immigration. Etrangers d'hier, Français d'aujourd'hui*. Paris: PUF.

Tribalat, M. (1995), *Faire France: Une enquête sur les immigrés et leurs enfants*. Paris: La Découverte.

Tribalat, M. (1996), *Vingtième rapport sur la situation démographique de la France*. Paris: Ministère du Travail et des Affaires sociales.

Van Selm, J. (2002), 'Comprehensive immigration policy as foreign policy?', in S. Lavenex and E. Ucarer (eds), *Externalities of Integration: The Wider Impact of the EU's Migration Regime*. Lexington MA: Lexington Books.

Venel, N. (1999), *Musulmanes françaises: Des pratiquantes voilées à l'université*, Paris: L'Harmattan.

Voisard, J. and Ducastelle, C. (1988), *La question immigrée dans la France d'aujourd'hui*. Paris: Calmann-Lévy.

Waever, O., Buzan, B., Kelstrup, M. and Lemaitre, P. (1993), *Identity, Migration and the New Security Agenda in Europe*. London: Pinter.

Wallet, J-W., Nehas, A. and Sghiri, M. (1996), *Les perspectives des jeunes issus de l'immigration Maghrébine*. Paris: L'Harmattan.

Walzer, M. (1997), *On Toleration*. New Haven: Yale University Press.

Weil, P. (1991), *La France et ses étrangers. L'aventure d'une politique de l'immigration*. Paris: Calmann-Lévy.

Wieviorka, M. (1993a), *La démocratie à l'épreuve. Nationalisme, populisme, ethnicité*. Paris: La Découverte.

Wieviorka, M. (ed) (1993b), *Racisme et modernité*. Paris: La Découverte.

Wieviorka, M. (1998), 'La production institutionnelle du racisme', *Hommes et Migrations*, 1211, pp. 5-15.

Wihtol de Wenden, C. (1988), *Les immigrés et la politique*. Paris: Presses de la fondation nationale des sciences politiques.

Wihtol de Wenden, C. (2002), 'La crise de l'asile', *Hommes et Migrations*, 1238, pp.6-12.

Wihtol de Wenden, C. and Leveau, R. (2001), *La Beurgeoisie: Les trios ages de la vie associative issue de l'immigration*. Paris: CNRS.

Yuval-Davis, N. and Anthias, F. (1989), *Woman-Nation-State*. London: Macmillan.

Zehraoui, A. (1996), 'Processus différentiels d'intégration au sein des familles algériennes en France', *Revue française de sociologie*, 37, 2, pp. 237-261.

Index

educational 146
gender 4, 113
immigrants' rights 4, 103
Muslims 137
Institut National de la Statistique et des
    Études Économiques (INSEE)
    18, 121
Institut National d'Etudes
    Démographiques (INED) 9, 11
institutional racism 5, 143, 146–9, 160
integration 3, 4, 8, 26–9
    citizenship 19
    contract of 52
    European vs non-European
        immigrants 17
    failure of 28, 29–30
    immigration policy aims 34, 35
    institutional racism 146, 147, 160
    Muslims 127, 129–30, 133, 141
    Pasqua laws 45
    'Republican pact' 49
    rights 89
    Sarkozy law reforms 51–2
    secular education 131
    women's role 107, 112–13
    see also assimilation; European
        integration
international agreements 13, 20, 21
    Amsterdam Treaty (1997) 23, 32, 33,
        154
    Dublin Convention (1990) 55, 56
    Geneva Convention (1951) 21, 61,
        63, 117, 118
    Maastricht Treaty (1991) 23, 55, 64,
        92
    Schengen Agreement (1985) 32–3,
        34, 44, 55, 56
    Single European Act (1986) 32
    see also legislation
International Labour Organisation (ILO)
    19
International Organisation for Migration
    (IOM) 1, 65
'invasion' myth 17–19
IOM *see* International Organisation for
    Migration
Iraqi asylum seekers 64, 65, 69
Islam
    affaire des foulards (headscarves
        affair) 4, 14, 27–8, 44, 52, 127–
        41, 159

family codes 114–15
fundamentalism 127, 130, 134, 135,
    159
Muslim population in France 128–30
    perceived as threat to national
    identity 3, 138, 140
    see also Muslims
Italian immigrants 11, 17

Jazouli, A. 156–7, 159
Jeanneney, Jean-Marcel 12
Jelen, Christian 27, 112–13
Jennings, J. 27
Jospin, Lionel 19, 48–9, 74, 75
    affaire des foulards 133
    defeat by Le Pen 7, 50, 95n
    homosexuals 112n
    voting rights 93
Juppé, Alain 18, 72, 73, 136
justice 147, 149

Khosrokhavar, Farhad 139–40
Koser, K. 56
Kosovo 61, 64
Kostakopoulou, T. 2, 53
Kurdish asylum seekers 58

Laacher, Smaïn 65–6, 67
labour market issues
    asylum seekers 57–8, 64
    black market 75, 80, 82–6, 109, 110,
        120, 124–5
    discrimination 99–100, 154–5
    Europe 2
    residence status uncertainty 79
    sans-papiers 79, 80, 82–6
    women 108, 109, 110, 119–25
    see also migrant workers;
        unemployment
labour migration 9–13, 22, 31, 34, 55,
    128
    see also migrant workers
language 10, 11
Lapeyronnie, D. 147
Lavenex, S. 33
Le Gallou, Y. 145, 146
Le Garrec, Jean 92
Le Pen, Jean-Marie 7, 38, 39–41, 50,
    95n, 144–5, 150
the Left 1, 27, 36–8, 39, 43, 48
    affaire des foulards 141